AF328524

# CONFLICT and LOYALTY

# CONFLICT
## and
## *Loyalty*

## JACOBITISM in EUROPE and BEYOND

ALLAN I. MACINNES

REAKTION BOOKS

*Til Karl Emil og Svend*

*Published by*
REAKTION BOOKS LTD
2–4 Sebastian Street
London EC1V 0HE, UK
www.reaktionbooks.co.uk

First published 2025
Copyright © Allan I. Macinnes 2025



EU GPSR Authorised Representative
Logos Europe, 9 rue Nicolas Poussin, 17000, La Rochelle, France
email: contact@logoseurope.eu



Printed and bound in Great Britain by Bell & Bain, Glasgow

A catalogue record for this book is available from the British Library

ISBN 978 1 83639 093 0

# Contents


Chronology  6

Introduction  13

1  The Cause of the Exiled Stuarts  21

2  Scottish Jacobitism  48

3  Risings and Reprisals  79

4  Jacobite Diaspora in Continental Europe  109

5  Adventuring in the American Colonies  141

6  Africa, Asia and Global Adventuring  173

7  Enlightenment and Romanticism  200

Valedictory: Conflicted Loyalties  225

REFERENCES  237
BIBLIOGRAPHY  240
ACKNOWLEDGEMENTS  255
INDEX  257

# Chronology

| YEAR | Scotland, Ireland, England | <u>Continental Europe</u> | *Beyond* |
|---|---|---|---|
| 1685 | Accession of Duke of York as James VII & II | | |
| 1686 | General Patrick Gordon Russian envoy to London | | |
| 1687 | Thomas Nicolson appointed vicar-apostolic for Roman Catholicism in Scotland | | |
| 1688 | Last clan battle at Mulroy in Lochaber<br>Arrival of William of Orange at Torbay<br>Revolution against James VII & II<br>Nine Years War (1688–97) | | |
| 1689 | Accession of William of Orange and Mary<br>First major Jacobite rising (1689–91)<br>Siege of Londonderry/Derry (Ireland)<br>Battles of Killiecrankie and Dunkeld (Scotland) | | |
| 1690 | Presbyterianism re-established at expense of Episcopalianism in Scotland<br>Battles of Aughrim and Boyne (Ireland)<br>Naval battle at Beachy Head<br>Battle of Cromdale (Scotland)<br>Massacre on island of Eigg<br>Attainders and forfeitures, first wave<br>Royal African Company loses trading monopoly | | |
| 1691 | Siege of Limerick | <u>Court in exile at Saint-Germain, France</u> | |

| YEAR | Scotland, Ireland, England | <u>Continental Europe</u> | *Beyond* |
|---|---|---|---|
| | Treaty of Limerick (Ireland) | <u>Earl of Melfort principal secretary</u> <u>at court in exile (Saint-Germain)</u> | |
| | 'Wild Geese' depart Ireland | <u>Irish brigades in France and Spain</u> | |
| | Treaty of Achallader (Scotland) | <u>Sir David Nairne private secretary</u> <u>to James VII & II</u> | |
| 1692 | Massacre of Glencoe | | |
| | William of Orange assassination plot | <u>Naval battle at La Hogue</u> | |
| | Licensing of English press lapses | | |
| 1693 | | <u>Earl of Melfort joint secretary of</u> <u>state with Lord Caryll at Saint-Germain</u> | |
| | Earl of Middleton becomes joint secretary of state at Saint-Germain | | |
| 1694 | Bank of England founded | | |
| 1695 | Bank of Scotland founded | | |
| | Company of Scotland trading to Africa and the Indies founded | | |
| | Famine in Scotland (1695–1700) | | |
| | Death of Queen Mary | | |
| 1696 | William of Orange assassination plot | | |
| 1697 | | <u>Peace of Ryswick</u> | |
| 1698 | Muscovy Company reincarnated as Russia Company | | *Darien venture (1698–1700)* |
| 1700 | | | *Battle of Tubuganti* |
| | Great Northern War (1700–1721) | | |
| 1701 | | <u>Death of James VII & II, Saint-Germain, Paris</u> <u>Jacobite succession, James VIII & III</u> | |
| 1702 | Death of William of Orange | <u>War of the Spanish Succession</u> <u>(1702–13)</u> | |
| | Accession of Queen Anne | | |
| 1703 | Scotch Plot | <u>Petersburg founded as capital of Russia</u> | |
| | George Lockhart of Carnwath director of covert Jacobite activities (1703–27) | <u>Nathaniel Hooke French agent</u> <u>to Scotland (1703–8)</u> | |
| 1705 | MacDaniel Plot | | |
| 1706 | Treaty of Union | | |

| YEAR | Scotland, Ireland, England | Continental Europe | Beyond |
|---|---|---|---|
| 1707 | Acts of Union | | |
| 1708 | Minor Jacobite rising (French backed) | | |
| | Treason Act | | |
| | East India companies merge | | |
| 1710 | Sacheverell trial | | |
| 1711 | Jacobite street protest in Edinburgh | | |
| 1712 | Acts of Toleration and Patronage | Dr Robert Erskine physician and political adviser to Peter the Great | |
| | Easy Club established in Edinburgh | | |
| 1713 | Attempt to repeal Union defeated | Treaty of Utrecht | |
| | Jacobite street protest in Edinburgh | | |
| | South Sea Company established | | |
| 1714 | Death of Queen Anne | | |
| | Hanoverian succession: accession of George I | | |
| 1715 | The Clan Act passed to encourage loyalty to George I | | |
| | Second major Jacobite rising (1715–16) | | |
| | Earl of Mar raises standard in Braemar | | |
| | Battle of Preston (England) | | |
| | Battle of Sheriffmuir (Scotland) | | |
| | Sacking of Strathearn | | |
| | James VIII & III lands in Peterhead | | |
| 1716 | James VIII & III departs from Montrose | Court in exile expelled from France | |
| | Disarming Act for clans | Courts in exile at Lorraine and Avignon | |
| | Treason trials and executions | Earl of Mar principal secretary at courts in exile: St Germain, Avignon and Rome | |
| | Show trials in England | | *Jacobite prisoners transported to America* |
| | Nonjuring rapprochement with Greek and Russian Orthodoxy (1716–28) | | |
| 1717 | Attainders and forfeitures, second wave | Swedish Plot | |
| | | Court in exile at Urbino | |

| YEAR | Scotland, Ireland, England | Continental Europe | Beyond |
|---|---|---|---|
| 1718 | Highlands refortified (1718–23) | Sir Henry Stirling Jacobite agent in St Petersburg (1718–41) | |
| | English nonjuring liturgy | | |
| 1719 | Minor Jacobite rising (Spanish backed) | | |
| | Battle of Glenshiel (Scotland) | Court in exile established at Rome | |
| 1720 | South Sea Bubble | | *Mississippi Project* |
| | Scottish Episcopal College of Bishops | Birth of Prince Charles Edward Stuart at Rome | |
| | Sir Robert Walpole becomes first prime minister | | |
| | Commission of Trustees for Scotland (1720–28) | | |
| 1721 | Ambush at Allt-na-mullach in Kintail | Peace of Nystad | |
| 1722 | | Ostend East India Company founded | |
| 1723 | Atterbury Plot exposed | | |
| | Grand Lodge of England reconstituted | | |
| 1724 | | Earl of Inverness principal secretary at Rome | |
| 1725 | Shawfield Riot, Glasgow | Birth of Prince Henry Benedict at Rome | |
| | Disarming Act for clans | Russian naval ships at Isle of Lewis | |
| | Earl of Islay (later 3rd Duke of Argyll) Whig manager for Scottish Affairs (1725–61) | | |
| 1727 | Accession of George II | Siege of Gibraltar | |
| | Royal Bank of Scotland founded | Earl of Dunbar principal secretary at Rome | |
| 1728 | General George Wade commences roads and bridges for Highlands | | |
| 1729 | | | *Argyll colony flourishing in Jamaica* |
| 1731 | Nonjuring field preaching in North Ballachulish | Swedish East India Company founded | |
| | Bishop Hugh MacDonald takes charge of Roman Catholic mission to the Highlands | | |
| | Charitable Company of London insurance fraud | | |

| YEAR | Scotland, Ireland, England | Continental Europe | Beyond |
|---|---|---|---|
| 1732 | | War of the Polish Succession (1732–4) | |
| 1734 | Lord Grange principal agent for Patriot party in Scotland | Battle of Danzig<br>Siege of Gaeta | |
| 1735 | | | *Jacobite frontier families in Georgia* |
| 1736 | Porteous Riot, Edinburgh<br>Grand Lodge of Scotland established | | |
| 1739 | Scottish Jacobite Association (1739–45)<br><br>Founding of Black Watch | | *Jacobite frontier families in North Carolina* |
| 1740 | General Keith Russian envoy to London | War of the Austrian Succession (1740–48) | |
| 1742 | Resignation of Sir Robert Walpole | | *Naval assaults on Cartagena and Havana<br>Russia Company reinstated in Persia* |
| | | Advert in *Amsterdam Gazette* exposes French designs for Stuart restoration | |
| 1743 | Black Watch mutiny | | |
| 1744 | Scottish nonjuring liturgy<br>Royal Scots Regiment formed in France<br>French invasion fleet blown off course | | |
| 1745 | Prince Charles Edward lands in Eriskay<br>Raising of standard at Glenfinnan<br>Battle of Prestonpans<br>Surrender of Edinburgh<br>Jacobite Army marches into England<br>Duke of Cumberland recalled from Continent<br><br>Retreat from Derby<br>Battle of Inverurie | Battle of Fontenoy<br><br><br><br>Irish and Scottish forces arrive from France | *Siege of Louisbourg, Cape Breton* |
| 1746 | Battle of Falkirk<br>Duke of Cumberland in Scotland | Swedish fleet trapped in ice at Gothenburg | *Fall of Madras* |

| YEAR | Scotland, Ireland, England | <u>Continental Europe</u> | *Beyond* |
|---|---|---|---|
| | Battle of Culloden | | |
| | Jacobites disband at Ruthven in Badenoch | | |
| | Prince Charles Edward departs from Loch nan Uamh in Lochaber | | |
| | State-sponsored terrorism in Highlands (1746–7) | | |
| | Treason trials and executions | | *Jacobite prisoners transported to America* |
| | Show trials in England | | *Carnatic Wars (1746–56)* |
| 1747 | Attainders and forfeitures, third wave | <u>Battle of Laffeldt</u> | |
| | Purge of local government and customs | | |
| | Disarming Act for clans | | |
| | Proscription of Gaelic, tartan and bagpipes | | |
| 1748 | | <u>Treaty of Aix-la-Chapelle</u> | |
| | | <u>Prince Henry Benedict becomes a cardinal</u> | |
| | | <u>Prince Charles Edward expelled from France</u> | |
| | | | *Jacobite prisoners venture to Ethiopia* |
| | | | *Siege of Pondicherry* |
| 1750 | Prince Charles Edward visits London, becomes an Anglican | | |
| 1752 | The Appin murder | | |
| | Abolition of heritable jurisdictions | | |
| | Commission for Annexed Estates (1752–84) | | |
| 1753 | Elibank Plot | | |
| | Execution of Dr Archibald Cameron | | |
| 1756 | Raising of Highland regiments | <u>Seven Years War (1756–63)</u> | |
| 1757 | Battle of Hochkirk | | *Battle of Plassey* |
| 1758 | | | *Battle of Ticonderoga* |
| | | | *Siege of Madras* |
| | | | *Recapture of Louisbourg* |
| 1759 | George Keith, Earl Marischal, Prussian envoy to London | | *Battle of Plains of Abraham (Quebec)* |
| | | <u>Naval battle in Quiberon Bay</u> | |
| | | | *Naval assaults on Guadeloupe and Havana* |

| YEAR | Scotland, Ireland, England | Continental Europe | Beyond |
|---|---|---|---|
| 1760 | Accession of George III | | *Battle of Buxar* |
| 1761 | Ossianic controversy instigated | | *Fall of Pondicherry* |
| 1763 | | <u>Treaty of Paris</u><br><u>James Edgar principal secretary at Rome</u> | |
| 1764 | Scottish Episcopal liturgy | <u>Andrew Lumisden principal secretary at Rome</u> | |
| 1765 | | | *Treaty of Allahabad* |
| 1766 | Death of James VIII & III, Rome | | |
| 1774 | Simon Fraser, Master of Lovat, restored to his annexed estate | | |
| 1775 | Raising of Highland regiments | | *War of American Independence (1775–83)* |
| 1776 | | | *Battle of Moore's Creek* |
| 1777 | | | *Battle of Princeton* |
| 1778 | Joseph Knight case against slavery in Scotland | | |
| 1783 | | | *Creation of the United States of America*<br>*Cherokee Wars (1783–92)* |
| 1784 | End of Whig ascendancy<br>Disannexation Act<br>Seabury consecrated at Aberdeen as bishop for United States<br>Board of Commissioners for India | | |
| 1788 | | <u>Death of Prince Charles Edward, Rome</u> | |
| 1789 | | <u>French Revolution</u> | |
| 1793 | Raising of Highland regiments | <u>Napoleonic Wars (1793–1815)</u> | |
| 1800 | Prince Henry Benedict receives annuity from George III | | |
| 1807 | Abolition of slave trading in empire | <u>Death of Prince Henry Benedict, Frascati</u> | |
| 1815 | Glenfinnan Monument erected | <u>Battle of Waterloo</u> | |
| 1817 | Stuart Papers sold to Hanoverians | | |
| 1820 | Accession of George IV | | |
| 1822 | George IV visits Edinburgh | | |

# Introduction

At Culloden in the Scottish Highlands, Jacobite forces commanded by Prince Charles Edward Stuart were defeated decisively by Hanoverian forces commanded by William Augustus, Duke of Cumberland, on 16 April 1746. That evening in the aftermath of the battle, 22 men drawn from the MacDonnnells of Glengarry and the Stewarts from Atholl were thrown aboard a ship in Cromarty Bay in the Black Isle. Next day the ship sailed for Portsmouth where the severely wounded men led by Donald MacDonnell of Scotus and John Stewart of Acharn were unceremoniously transferred to another ship, an Indiaman bound for the British colonies in the Americas. No effort was made to validate this transportation by judicial proceedings. Sometime later in the course of their Atlantic crossing, the Indiaman was captured by a 'Salle Rover'. Its Turkish adventurers strangled the captain and crew of the Indiaman. But the Gaelic-speaking, tartan-clad Highlanders were spared by the Turks, 'since they had never seen their habit, nor heard their language before'. Their onward passage to the Isle of Lemnoa on the coast of Ethiopia is somewhat problematic. It is more likely that the Turkish ship rounded the Cape of Good Hope to reach markets in Sudan or Egypt rather than through the Mediterranean and along the River Nile to arrive at an Ethiopian island. It is unknown whether it was blown off course, or had escaped from attack by other naval vessels, or had used this route to markets before. It may even have engaged in prolonged piracy in the Atlantic and Indian oceans. However, when their ship eventually arrived at Lemnoa in 1748, it was visited by the island's governor. The Highlanders were greatly surprised when he conversed with them in Gaelic. For the governor was a Stewart, also from Atholl, who as a youth had gone on the ill-fated Darien expedition, the brief Scottish colonial venture between 1698 and 1700. Rather than return home when the colony on the Isthmus of Panama failed at the outset of the eighteenth century, he had continued his adventures (probably in the East Indies) before navigating his way through the ethnic, regional and religious factions that beset the Solomonic Empire of Ethiopia as Christianity continued to give way to Islam.[1]

Governor Stewart was also 'a remote cousin' of Stewart of Acharn. Once the Highlanders were taken ashore under the governor's protection, Acharn persuaded his kinsman to write letters to Scotland asking for overtures to be made to Louis XV of France that he order his ambassador in Constantinople to intercede for the release of the 22 Highlanders. The pope was also to be approached to see if their ransom could be facilitated. Their chosen contacts in Scotland were Duncan Stewart of Glenbuckie and William Henderson (or Harryson), a Benedictine monk resident among the MacDonalds of Clanranald. The latter had been in correspondence with the Stuart court in exile in Rome in 1737 in an unsuccessful attempt to secure a 'chanonry' at the Scottish monastery at Regensburg in Bavaria. However, his cousin was Peter Grant from Glenlivet, who had served for two years as a priest in Glengarry before leaving for Rome in 1737 to become the agent at the Sacred College of Propaganda for the Catholic mission in Scotland. As Abbé Grant he built up a notable track record in securing papal audiences. The letters from Governor Stewart took two years to arrive by an Irish ship to the River Clyde, by which time Stewart of Glenbuckie was debilitated by tuberculosis. On 8 October 1750, Henderson wrote to Rome from Kinlochmoidart to the exiled monarch (and father of Prince Charles Edward) James VIII & III, with a covering letter to Abbé Grant, to expedite assistance from the king of France and the papacy. At this point the trail goes cold. The fate of the 22 Highlanders remains unknown. MacDonnell of Scotus is reputed to have died in captivity and Stewart of Acharn seemingly never returned to Scotland.[2]

This Ethiopian episode was first discovered in the Stuart Papers, purchased by the Hanoverian monarchy and lodged at Windsor Castle from 1817, by Andrew Lang in the course of his research into the Jacobite spy who had passed information to the Hanoverians on the movements of Prince Charles Edward in France from 1747 and betrayed the last Jacobite plot in 1753. Lang was to identify the spy, codenamed 'Pickle', as Alasdair Ruadh MacDomhnaill (red-haired Alexander MacDonnell), the heir to the chiefship of Glengarry, to which he succeeded in 1754. Lang, who originally hailed from Selkirk in the Scottish Borders, was a prolific folklorist and historian as well as a poet, novelist and literary critic. The Ethiopian episode lost all historical traction after Lang published his revelations on *Pickle the Spy* in 1897. But it resurfaced among 'Scraps on the Jacobite Episode, 1688–1746' in the Macbean Collection. This collection, second only to the Stuart Papers at Windsor for Jacobite studies, was gifted to the University of Aberdeen by the New York entrepreneur William Munro Macbean in 1919. Ethiopia's featuring in this book serves both to introduce and contextualize the global impact of Jacobitism as it spread from Scotland, Ireland and England not just throughout Europe from Iberia to Russia, but on to the Americas, Africa and Asia. It also highlights unexpected aspects of Jacobitism that distance the Stuart cause from the Enlightenment and Romanticism.

In varying and lesser degrees with respect to Ireland and England, Jacobitism was an issue of substance as long as there was any prospect of restoring the Stuart monarchy exiled at the Revolution of 1688–91. However, there was undoubted political substance to the appeal of Jacobitism in Scotland that stretched over seven decades from the late seventeenth to the mid-eighteenth century. The cultural dimension of this appeal was subsequently extended through the Enlightenment and Romanticism well into the nineteenth century. Distinctively in Scotland, Jacobitism had a patriotic agenda that engaged Scots politically and culturally as well as militarily and subversively. Accordingly, this book aims to shift the focus of Jacobite studies. The Stuart courts in exile on the European continent, dynastic and confessional identification with their cause, and espionage and diplomacy on their behalf are of secondary consideration. Priority is given to Jacobite communities at home and in exile as old European horizons were broadened by trans-oceanic adventuring. New horizons were intellectual as well as geographic. Scottish patriotism was bolstered by writings of Jacobite exiles on state formation and political economy as aspects of applied Enlightenment and subsequently given new direction at home through Romanticism.

The first chapter, 'The Cause of the Exiled Stuarts', traces Jacobitism from the removal of James VII & II as king of Scotland, Ireland and England by the Revolution of 1688–91 to the death of his grandson, Prince Henry Benedict, as the last direct Stuart claimant to the three kingdoms in 1807. The propaganda for and against the Jacobites is examined in depth with further scrutiny given to the direction of Jacobitism, especially under James VIII & III from his courts in exile in France and Italy. Particular attention is given to the lack of co-ordination between the courts in exile and to their followers in the three kingdoms before touching on the comparative standing of episodic Jacobite organization in Ireland and England, which stood markedly in contrast to that of a more cohesive movement in Scotland. Accordingly, the main theme of the second chapter is the distinctiveness of Scottish Jacobitism. Here the focus is on Jacobite agents and agencies and on their covert organization for the cause in town and country. The commitments and priorities of Scottish Jacobites set the dynastic and confessional against the patriotic, particularly after the accomplishment of parliamentary union between Scotland and England in 1707. Conflicting commitments occasioned political divisions and religious differences within and among Scottish Jacobites that affected their ability to effect counter-revolution and a Stuart restoration.

As Scotland bore the brunt of the fighting, dying and punishment for Jacobitism, the third chapter deals with 'Risings and Reprisals'. The Scottish theatre was certainly secondary to that of Ireland in the first major rising of 1689–91. Thereafter, all subsequent major risings in 1715–16 and 1745–6, as well as minor risings in 1708 and 1719, began and ended in Scotland. In the major risings known as the Fifteen and the Forty-Five, Jacobite strategy was affected adversely by the clash between British dynastic and Scottish patriotic objectives. Both the major and minor risings were marked by punitive reprisals in Scotland. Ireland suffered comprehensively in the first major rising, while the few English participants in the Fifteen and the Forty-Five were marked out for exemplary punishment. The escalation of punitive reprisals in the Forty-Five was marked by state terrorism with a genocidal intent in the Scottish Highlands that commenced before Culloden and continued subsequently for eighteen months. Jacobites were also expelled. Some who avoided capture fled to the European continent; others were transported as prisoners to the British American colonies. Not all of the latter arrived. A few ships were taken over by prisoners and returned to voluntary exile in France. Some ships were seized by pirates who sold prisoners into slavery from North Africa to Turkey or, exceptionally, took them in bondage to Ethiopia.

The fourth chapter deals with the Jacobite diaspora in continental Europe, where studies of Scottish exiles lag behind those of the Irish in commercial, military and religious networking. English exiles remain a peripheral interest. Scottish networking among continental exiles was certainly as extensive and influential as the Irish. Its clannish character, based on kinship and local association, was reinforced by high degrees of literacy, by a willingness to circumvent legal restrictions on trade, and by a readiness to promote fellowship through Freemasonry. Nevertheless, the majority of Scottish émigrés were not active courtiers and, even if involved in commercial networking, were largely passive in their Jacobite commitment other than those who returned to fight in the minor rising of 1719 and the major rising of the Forty-Five. Émigrés returning from France and Spain for these engagements were prepared to compromise their prospects of a pardon from the Hanoverian dynasty which succeeded to Scotland, Ireland and England in 1714. But the majority of those exiled for their participation in the Fifteen pursued conditional pardons to secure their return to their families in the hope of reclaiming their forfeited estates. The same situation prevailed for émigrés who fled Scotland after the Forty-Five, which diminished viable prospects of another major rising. Nevertheless, Jacobites exiled from France to Russia, including some in Iberia, the Netherlands and Scandinavia, became active in their host country's plans for state formation and ambitions for imperial expansion. Freemasonry reinforced such service, but purely Jacobite fellowships, such as the Order of Toboso, can be deemed as effective as tilting at windmills.

Jacobites repatriated capital from the Caribbean and North America through the sugar, tobacco and fur trades. Nonjuring Episcopalians in

Scotland, who faced penal sanctions for declining to take oaths to abjure the exiled Stuarts, received bequests from such commercial ventures. Yet active Jacobite commitment in the Americas was less pronounced than in continental Europe. The fifth chapter on adventuring in the American colonies charts the foundation of a Jacobite presence through the creation of Scottish colonies by James VII & II. Less enduring was the Darien venture on the Isthmus of Panama, which his successor at the Revolution, William of Orange, authorized reluctantly and compromised pragmatically. Nevertheless, once Scots secured unrestricted access to the American colonies at the Union of 1707, Jacobites became prominent frontier fighters and traders while continuing to indulge in occasional piracy. But the contribution of colonial exiles to the Jacobite cause was more a matter of smoke and mirrors than of substantial commitment. Indeed, with the outbreak of the Seven Years War in 1756, the vanquished at Culloden were recruited into Highland regiments to fight against the French in Canada and the Caribbean. In the process, Scottish Jacobites became British imperialists, with further Highland regiments raised from 1775 to fight against the colonists in the American War of Independence. Jacobites who had settled in the southern colonies after the Fifteen were more inclined to fight alongside the colonists, as did some escapees from the Forty-Five. However, Scottish settlers after the Forty-Five were more prone to side with the British. Some Highland Jacobites were less enthusiastic enslavers of Africans than the bulk of the Scottish settlers in the southern colonies and the Caribbean. Other Highland Jacobites were also noted for their integration with Native American tribes, particularly the Cherokees and the Creeks, fighting with them against land grabs by other American colonists during the War of Independence and after the creation of the United States in 1783.

Chapter Six on Africa, Asia and global adventuring deals with Jacobite engagement in chartered companies as much as individual endeavours as free traders. The Company of Scotland trading to Africa and the Indies, which had promoted the Darien venture, also engaged in trading ventures to West Africa and the East Indies and met with mixed but limited success. However, the Treaty of Utrecht that concluded the War of the Spanish Succession in 1713 allowed Scots to break into slave trading to Latin America, mainly through the Royal African

Company in association with the South Sea Company. Scottish involvement in slave trading from Africa was a much less rewarding endeavour than tramp trading from Arabia to China, usually under the auspices of the English East India Company. However, Scottish Jacobites were prominent initially in the Ostend East India Company and then in the Swedish East India Company. They also served in French and Dutch, and to a lesser extent in Spanish and Danish, commercial and military ventures to the East Indies. Jacobite families were prominent in freelance global ventures, moving funds from the West Indies to the East Indies then back to the Caribbean, and repatriating considerable funds from the Swedish and the Spanish as well as the British empires. The most lucrative phase of capital repatriation from India occurred after the conclusion of the Seven Years War in 1763, when the British defeat of the French and their Indian allies opened up territorial acquisitions for the English East India Company, most notably control over Bengal. Highland regiments were again deployed for British imperialist ventures. Scottish families with a Jacobite hinterland who progressed through the civil and military ranks of the English East India Company gained a substantive imperial dividend through the massive repatriation of capital not only to acquire and reclaim estates in Scotland but to purchase sugar plantations in the West Indies. No thought was given to revitalizing Jacobitism as the courts in exile wound down in 1766.

Before the demise of Jacobitism as a political force, new horizons were opening up that were intellectual and cultural rather than geographic and political. As Chapter Seven on the Enlightenment and Romanticism demonstrates, these alternative new horizons lasted throughout the eighteenth century and well into the nineteenth, revitalizing Jacobitism culturally as its political impact sundered. Jacobites were prominent in the intellectual reawakening, the Republic of Letters, from the late seventeenth to the mid-eighteenth century. Scots of a Jacobite persuasion achieved prominence in architecture, medicine, mathematics, political economy, history, deism and liturgical innovation. Despite Whig intellectuals, primarily based in Edinburgh, laying claim to the Scottish Enlightenment in the mid- to later eighteenth century, exiled Jacobites made distinctive contributions by experiments in electricity and artistic engraving and, above all, furthered the pursuit of political virtue through state formation and political economy. Applied Enlightenment went hand in glove with redefined patriotism and technological innovation. The Enlightenment's tempering of reason with emotion was fundamentally questioned by Romanticism's fascination with the primitive and the irrational. Polemicists and historians who were drawn from Jacobite families or who had an emotional commitment to Scotland's Jacobite past were prominent in the European shaping of Romanticism from the mid-eighteenth century. Their path-breaking work was sustained into the mid-nineteenth century by poetry and songs that acclaimed the Jacobite cause, now sufficiently sanitized and dressed up in tartan to win the approval of the Hanoverian George IV and his niece Queen Victoria.

# 1

# The Cause of the
# Exiled Stuarts

The Revolution of 1688–91 was of seismic importance for the house of Stuart and the three kingdoms of Scotland, England and Ireland. James VII (of Scotland) & II (of England and Ireland) was removed in favour of his eldest daughter, Mary, and her Dutch husband, William of Orange. This relatively bloodless accomplishment in England from 1688 encountered armed resistance in Ireland and Scotland that was not dispersed until 1691. Jacobitism, support for the now exiled James VII & II, was far from vanquished, however. While the major theatre of resistance to William of Orange was initially in Ireland and while England remained the main locus of Jacobite plotting, Scotland proved the more enduring Jacobite heartland, staging major risings in 1715–16 (the Fifteen) and in 1745–6 (the Forty-Five), with minor risings in 1708 and 1719. Jacobites in all three kingdoms were outraged by the Hanoverian succession. The death in 1714 of Queen Anne, the younger daughter of King James, in Scotland led to the accession of her distant cousin, the Elector of Hanover, as George I rather than her half-brother, the Prince of Wales, who had been recognized by France as James VIII & III on the death of his father in 1701. Although the Jacobite cause was also recognized by the papacy and intermittently in other European courts, it had largely run its political course by the death of James VIII & III in 1766. Nevertheless, it still gained some traction from the Enlightenment, Romanticism and Freemasonry until the leader of the last major rising, Prince Charles Edward Stuart, died in 1788. The direct Stuart line in exile did not actually expire until the death in 1807 of his brother, Henry Benedict, called the Cardinal Duke of York, as he was a long-serving Italian cardinal in the Roman Catholic Church as well as the titular duke in the Jacobite peerage.

## Polemics and Plots, 1690–1725

The proclaiming of the Revolution as 'Glorious' was a polemical act that demonstrated the importance of the pen as well as the sword to the supporters of William of Orange. The licensing of the English press, which James VII & II had confirmed in 1685, was allowed to lapse in 1692 and had effectively expired by 1695. Nevertheless, successive British governments could and did instigate prosecutions for libel against authors, printers and booksellers for publishing and distributing books deemed seditious, treasonable or overtly critical of governance in England and Ireland. In Scotland the corresponding legal action, for defamation, was used less assertively. Indeed, the noted Jacobite printer Robert Freebairn, who was to publish the manifestos for James VIII & III issued at the Fifteen, had been able to operate openly in Edinburgh in the years prior to that rising. Given that Jacobites were intent on counter-revolution, their polemicists in all three kingdoms were right at the margins of legality, if not wholly beyond the pale, from the 1690s to the 1750s. Given the perennial prospect of legal harassment from British governments, most authors preferred to remain anonymous, be they Whig, Tory or Jacobite. Overwhelmingly, polemics were an anti-Jacobite pursuit throughout the successive reigns of William of Orange, Anne, George I and George II.

Under William of Orange, 1692 proved to be a critical year. Given that William was opposed to France in the Nine Years War, the Jacobites, through the Anglo-Irish polemicist Charles Leslie, were able to use the French press, specifically the *Paris Gazette*, to leak orders for the Massacre of Glencoe. This atrocity was stage-managed by Sir John Dalrymple, Master (later 1st Earl) of Stair, as a secretary of state for Scotland; carried out by the Argyll Regiment, staffed mainly by the Clan Campbell; and condoned by William himself. But failed French invasions in 1692 and again in 1696 led to assassination attempts by Jacobite plotters, approved by the court in exile, which unleashed a spate of Whig polemics mainly from London and supplemented from Edinburgh. Jacobites and their cause were castigated for treachery, perjury, villainy, subversion, conspiracy and tyranny – with an intent to enforce popery and slavery to France thrown in for good measure. Despite the Revolution being the accomplishment of Whigs and Tories, efforts were made by the former to tar the latter with the same Jacobite brush. Any Jacobite vindication of their principles was given short shrift.

Jacobite criticism of the maladroit reign of William in Scotland merged with the general outcry raised by the Country interest against the Court for William's reneging on his endorsement of the ill-fated Scottish colonial venture to Darien on the Isthmus of Panama. William effectively withdrew his backing for a venture that started as a colonial confederation of Scottish with English, Dutch and Hanseatic commercial interests. In doing so, he succumbed to diplomatic pressure from Spain, which claimed Panama, and to the corporate power of the East Indian vested interests in the English Parliament, in both the Commons and the Lords. Deprived of foreign mercantile expertise and capital, the Darien scheme initiated in 1695 and launched in 1698 had become a fiasco by 1700. William, however, was entirely innocent of prolonging the famine that afflicted Scotland during these years. Nonetheless, biblical allusions triumphed over arithmetical accuracy when the famine was dubbed as the 'Seven Ill Years' of William, who further pushed the disaffection of the Country from the Court with his endeavours to strengthen bonds between England and Scotland by a parliamentary union as hostilities with France were set to resume in the War of the Spanish Succession.

The determination of Queen Anne to press ahead with Union led to the Jacobites continuing their association with the Country interest, now a more formidable party in the Scottish Parliament as part of a confederated opposition to political incorporation. But the Jacobites' engagement with the Country party was compromised by two plots in 1703 and 1705. In both plots, Queen Anne was to be replaced by her half-brother, James VIII & III, with armed assistance of Louis XIV of France, on the first occasion through an initial invasion of Scotland, in the second through Ireland.

The 'Scotch Plot' of 1703 was the fabrication of Simon Fraser of Beaufort, who had been convicted in his absence of treason in 1698 for attempting to acquire the vacant title and estates of the Lord Lovat and the chiefship of Clan Fraser by kidnap, rape, forgery, fraud and extortion. The court in exile at Saint-Germain was not enthusiastic. But Beaufort had turned Roman Catholic after escaping to France from Scotland and managed to ingratiate himself at Louis xiv's court at Versailles through the patronage of Cardinal Francesco Gualterio, the papal nuncio. Although there was scepticism at Versailles as well as at Saint-Germain about Beaufort's capacity to mobilize the Highland clans, the court in exile was prevailed upon to support an exploratory mission to Scotland by Beaufort. After his arrival in London, Beaufort contacted the leader of the Court party in Scotland, James Douglas, 2nd Duke of Queensberry, conveying information designed to implicate James Douglas-Hamilton, 4th Duke of Hamilton, the leader of the Country party, long suspected for his covert association with Saint-Germain. Also in Beaufort's sights was John Murray, 1st Duke of Atholl, a leading Cavalier (parliamentary Jacobite) who was the brother of the dowager Lady Lovat, whom Beaufort had raped. Atholl, in turn, was able to use information gleaned from contacts among Jacobites in London not just to discredit Beaufort but to expose Queensberry's role in facilitating Beaufort's escape to France. While his dealings as a double agent destroyed any credibility at Saint-Germain, they did pave the way for Beaufort's recognition as Lord Lovat on his return to Scotland.

In the interim, Hamilton and Atholl were again compromised by a plot leaked to John Campbell, 2nd Duke of Argyll, who had replaced Queensberry as leader of the Court party. Argyll's informant was James MacDaniell, an Irish participant in a putative plot led by his uncle John Mullany, the Roman Catholic Bishop of Killalie. Large contingents of French forces were to be landed initially in County Cork, then through Dundee. Hamilton, Atholl and other leading Scottish Jacobites were to join forces with prominent English Tories. But MacDaniell's claims of concerted action in all three kingdoms were highly embellished and unsubstantiated. Whig polemicists rejoiced at the dashing of Jacobite hopes by the exposure of their plots prior to the Act of Union in 1707 and by the aborted French invasion to support Jacobite insurgency in 1708. Nevertheless, this minor rising clearly marked out the willingness of Scottish Jacobites to pursue armed struggle and, if necessary, the invasion of England to restore the exiled house of Stuart.

Whigs and Tories rigorously contested prospects for peace with France to end the War of the Spanish Succession, for a settled religious accommodation of Anglicans with Dissenters within the Church of England, and for a British political realignment post-Union. However, party labelling was becoming more flexible as Tories as well as Whigs now sought to tinge their rivals with Jacobite faction, disruption and desperation. The British unionism of the Whigs was more evident in appeals to concerted action in North and South Britain, which came from Glasgow and Edinburgh as well as London. According to the Anglo-Irish Whig intellectual John Toland, the Revolution was the common bulwark against absolutism, Roman Catholicism and incivility. His pamphlet of 1710 was titled more pejoratively as 'The Jacobitism, Perjury and Popery of High-Church-Priests'. Whigs found themselves on the defensive with their impeachment of Henry Sacheverell, whose advocacy of non-resistance to (lawful) monarchy, indefeasible hereditary right and no toleration for Dissenters was a potent mixture of clerical certainty and academic arrogance. His subversion of the Revolution's principles in pamphlets and sermons, particularly before the magistrates and council of the City of London in St Paul's Cathedral in November 1709, certainly did not endear him to the Whigs, though he did attract a measure of Tory support for his antipathy to the forced abdication of James II in England, to the Union which confirmed the Presbyterian establishment in Scotland, and to the protracted and expensive wars with France. Whigs were the driving force for his impeachment, insti-gated by the Commons in January 1710, and his trial before the Lords at Westminster in February. Sacheverell attracted considerable extra-parliamentary support as his trial wound to its conclusion in March. He was given the relatively lenient sentence of a few weeks in prison and a three-year ban from preaching. His trial and conviction helped carry the day for the Tories in the subsequent general election.

Although Sacheverell was determined to penalize both Dissenters and Catholics, he was counted along with other English nonjurors and papists as being among the 'Pretender's clergy' for his refusal to abjure the exiled Stuarts. Sacheverell briefly flirted with Jacobitism in the wake of his impeachment, a situation not untypical of other English non-jurors, a distinct minority within the Anglican community in England and Ireland. In 1712, the Tory administration imposed the Toleration Act upon Scotland. Toleration for Episcopalians was conditional on abjuring the exiled Stuarts. While this was acceptable to the minority deemed jurors, it was not to the majority of Scottish Episcopalians deemed nonjurors, who became liable to the penal laws imposed on Roman Catholics. In marked contrast to their English colleagues, Scottish nonjurors actively prayed, planned and fought for a Stuart restoration. They were active in street protests in Edinburgh in 1711 that were repeated in 1713 with no official backing from Saint-Germain. Such protests drew on Scottish dissatisfaction with the Treaty of Utrecht, which concluded the War of the Spanish Succession. Although this treaty offered imperial opportunities for Scots as well as English in the Americas, there was no immediate removal of trade restrictions with France, which was particularly damaging to Scottish wine imports and to fish and textile exports.

The conclusion of the War of the Spanish Succession coincided with the circulation of rumours, not particularly well founded, that Queen Anne wished to be succeeded by her half-brother, James VIII & III, rather than the Electoral house of Hanover as prescribed in the Treaty of Union. These rumours unleashed a polemical torrent against the curse of Jacobitism and the centrality of Scottish engagement in intrigues, schemes and plots to prevent a Hanoverian succession and end the Union. Indeed, an anonymous Scottish Presbyterian with a radical Covenanting heritage claimed that if the Pretender at Saint-Germain prevailed, Britain would be exposed not only to tyranny and arbitrary government, but to slavery and oppression that would lead to the utter ruin of Britain. He compared James VIII & III to the puppet king, John Balliol, set up by Edward I of England in 1296 at the outset of the Wars of Independence: 'Baliol submitted us to England, the Pretender enslaveth us to France and Rome. Baliol endangered our Liberty, the Pretender our Liberty and Religion both.' But there was no guarantee that a Stuart restoration would sever the Union from which Jacobites in Scotland wanted liberation.[1]

However, before the accomplishment of the Hanoverian succession, the noted British unionist Daniel Defoe sought to vindicate the

Scottish nation from overidentification with Jacobites, the only people in both England and Scotland who wished to sunder the Union. In the aftermath of the succession, the British imperialist John Oldmixon praised the Scottish nation for always being zealous in their defence of the Protestant religion and liberty. He also claimed that the popular charges of betraying independence levelled against the Scottish commissioners who negotiated Union with England in 1706 were groundless. Such magnanimity ceased with the outbreak of the Fifteen, which Daniel Defoe viewed as the Scots Rebellion. As it lost momentum, which James VIII & III could not revitalize after he arrived belatedly in Scotland in 1715, Whigs called for the reinforcement of the British bulwark, notably the penal laws against nonjurors and Catholics. On the rising's defeat, English Dissenters published sermons of thanksgiving to affirm their loyalty to the British state. The plot instigated in 1717 by the Swedish ambassador in London, Count Gyllenborg, which drew on Scottish sympathies but lacked co-ordination with the other two kingdoms, was written off as a Jacobite factional endeavour of no serious purpose. The failure of the Spanish-backed minor rising in 1719 was hailed as Britain's delivery from popery and arbitrary power. At the same time, the loyalty of Scottish Tories was questioned.

Two years later, claims emanating from Edinburgh affirmed the growth of popery and the insolence of papists and Jacobites in Scotland. Much of this propaganda was designed to entrench the electoral success of the Whig ascendancy after the Tories had been removed from government at the Hanoverian succession. The crash in financial stocks and shares brought about by the South Sea Bubble in 1720 led James VIII & III to issue a public declaration from his court in exile, now at Rome, affirming his paternal concerns for the sufferings of his people. However, his desire for a British restoration was frustrated by the failure of the plot to invade England in 1721–2 associated with Francis Atterbury, Bishop of Rochester. Scottish Jacobites belatedly attached themselves to this endeavour, which had been afflicted by English Jacobite inertia after Atterbury was impeached in the Lords and banished perpetually overseas in 1723.

In the following year, loyalty in North Britain to George I and the Whig ascendancy was brought into question from Edinburgh by the practice of trimming. Ostensibly, considerable numbers of the political elite in Scotland disguised their Jacobite sympathies by swearing and subscribing oaths of allegiance and abjuration in order to hold office in town and country: a practice first evident under William of Orange but reputedly intensified after the Hanoverian succession. Jacobite trimmers distinguished between de facto and *de jure* government. They abjured the Pretender on the understanding that as he was the rightful James VIII & III, he was no Pretender. Therefore, when they abjured the Pretender, they abjured nobody. The legal right of governing in the Hanoverian interest did not eliminate or suborn the natural right of the exiled Stuarts to rule Scotland and their two other kingdoms. Such equivocation, compounded by the patronage of leading families in Scotland, facilitated deep Jacobite penetration of government posts, such as justices of peace and commissioners of supply in the shires, magistracy in the towns, and the postal and even the customs services, especially after the accession of George II in 1727.

## Polemics and Plots, 1725–53

This accession was preceded by the failure of another plot conceived at the court in exile, this time to secure military assistance from Peter the Great of Russia and instigate a rising in the Highlands of Scotland. Its only meaningful impact was to offer up military and mercantile opportunities in Russia for Scottish Jacobites exiled since the Fifteen. The threat of rioting, which had led the British government to postpone the implementation of an augmented malt tax in 1713, duly became a reality in 1725. When a revised malt tax was introduced, it occasioned strikes by brewers in west and central Scotland. The most notorious protest was the Shawfield Riot in Glasgow, where the mansion of the local Member of Parliament and transatlantic trader Daniel Campbell of Shawfield was razed because he had not vociferously opposed the imposition of the tax. Reports of endemic rioting in the city were grossly exaggerated, but disorder certainly spread on account of the inept handling of the mob by the military. The British government, which despatched reinforcements from England under the command of General George Wade, blamed the magistrates and the town council, who, after a brief period of incarceration in Edinburgh, were punitively fined by the Scottish judiciary. Wade went on to enforce a military occupation of the Highlands to contain Jacobitism, which had not been a clearly identifiable feature in the rioting. This was also the case with the Porteous Riot in Edinburgh in 1736, after the city guard opened fire on a mob attempting to free a convicted smuggler. The mob regrouped, then seized and lynched John Porteous, captain of the city guard. Although the mob had included contingents from Fife and other contraband districts, political reprisals were less pronounced than after the Shawfield Riot. Order was restored without punitive action being taken against the magistrates and town council. Instead, the Porteous Riot was attributed to a lack of co-ordination between the military and the Scottish judiciary. Jacobites claimed, with some merit, that the main perpetrators of mobbing and rioting in Scotland were Presbyterians opposed to the intrusion of ministers in parishes at the behest of their patrons, whose rights had been removed at the Revolution but restored by parliamentary enactment in 1712.

Jacobitism, however, was a convenient label to apply to financial irregularities as well as political disturbances. Towards the end of 1731, an insurance fraud was perpetrated by John Thomson and a few associates in the Charitable Company of London. Thomson, who was a warehouse keeper, absconded with funds rumoured to be as much as £80,000, though half this sum would be a more than generous estimate, with £25,000 probably being nearer the mark. Thomson, from a mercantile family in Edinburgh, went first to Paris and duly turned up in Rome by May 1732, which fuelled rumours within British diplomatic circles that his embezzled funds would finance Jacobite plotting to restore the exiled Stuarts. Monitoring of Thomson's movements ended in September with the realization that his family's extensive mercantile links from Lisbon in Portugal and Alicante in Spain to (St) Petersburg in Russia were primarily concerned with trade.

Not the Jacobites but the emergent Patriot party was the main beneficiary of British government overreaction to rioting and fraud. The party, which drew support from all three kingdoms and the American colonies, was intent on the pursuit of probity in public life during the particularly corrupt tenure of Sir Robert Walpole, who had become

Britain's first prime minister in the wake of the South Sea Bubble. Among the Scots who identified as Patriots opposed to Walpole's manipulation of place and profit on behalf of the Whig ascendancy were John Dalrymple, 2nd Earl of Stair, a military commander turned diplomat; James Erskine, Lord Grange, a prominent member of the Scottish judiciary and brother of John, 6th Earl of Mar, who had led the Fifteen; and Andrew Buchanan, a prominent transatlantic trader and a funder of nonjuring Episcopalianism who became lord provost of Glasgow. Polemicists favourable to Walpole attacked the Patriots as 'apostate Whigs' embroiled in the schemes of the Jacobites. Unlike the Jacobites, however, the Patriots sought to strengthen not to sunder the Union.

They opened a new phase of anti-Jacobite polemics in targeting the clans whom General Wade had sought to contain through a building programme for roads, bridges and fortifications. An Ayrshire laird (landowner), William Logan of Logan, claimed in 1733 that clansmen were on the side of popery and slavery, and kept there by the feudal superiorities and heritable jurisdictions of their chiefs and leading clan gentry. Notwithstanding that few chiefs had regalities, stewartries or heritable sheriffships which operated independently of royal courts, Logan was deliberately confusing institutional with personal authority: a stance subsequently taken up and embellished by Sir Alexander Murray of Stanhope, an active Jacobite in the shire of Peebles during the Fifteen. Having acquired a forfeited Jacobite estate in the West Highlands on the Ardnamurchan peninsula in 1722, he attempted to demonstrate exemplary landed enterprise through extractive industries linked to canal building. His timber, lead and copper mining endeavours met with blatant and even violent obstruction from clansmen Macleans, MacLachlans and especially Camerons, all incorrigible Jacobites unwilling to accept removal from their traditional lands for a migrant workforce. Their behaviour allegedly confirmed that heritable jurisdictions in the Highlands were abused by the clan elite to keep their lands and people in a state of slavery and misery compounded by barrenness, theft and robbery. This claim was made in a pamphlet of 1740, which proposed that the Union of Scotland and England be extended not only to Ireland but to all the British colonies in America. To facilitate this and resolve his local difficulties, he advocated that all Highlanders be transported to the West Indies to strengthen the colonies. The Highlands should be repopulated with industrious and laborious people from the southern parts of Great Britain.

Clans prepared to support the Forty-Five were entirely ignorant of the principles of religion and virtue, claimed an anonymous gentleman from Edinburgh, taken aback by the audacity of Prince Charles Edward Stuart's landing in the Highlands in the late summer of 1745. Their idleness, poverty and preference for the Gaelic over the English language gave them an imperfect grasp of liberty. Brought up in support of tyranny and arbitrary government, and dependent upon support from foreign papists, clans were the source of all the rebellions and insurrections since the Revolution. However, their supplies of fish, timber and black cattle offered a considerable accession of power and wealth to Great Britain, especially if their martial vigour could be redeployed from Jacobite to Hanoverian service. An attempt had already been made in this direction with the formation of the Black Watch as a regiment of foot in 1739 from the Independent Highland Companies reinvigorated by General Wade to patrol the Highland–Lowland peripheries to contain thefts of livestock and other bandit activities (usually undertaken sporadically by cateran bands rather than systematically by clans). However, well-founded fears within the regiment on being taken to London that they were to be transported overseas, either to North America or to continental theatres of war, had led the Black Watch to mutiny in 1743. Although the Black Watch were to be brought back from Flanders in November 1745, trust in their loyalty to Hanoverian Britain was undermined by continuous desertions from Scottish regiments in Dutch service to join the Jacobite forces then advancing into England. The Black Watch were confined to barracks outside London at Camberwell, where their chaplain, Adam Ferguson, later a leading figure in the Scottish Enlightenment, preached to them on the virtues of British civil and religious liberties over clannish affinities to Jacobitism:

> Every subject of Britain enjoys all the Advantages that arise from a well-ordered state, and . . . this good Order of Government is in danger of being subverted unless we exert ourselves in its Support.

> If any Man is insensible of the Advantages we Enjoy as Subjects of Britain it must be owing to his want of Experience, and his being a Stranger to Oppression.[2]

This sermon, which was translated into English for publication, was preached on 18 December, thirteen days after the Jacobite Army had commenced its retreat from England. It was preceded by two other sermons of note from Scottish Presbyterians. David Plenderleith, minister of Ormiston in East Lothian, had recourse on 8 November to a well-worn Whig trope in describing the Forty-Five as an 'unnatural rebellion', carried on mainly by Highland clans who had already threatened great devastation since their seizure of Edinburgh. They were now on their way to England intent on subverting religion, property and enterprise and destroying the free and wise constitution that Britain has enjoyed since the Revolution. Coinciding with the withdrawal of the Jacobite Army from England, James How, from Blackfriars Church in Glasgow, railed against sedition and rebellion on 6 December. Jacobites from North Britain had perpetrated civil war for a degenerate cause. They were mainly desperate men of sinking fortunes oppressively intent on imposing misery, slavery and destruction on Great Britain and Ireland. No true Briton could support a 'Popish Pretender'. English sermons of thanksgiving for deliverance from enemy hands gained momentum from the Jacobite retreat from Stirling in February 1746. The emphatic Jacobite defeat at Culloden on 16 April 1746 occasioned a plethora of sermons published in London extolling victory over the rebels. Sermons giving thanks for deliverance were issued on behalf of Anglicans, English Dissenters and Scottish Presbyterians, a practice extended to the American colonies with prominent preachers having their thoughts published in Boston and Philadelphia in the run-up to 9 October, the day for a general thanksgiving prescribed by the British government. Some sermons were notably pejorative, claiming that rebellion and treachery had been defeated by bravery and courage; others called for retribution, stressing the lawfulness of making destruction on George II's enemies and that suppression was a proper improvement for savage Highlanders.

In addition to the proliferation of sermons for Whig thanksgiving, there was an increased output on the Jacobite side of purported speeches from the scaffold in defence of the exiled Stuarts, religious persuasions and commitment to country. In part, this can be attributed to the greater number of executions after the Forty-Five – 120 as against 6 in the Fifteen – but also to Jacobites publishing the purported thoughts of the condemned from papers they had submitted to the sheriffs who presided over their execution. The first published scaffold statement of note was that of Sir William Parkins, executed in London for his involvement in the assassination plot against William of Orange in 1696. He died a committed Anglican, persuaded of the justice of the cause of James II and his duty as an Englishman to aid the exiled king's restoration. The two peers executed after the Fifteen, in February 1716, were held to have boldly affirmed the Jacobite cause and their respective commitments: James Radcliffe, 3rd Earl of Derwentwater, to Roman Catholicism and Northumberland and William Gordon, 6th Viscount Kenmure, to non-juring Episcopalianism and Galloway. Their oratory, particularly that of the more charismatic and unapologetic Derwentwater, reportedly swayed the crowd witnessing their execution on to their side, much to the concern of the magistrates. Crowd control was more evident in executions in the aftermath of the Forty-Five. The *Scots Magazine* provided extensive accounts of the speeches made at the joint trial of Arthur Elphinstone, 6th Earl of Balmerino, and William Boyd, 2nd Earl of Kilmarnock, whereas the *London Magazine and Monthly Chronicler* for August 1746 reported merely that the pair justified their military conduct as Jacobites and exonerated each other from any involvement in atrocities.

Balmerino, a far more ideologically committed Jacobite than the pragmatic Kilmarnock, was responding to a claim, initially slipped into the same newspaper on 25 April, that the Jacobite orders issued on the eve of the battle of Culloden instructed both foot and horse to give no quarter to the Hanoverian troops. This denial of quarter under any circumstances was a deliberate falsification by the Hanoverian army's high command to justify the slaughter of wounded Jacobites, especially clansmen, either as they lay on the field or as they attempted to escape from Culloden. This black propaganda was subsequently circulated in newspapers throughout Britain and its American colonies. In the interim, Balmerino had stopped his coach to buy gooseberries at Charing

Cross when returning to the Tower of London after hearing his death sentence at Westminster.

The most spirited speech from the scaffold was delivered at Penrith on 28 October 1746 by David Hume, the brother of the laird of Manderston in Berwickshire. He had been captured at Culloden along with his younger cousin, William Hume of Broomhouse, who had joined the Jacobite forces at Edinburgh when not quite fourteen years of age on the promise of a fine uniform and the role of a standard bearer, which he had fulfilled at the battles of Falkirk and Culloden. Both Humes were tried and convicted of treason at Carlisle, but the younger William was still languishing in jail in August 1747 pending his inclusion in an indemnity for his youthful indiscretions. David Hume, in an unrepentant speech from the scaffold addressed to 'My Dear Countrymen', upheld the hereditary succession of the Stuarts, whose removal at the Revolution had led to the heaviest load of oppression and tyranny to be inflicted upon Scotland. He affirmed that he had embraced the Jacobite interest frankly and cheerfully, 'with my Sword in one hand and my Heart in the other'.[3]

The most eloquent defence of Scottish Episcopalianism came at the execution of Robert Lyon at Penrith in October 1746. Sharing the same fate as Lyon from Forfar in Angus was another nonjuring priest acting as an army chaplain, Thomas Coppock, one of the 24 officers and men executed from the Manchester Regiment, nine of whom had their last letters sold by publishers and pamphlet sellers in London. The last Jacobite execution in Britain was of Dr Archibald Cameron, a brother of the chief of Clan Cameron, a veteran of the Forty-Five and subsequently a close political associate of Prince Charles Edward Stuart in exile. He was executed in June 1753 for his involvement in the Elibank Plot, which projected a rising in the Highlands to facilitate a *coup d'état* in London in which the Hanoverian royal family was to be assassinated. This, the last of the Jacobite plots, was finalized by Alexander Murray, from the noble house of Elibank in the Scottish Borders, who had joined Prince Charles in exile after his political agitation against electoral patronage in London faced punitive reprisals. The Elibank Plot was condoned by Prince Charles and sought to attract military support from Prussia. Not only did this fail to materialize, but the Highland rising never got off the ground and the English Jacobites backed off. Dr Cameron was arrested by government forces in his native Lochaber and brought to London for trial. Although he was denied paper to write to the sheriff of Middlesex before his execution, he put down his last thoughts on scraps of paper which his wife smuggled out of the Tower and gave to sympathetic printers. His unstinting commitment to Jacobitism was delivered to at least five printing firms for prompt publication.

The Elibank Plot and Dr Cameron's last thoughts demonstrated that the Jacobite cause in the aftermath of Culloden was not yet redundant or defunct. It did derive a limited measure of public sympathy from the conspicuous and wanton destruction of life and livelihoods unleashed by the victor, William Augustus, Duke of Cumberland, which polarized public opinion as to whether this younger son of George II was a conquering hero or a psychopathic butcher. Reminiscences of apologists and participants, some of which were not published until several years after the battle, were complemented by lively debates in British newspapers and journals on whether to bring an end to reprisals targeted particularly against the clans. Views for and against were collated in the *Scots Magazine* for October and November 1746, which reproduced a contribution to the *Craftsman*, a London newspaper favourable to the Patriot party: 'How ill-designing against our government must those people appear, who advise or wish to multiply slaughter, and kill those people in cold blood? Kill them! For what?'[4]

Considerably less favourable to Jacobitism and more than hinting, if not heralding, its passing was the trend towards writing histories rather than memoirs or narratives of the risings. This trend, initiated in the aftermath of the Fifteen, was undoubtedly polemical. *The History of the Late Rebellion* (1717) was written by Robert Patten, an Anglican curate at Allendale in Northumberland, who had led a party of local volunteers, supplemented by Scots, to join up with the Earl of Derwentwater and Thomas Forster, MP for Northumberland, who were leading the rising in the north of England. But after his capture in the aftermath of the Jacobite defeat at Preston in November 1716, he offered to turn king's evidence against his associates and became a vociferous anti-Jacobite. His first edition was subsequently enlarged, and two further editions were published in support of the Hanoverians during the Forty-Five.

Peter Rae, a printer and Presbyterian minister in and around Dumfries who specialized in religious tracts and chapbooks containing ballads, folk tales and popular histories, researched, wrote and published *The History of the Rebellion rais'd against His Majesty King George I by the Friends of the Popish Pretender* (1718). Although Viscount Kenmure raised forces for the Jacobites in Dumfries, the town and shire were on the fringes of the rising. Rae was not himself actively involved. But his work was also republished for the Whig ascendancy in 1746.

James Wray from Whitehaven described himself as an 'Egyptian', presumably for his activities as freelance undercover agent monitoring the progression of the Jacobite forces into England in 1745 before he joined up with Cumberland in the Midlands. Having fought at Culloden, he promptly published a pamphlet entitled the 'Acts of the Rebels', which he enlarged into *A Compleat History of the Rebellion, from its first Rise in MDCCXLV, to its total Suppression at the Glorious Battle of Culloden, in April 1746* (1750); it passed through nine editions by 1760. Dugald Graham from Stirling, a prolific author of chapbooks – coarsely bound reading material for a popular market – had embedded himself with the Jacobite Army as a non-combatant during the Forty-Five. His *A Full, Particular and True Account of the Rebellion in the Years 1745–46*, published in late 1746, was primarily concerned with reporting rather than editorializing the campaign, and went to a second edition in 1752. His third edition of 1774 was enlarged and republished as *The History of the Rise, Progress and Extinction of the Rebellion in Scotland, in the Years 1745 and 1746*. Graham, now the town crier of Glasgow, was notably sympathetic to the hardships the Young Pretender suffered after the battle of Culloden until his escape to France by October. John Hume, who served as a volunteer against the Jacobites, first for Edinburgh students and then as an officer for Glasgow, went on to become a Presbyterian minister, and subsequently a playwright and man of letters closely associated with leading figures of the Scottish Enlightenment. *The History of the Rebellion in the Year 1745*, which he began in 1746, lay dormant for three decades, and his endeavours were not published until 1802. His scholarly approach endorsed the main thrust of Whig polemics after Culloden, contrasting progressive support for British patriotism, based on union and empire, with regressive Jacobite engagement in the cause of the exiled Stuarts. In doing so, Hume not only took advantage of hindsight, but set the benchmark for Whig polemics masquerading as history.

## Promoting the Courts in Exile

British historiography, from the eighteenth century even to the present day, has been heavily influenced by Whig polemicists who viewed the Revolution as 'Glorious' for its constitutional settlement promoting Protestantism, property and progress. Certainly, James VII & II, a convert to Roman Catholicism and a close ally of Louis XIV of France, was no great supporter of constitutional assemblies in Church and State, was not averse to the suppression of religious dissent by militant Protestants and was much inclined to commercial constraints, especially on overseas trade. However, the proclaimed achievement of constitutional monarchy in place of autocracy glossed over the continuation of the fiscal-military state instigated in the Stuart dominions beyond England in the later seventeenth century: a state with standing forces supplemented by shire militias that was sustained by taxation exacted, if necessary, by these same forces. The removal of commercial constraints, which ostensibly laid the foundations for the expansive British Empire in the eighteenth century, entrenched oligarchic power that was bolstered by ecclesiastical establishments that were far from accepting of religious pluralism. Moreover, British imperialism was moderated, not constrained, by parliamentary votes of supply, and fructified by the creation of the National Debt in 1693 that financed military engagements overseas while finance at home was regulated through the Bank of England from 1694. The English notion of the sovereignty of the Crown in Parliament triumphed over Scottish claims for rights of the commonwealth over the Crown and Irish aspirations to be delivered from constitutional if not colonial subjection. These purported attainments were consolidated by the Hanoverian succession in 1714, which facilitated a political ascendancy of Whig interests that endured until challenged by the American Revolution in 1775.

Despite Jacobitism outlasting the Whig ascendancy, the norms of Whig historiography remain commonplace with respect to the cause of the exiled Stuarts. They are deemed to be Pretenders, not the rightful claimants to the three kingdoms. Risings on their behalf are castigated as rebellions against legitimate government. As the antithesis to the patriotic and progressive development of Britain and its global empire, Jacobites have been decried as opportunist hijackers of national grievances or as deluded individuals prone to foibles rather than purposeful action, and generally out of touch with the silent majority in their pursuit of personal gain through insurrection. In particular, the association of clans with Jacobitism had been attributed to mercenary impulses, feuding and banditry. The last clan battle to settle a feud occurred just before the Revolution, at Mulroy on the Braes of Lochaber on 4 August 1688, between the Clan Chattan and the MacDonalds of Keppoch, both of whom became active Jacobites in the rising of 1689–91, by which time banditry was predominantly the activity of cateran bands that operated on the margins of clanship.

In substance and on principle, Jacobite support within the three kingdoms remained traditionally based on dynastic legitimacy, confessional allegiances and patriotism, especially enhanced in Scotland by opposition to the incorporating union with England in 1707. Notwithstanding a historiographical focus on the courts in exile, diplomacy and political clientage in Jacobite as well as Whig historiography, Jacobitism was not a homogenous movement. It was a distinctive development in all three kingdoms that had little common cause other than a wish to restore the Stuarts to their rightful thrones. Diverse international recognition from France, the papacy, Sweden, Spain, Poland-Lithuania, Russia, Bavaria and Prussia gave continuous credibility to Jacobitism. These countries also provided employment and succour to Jacobites forced into exile after failed risings and plots. But so too did Denmark-Norway and the Dutch Republic, which provided military assistance to William of Orange and the Hanoverians. Diplomatic engagement with the courts in exile was unreliable, manipulative and expendable. British governments not only were adept at intercepting letters to and from Jacobites through the postal services, but could depend on the haemorrhaging of information about Jacobite activities through espionage and double agents, as well as through leading Jacobites turning king's evidence against their erstwhile colleagues to safeguard their own lives and fortunes. The most egregious example of the latter informant was

John Murray of Broughton, a laird from the shire of Peebles. From 1740, he was the official correspondent between the Scottish Jacobites and the Charles court in exile in Rome. He subsequently served as chancellor to Prince Edward Stuart during the Forty-Five. He wrote his memoirs around 1757, primarily to vindicate himself from being a turncoat. Some informers were never unmasked in their own lifetimes. The Elibank Plot of 1753 was exposed to the British government by Pickle the Spy, reputedly Alexander MacDonnell of Glengarry, chief of a clan with a strong Jacobite pedigree. Suspicions about his duplicitous conduct, substantiated in the mid-nineteenth century, were not generally accepted by antiquarians sympathetic to Clan Donald.

Of greater significance than international backing for Jacobitism was the sustained assistance provided to British governments by factional infighting among European powers offering expedient support to the exiled Stuarts. For the French in particular, Jacobitism was a useful tool with which to embarrass British governments. But they were reluctant to mount and sustain a full-scale invasion, fearing that if the Jacobite cause was successful, the Stuarts would perpetuate British imperial expansion. Indeed, after the death of Louis xiv, the government of France passed to Philippe, Duke of Orléans, a younger son who on becoming regent withheld support for the rising of 1715. In a further effort to gain British recognition for his claim to be heir-apparent to the French throne, Regent Orléans sent over troops to oppose the Spanish-sponsored rising in 1719. Orléans also had the Jacobite court expelled from France. Its subsequent re-establishment at Rome, with pensions from the papacy, was essentially a propaganda exercise. Papal support was intended as much to disconcert France as to succour the Catholic Stuarts. Louis xiv had promoted Gallican autonomy as a counter to the Ultramontane centralizing authority of Rome. James vii & ii's support for Gallicanism had alienated the papacy, which had backed William of Orange at the Revolution. After the death of James viii & iii in 1766, no papal recognition was forthcoming for Prince Charles Edward Stuart, who remained an uncrowned king. Probably the most blatant factional indiscretion occurred when France was attempting to get concerted Spanish and Swedish support in 1741 for another campaign for the court in exile in Rome. Elizabeth Farnese, Queen of Spain, fearing that her country would thereby become a French satellite, took out an advertisement in the *Amsterdam Gazette* to expose the French designs on Britain. In the last fling of this diplomatic sideshow to support plots and risings, Prince Charles Edward Stuart was not actively consulted in 1759 when French plans to invade Britain during the Seven Years War came to grief at Quiberon Bay, where the progress of their fleet across the Channel was arrested by the Royal Navy.

Historiographical preoccupations about rivalries within the courts in exile have derailed considerations about the effectiveness of their liaison with the constituent kingdoms of the British Isles. Scots were initially well placed at the court of Saint-Germain, with their leading actors being the Drummond brothers: John, 4th Earl of Perth and William, 1st Earl of Melfort. Both had converted to Catholicism before the Revolution to affirm their loyalty to James VII & II. Melfort, made duke in the Jacobite peerage, became principal secretary of state to James VII & II at Saint-Germain in 1691 and the dominant presence pushing for a French invasion of England in 1692 that was terminated by Anglo-Dutch naval victory off La Hogue. Melfort's subsequent loss of support at the French court was compounded by his reluctance to compromise on the royal prerogative and Roman Catholicism, which marked him as a non-compounder at Saint-Germain. Concerned that his intransigence would make a restoration impossible, his English critics gained a powerful voice at Saint-Germain after Charles Middleton, 2nd Earl of Middleton, arrived from England to become a joint secretary of state in 1693. Middleton's position as the pragmatic leader of the compounders was further strengthened in 1694 when Louis XIV requested Melville's removal from office. Melfort retained the confidence of James VII & II but was obliged to withdraw from Saint-Germain. He was partially rehabilitated by James VIII & III in 1705, but was unable to participate in the minor rising in 1708. In the meantime, his brother, Perth, elevated to duke in the Jacobite peerage, had been appointed governor to James while Prince of Wales in 1698. Perth was the main supplier of contacts for Captain Nathaniel Hooke on his journeys to Scotland between 1703 and 1708. Indeed, Hooke's reliance on contacts in the noble houses of Gordon, Marischal and Erroll, all connected by marriage to that of Perth, made it appear that he was acting for the Drummond interest at the court in exile rather than Louis XIV of France, who was his principal sponsor, or, indeed, of Louis' client, James VIII & III. Although Perth did support James in his unsuccessful attempt to invade Scotland in 1708, he felt particularly neglected at Saint-Germain after 1694 when the English Catholic John Caryll, created 1st Lord Caryll of Durford in the Jacobite peerage, was confirmed as joint secretary of state with Middleton.

Perth, who lived to witness the failure of the Fifteen, was the first prominent Jacobite to claim that, after the death of James VII & II in 1701, the courts in exile tended to give less weight to Scottish over English and Irish influences and personalities, notwithstanding the disproportionate contribution of Scots to subsequent major and minor risings. But this claim mainly has force in relation to principal courtiers connected to leading noble families, such as the Drummonds. Certainly, when James VIII & III moved from Saint-Germain to Lorraine, Avignon, Urbino and then to Rome in the wake of the Fifteen, some of his principal Scottish adherents preferred to stay at Paris, where their activities were monitored if not always managed by the Irish military veteran General Arthur Dillon, who had fought in French service in the Nine Years War and the War of the Spanish Succession. Dillon was notably active in preparations at Saint-Germain for the Fifteen and (as ambassador in Paris to the French court for James VIII & III) was cognisant of the Swedish Plot in 1717 and charged to lead the invasion of England if the Atterbury Plot of 1722 had succeeded.

Growing frustrations among Scottish Jacobites at home and abroad that were to build up over the court in exile cannot credibly be attributed to a lack of a Scottish presence around the exiled Stuarts. For in the 72 years from the fall of Melfort in 1694 to the death of James VIII & III in 1766, the office of principal secretary of state was held for 53 years by Scots: that is, for 74 per cent of the time stated. Although Middleton enjoyed and largely retained the confidence of English Jacobites, he cannot be seen simply as an English presence, notwithstanding his disputes with Melville and Perth. It must be remembered that Middleton was a Scottish peer whose financial security continued to be based on his inherited estates in Angus and the Mearns. Much of his early career was spent in exile in continental theatres of war. He did marry into the

English aristocracy and was a confirmed Anglican until converting to Roman Catholicism in 1700. It was not his standing as an Anglo-Scot but his acceptability at the French court of Louis XIV that sustained his official position. Sole secretary of state after the death of Caryll in 1711, Middleton accompanied James VIII & III to participate belatedly in the Fifteen, but his influence had waned by 1719 after the arrival at the court in exile of James Erskine, Earl of Mar, who had led the second major Jacobite rising to defeat.

Mar's arrival sidelined not only Middleton but Henry St John, Viscount Bolingbroke, who had fled England in the wake of the Hanoverian succession to become the main planner for the Fifteen. His return to England and his securing a pardon served as an exemplar for Mar's future conduct at the courts in exile between 1716 and 1724. St John had worked well with James Butler, 2nd Duke of Ormonde, an Anglo-Irish noble who had supported the Revolution, served Queen Anne occasionally as Lord Lieutenant of Ireland and, after he was impeached and attainted for his opposition to the Hanoverian succession, became the most prominent English Jacobite in exile. But projected risings in the south as well as the north of England were never properly co-ordinated with that in Scotland under Mar. As principal secretary, Mar blamed Bolingbroke for the failure of the Fifteen and sought to purge the growing number of exiles who had taken refuge at the Stuart court. His partiality for his own relations first aroused suspicions about the probity of his dealings on the part of Ormonde and the most accomplished if not the most prominent Scottish exile from the Fifteen: George Keith, 10th Earl Marischal. Mar's endeavours to support the Swedish Plot of 1717 and subsequently to establish contact with Peter the Great of Russia proved fruitless. His divisions with Ormond and Marischal after their despatch to Madrid severely constrained Spanish support in 1719, turning plans for a major invasion of Britain under Ormonde into a minor rising with Marischal initially in charge. However, Mar, now ensconced in Rome, did not resist the overtures of the Scottish rump of exiles in and around Paris to have one of their number, William Murray, Marquess of Tullibardine, share the command. Although Tullibardine's elevation was not opposed by General Dillon, his joint command with Marischal was a major contribution to the eventual failure of the rising.

At the same time, Mar, who was continuously short of financial resources, had opened back channels of communication with the British ambassador in Paris and long-standing Scottish acquaintance, John Dalrymple, 2nd Earl of Stair. Mar's duplicity in pursuit of a pardon from George I was exposed by his leaking of the Atterbury Plot, especially after Francis Atterbury, Bishop of Rochester, came to Rome and firmed up his correspondence with the Earl Marischal, now ambassador for James VIII & III at the Spanish court. In receipt only of a partial pardon, Mar continued in exile when dismissed from Jacobite circles at Rome in 1724. Although he fleetingly proposed a union of Ireland and Scotland based on their common Celtic culture, his remaining eight years after his enforced retirement were taken up with architectural projects ranging from imaginative garden designs for his forfeited property in Alloa through visionary proposals for a Forth–Clyde canal to his ornate plan for a new town in Edinburgh and a grand palace in London to honour a Stuart restoration.

Mar's downfall was also expedited by John Hay of Cromlix (Duke of Inverness in the Jacobite peerage), by his wife Marjorie, a daughter of the Jacobite-inclined David Murray, 5th Earl of Stormont, and her brother, James Murray (Earl of Dunbar in the Jacobite peerage). Hay of Cromlix, who had been a commander in the Fifteen, was also brother-in-law of Mar, while James Murray had been a close ally of Bolingbroke. Both Inverness and Dunbar would serve as secretary of state, the former for three years after Mar and latter for twenty years from 1727. Marjorie Murray had initially become a close confidant of Clementina, daughter of the Polish prince, James Sobieski, after she married James VIII & III in 1719. However, the highly strung Clementina was to blame the subsequent crisis in their marriage to an affair between her husband and Marjorie Murray: an affair more fabled than substantiated. With papal backing for Clementina, James moved his court from Rome to Bologna from 1726 to 1729. Hay resigned as secretary in 1727 but remained close to James VIII & III. Reconciliation was a tortured process that taxed the philosophical bent of Alexander Forbes, Lord Forbes of Pitsligo, an occasional Jacobite courtier after the failure of the Fifteen and a religious ecumenical who tempered his Scottish Episcopalianism with Flemish mysticism. Inverness and his wife converted to Roman Catholicism in 1731, an acknowledgement that reconciliation had been achieved. Nevertheless, Inverness was not a functioning member of the court in exile until Clementina died in 1736. In the interim, and with international backing for Jacobitism effectively dormant, James VIII & III drew upon his wife's family connections to consider standing for the elective kingship of the Polish-Lithuanian Commonwealth in 1734. But speculation within the Jacobite court in exile gained no international traction from France or Austria, the most significant electoral influencers, nor from the nobility who constituted the Commonwealth's electorate.

Inverness was obliged to remove to Avignon in 1740, as his presence was seen as particularly challenging to Dunbar's continuance as principal secretary. Dunbar had commenced his political career as MP for the shire of Dumfries in 1710, moving to the court in exile at Saint-Germain with his Tory mentor Bolingbroke in the wake of the Hanoverian succession. Having aligned himself with Mar, he returned covertly to London in 1718 as the Jacobite agent charged to co-ordinate the correspondence between the court in exile (now in Urbino) and leading Jacobites in England and Scotland – a task in which he proved more acerbic than effective. On his return to the court as it moved from Urbino to Rome, he built up his influence as governor, first to the Jacobite heir-apparent, Prince Charles Edward, and then to his brother, Prince Henry Benedict. His twenty-year tenure of the office of principal secretary from 1727 was marked by the steady deterioration of his occasionally violent relationship with Prince Charles Edward. Yet in the aftermath of the Forty-Five, amid not entirely unfounded rumours of a growing split between Prince Charles and his father, Dunbar's vigorous defence of the prince's wayward behaviour, which the French court deemed irresponsible, led to his dismissal by James VIII & III in 1747. He also retired to Avignon where he remained despite his belated conversion to Roman Catholicism in 1751. Two more Scots served briefly and successively as principal secretary: James Edgar, 1763–4, and Andrew Lumisden, 1764–8. Both had served as private secretaries to James VIII & III in an unbroken line of Scots that stretched back to Sir David Nairne enrolling in the service of James VII & II in 1691. The actual dismissal of Lumisden by Prince Charles Edward in 1768, two years after the death of his father and the refusal of the papacy to recognize him as Charles III, signified his personal recognition that the Jacobite cause was now a diplomatic and military irrelevance.

This recognition had been foreshadowed by the gradual but irrevocable alienation of the Earl Marischal from the court in exile in Rome. Marischal had declined to serve as commander-in-chief in Scotland after a planned but abandoned French invasion of Britain in 1744, having become convinced that Prince Charles Edward was a rash adventurer. Although he was integrally involved in negotiations at the French court in Versailles to launch the Forty-Five, he took no part in the last major rising. In 1749, he rejected an offer to serve Prince Charles as his secretary of state. Having moved to the court of Frederick II of Prussia, he agreed to meet with the prince at Potsdam to promote the Jacobite cause, but he prioritized his own departure to Paris as Prussian ambassador to France. In 1753, shrewdly questioning the commitment of the English Jacobites, he effectively terminated Prussian engagement in the Elibank Plot. Stating that his services were now entirely at the disposal of Frederick II, Marischal refused any further meeting with Prince Charles in 1754. He went on to become Prussian ambassador to Spain in 1759. After he informed the Whig government of Spanish preparations to enter the Seven Years War on the side of France against Britain and Prussia, he received a pardon for his past Jacobitism from George II.

## Disparate Endeavours

Scottish frustrations with the courts in exile had less to do with any lack of controlling interest than with the energies wasted on courtier intrigues that could have been applied more productively and purposefully to advancing the Jacobite cause in war and peace. Not only was there a persistent and patent lack of co-ordination between the courts in exile and the three kingdoms, but there was a persistent and patent lack of co-ordination between Jacobites in Ireland, in England and in Scotland. A further complication for the co-ordination of Jacobite endeavours by the courts in exile was the comparative standing of the cause in the three kingdoms.

Although Ireland was the primary theatre for Jacobite military operations only in the 1690s, Irish Jacobites remained consistently well represented overseas, a situation attributable primarily to the international connections of the Catholic clergy, but also supported by the Irish brigades in the military service of France and Spain and Irish commercial networks throughout Western Europe. Irish brigades in Spanish service did feature peripherally in the minor rising in 1719 and provided a limited but effective military presence as professional troops released from France in the Forty-Five. Analysis of Irish Jacobitism has until recently suffered from the apparent finality of the first rising and its subsequent suppression by the ruling English interest, acting as an Anglican ascendancy for its enforcement of a Protestant supremacy in governance. Catholics were rigorously excluded from power in Ireland. Yet Irish Jacobitism was sustained covertly by the Catholic clergy, by the vernacular Gaelic poets and by sympathetic members of the landed and mercantile elites. Gaelic Ireland especially continued to dream of deliverance through Jacobitism well into the eighteenth century. A less convincing aspect of Irish Jacobitism was the prevalence of rapparees who used the mantle of the cause as cover for their predatory activities as bandits, which were not confined to reprisals against members of the Anglican ascendancy.

At the other end of the social spectrum, Anglo-Irish nobles such as the Duke of Ormonde, as well as English peers such as Viscount Bolingbroke, were key figures periodically at the courts in exile, which became a bolthole for political opportunists thrown out of office in England. Their prominence in the counsels of the exiled monarchy stood in marked contrast to marginal English involvement in the major Jacobite risings. Anglocentric revisionists have tended to become embroiled in the parliamentary enumeration of Jacobite influence among the Tories, as the principal party interest opposed to the Whig ascendancy. The fluid political structure of party and patronage promoted in British polemics has been translated into parliamentary historiography as a peripheral debate about the extent to which Jacobites and Tories were compatible as unplaced political interests. Parliamentary agents for English Jacobites were notably prone to accepting blandishments for place and profit, particularly during the political hegemony of the Whig prime minister Sir Robert Walpole. More substantively, Jacobitism has been identified as a significant, if disruptive, aspect of

English political culture. The plethora of clubs, societies and associations for improvement and learning, welfare and conviviality even suggests that England had a distinctive Jacobite political culture. Large groups of armed gangs engaged in smuggling along the eastern and southern seaboards highlight its clandestine element. English Jacobitism certainly has attracted more attention for its drunken conviviality than its campaigning potency. England, particularly London, remained the focus of Jacobite plotting. But English involvement in the Fifteen was noted more for its disruptive than its harmonious contribution on the Borders. English troops were recruited in Manchester in the Forty-Five, an occurrence mainly commemorated for the use of ladies paid for pleasure in the recruitment process being translated into the Scottish country dance the Dashing White Sergeant.

There was political substance to the appeal of Jacobitism in Scotland that was not replicated in Ireland or England. After 1689–91, Scots formed the bedrock of Jacobite forces in the next four risings. Between the attempted assassination of William of Orange in 1692 and the Elibank Plot in 1753, Scots were involved in another five plots to effect changes of government. The Highland clans remained the main military source of Scottish support for the exiled Stuarts and bore the brunt of the fighting and dying in the front lines during the risings. However, Jacobitism had vitality in Scotland north of the Tay, not just in the Highlands. Recruitment patterns, prisoner lists, protest songs, papers from agents, accounts and ledgers of merchant houses, and subscription lists to historical and religious books demonstrate that Jacobitism was a sustained national endeavour. But Scottish Jacobites were also afflicted by distinctive organizational, ideological and campaigning problems that debilitated their disparate endeavours to restore the exiled Stuarts.

# 2

# Scottish Jacobitism

Split centres of power between the courts in exile and each of the three kingdoms compounded distrust rather than promoted harmony within Jacobite circles. More so than in Ireland and England, Scotland – as the main launching pad for risings – was over-reliant on agents who tended to be of dubious political provenance or of extremely doubtful repute. This had profound consequences for Jacobitism in peace and war. At the same time, ideological and political differences between Jacobites and Whigs caused Scotland to erupt periodically in civil war during the Revolution, the Fifteen and the Forty-Five. The polarizing impact of Jacobitism over six decades impacted throughout Scottish society. Not only were families divided, but they frequently switched sides and were increasingly drawn to neutrality. Differing campaign strategies also reflected inherent tensions within Scottish Jacobitism. Dynastic and confessional objectives, shared with Irish and English proponents of restoration for the exiled Stuarts, lost ground to the distinctive Scottish promotion of patriotism fuelled by the making of the Union in 1707 and sustained by its subsequent management in the first half of the eighteenth century.

### Jacobite Organization: Agents and Agencies

Only Scotland within the three kingdoms had central agencies to co-ordinate parliamentary and extra-parliamentary activity. Despite their failure to prevent James VII from being forfeited in 1689, the Jacobites maintained an overt presence in the Scottish Estates after the Revolution. Although they associated with the Country party, created to obtain reparations from William of Orange for his maladroit handling of the Darien scheme, their parliamentary performance was noted more for shifting alliances than the pursuit of principled opposition: a feature particularly evident in the parliamentary session which enacted the Union in 1706–7. A small cohesive grouping associated with Charles Hay, 13th Earl of Errol, and William Keith, 9th Earl Marischal, voted consistently against Union as antipathetical both to Scottish independence and to principles of constitutional reform. However, a larger grouping led by John, Duke of Atholl became exasperated with James, Duke of Hamilton's intent to oppose the accomplishment of political incorporation. They abstained in protest when the treaty was eventually ratified – despite their initial vote against the principle of Union. Indeed, throughout the last parliamentary session, these Jacobites exhibited a high indulgence in cross-party voting and limited enthusiasm for parliamentary as distinct from extra-parliamentary protest through risings and plots.

Jacobite commitment to and enthusiasm for extra-parliamentary protest in Scotland was revealed as often by informers as by the testimony and actions of instigators. The first significant revelation, in the wake of the first assassination plot against William of Orange, was made to the Scottish Privy Council by James McGill, an officer in the British forces in the Flanders theatre of the Nine Years War. McGill suggested that Jacobites in Scotland and England were operating sophisticated espionage networks using civilian and military couriers. The civilian couriers, who delivered and collected letters to and from Scottish and English Jacobites, were mainly women employed by or associates of Elizabeth Murray, dowager Countess of Lauderdale. The letters were concealed or even sewn into voluminous dresses. Some of the letters were written in lemon juice, their content only being readable when exposed to a naked flame. Letters for leading nobles and gentry were delivered to and collected from safe houses owned or rented by trusted acquaintances or servants in London, from where they were distributed to Scotland under the auspices of the Countess of Lauderdale. In one tranche, she had letters from James VII & II delivered to 36 Scottish nobles. On the Continent, letters were dispatched to drop boxes before being moved on by women couriers to Saint-Germain. The two most noted boxes were under the charge of the abbess of the English nunnery at Douai and of the abbot of the neighbouring Scots College. McGill himself was primarily a military courier carrying commissions from James VII & II for promoted posts for Scottish officers and reporting back on the inclination of others to serve the Jacobite cause. Among those whom McGill specifically named and compromised as correspondents with Saint-Germain were the military commander John Churchill, Earl (later 1st Duke) of Marlborough, and two prominent politicians, John, Earl (later 1st Duke) of Atholl, and James, Earl of Arran (later 4th Duke of Hamilton).

The last (Earl of Arran) was to be further compromised in a report of a visit to Saint-Germain by his kinsman and political associate, John Hamilton, Lord Belhaven, in the months prior to William of Orange's death in March 1702. The report by an anonymous inform- ant at the court in exile was leaked two months later to James, Duke of Queensberry, the leader of the Court party intent on promoting Union as desired by the new monarch, Queen Anne. Belhaven claimed to be acting under instructions from the Duke of Hamilton to circumvent the English Act of Settlement in 1701, which had prescribed a Hanoverian succession rather than that of the exiled Stuart Prince of Wales. In audi- ences with the Queen Mother, Mary of Modena, Belhaven claimed that the prince would be called back to Britain as James VIII & III if he would renounce Roman Catholicism and turn Protestant. As the Queen Mother was inflexible on this point, Belhaven brought into play a counter-proposal from Hamilton: if the prince would not change his confessional commitment, he would restrict himself to a small number of Catholic courtiers and counsellors and he would make a binding commitment never to attempt anything detrimental to Protestantism. Hamilton's promotion of constitutional limitations, which gave a dis- tinctive dimension to Scottish over Irish and English Jacobitism, was not sustained in the making of Union, even though the duke retained his own female courier, Lady Largo, to liaise with Saint-Germain and prominent Jacobites exiled overseas.

At the same time as their parliamentary endeavours to prevent Union and an eventual Hanoverian succession were running out of traction, the Scottish Jacobites overestimated their capacity to prevent political incorporation by extra-parliamentary means. In no small measure this was due to a military and political survey of Scotland undertaken by the resident Jacobite agent in Edinburgh, Captain Henry Straton, which he personally delivered to Saint-Germain in July 1706. According to Straton, the British forces available for the defence of Scotland in field and in garrison amounted to no more than 2,860 men, a figure matched by Jacobite forces that could be raised in the Lowlands and easily surpassed by 8,000 clansmen that could be mobilized in the Highlands. Moreover, within the military high command in Scotland and regiments of foot, cavalry and Independent Companies at their disposal, there were well-placed loyal or well-disposed officers who would take no action to resist the restoration of James VIII & III. However, Straton had conducted his survey mainly in the central Lowlands. Other than a cursory visit to Aberdeen, he had not set foot in the Jacobite heartlands of the northeast and the Highlands. His survey was no less marked by misplaced optimism. Other than Argyll, he reckoned that the majority of commissioners for the shires and burghs in the Scottish Estates were committed to the Country party, which led the opposition to Union. He went so far as to claim that most of Scotland was committed to the Jacobite interest, with only those areas under the pernicious influence of the Presbyterian ministry virulently opposed to the exiled Stuarts. Even in Fife and the western shires, a substantial number of gentry were supportive. The most militant of the Presbyterians, the Cameronians in the southwest, were prepared to rise in opposition to the Union with the Jacobites. No such conjunction occurred to seriously prevent the passage of Union in the Scottish Estates in 1706–7, despite the possibility of the Jacobites and Cameronians concerting a *coup d'état* being hyped up by Daniel Defoe and John Ker of Kersland. Defoe, the polemicist and novelist, wished to enhance his own importance as a spy for the English ministry. Kersland, from Ayrshire, wanted to demonstrate his worth as a Cameronian activist whose covert liaison with Jacobites merited reward from the Court party. Over the next two decades, Kersland was to operate as a double, if not triple, agent meandering between Hanover and the courts in exile to the detriment of Jacobitism. His wholly unreliable memoirs were published in 1727.

As evident from Kersland's career, the Jacobites were afflicted by agents provocateurs. Queensberry, as leader of the Court party, made judicious use of another Ayrshire exponent of the black arts of espionage, Major James Cunningham of Aiket, who apparently countermanded a rendezvous outside the town of Hamilton in Lanarkshire at the outset of December 1706 by an anticipated force of up to 8,000 Jacobite clansmen and militant Cameronians. Extraordinarily bad weather from the onset of winter had limited both the scope and the enthusiasm for extra-parliamentary mobilization. Disaffected tradesmen from Glasgow did issue a declaration against the Union and paid wages to those recruited for a proposed march to the Scottish Estates in Edinburgh. In the event, far fewer than five hundred men turned up in Hamilton, only for the duke to take fright at the prospect of the Estates being dissolved by force of arms. A few weeks later, Hamilton again proved an unexpected ally of the Court party. Jacobites, at the urging of George Lockhart of Carnwath, had attempted to regain the political initiative by organizing a mass lobby on the Scottish Estates by over five hundred gentry who had been party to addresses from the shires against the Union. They were to demand, as freeholders and parliamentary electors, that the Estates suspend proceedings until Queen Anne was acquainted with the extensive public antipathy towards the Union. Unwilling to admit his Jacobite machinations, Hamilton forestalled this lobby by insisting that any address to the queen must accept the Hanoverian succession.

Attending the Scottish Estates as a commissioner for Lanarkshire, Lockhart of Carnwath became the main director of covert Jacobite activities in Scotland, a position he held from 1703 until his flight to the Continent on being exposed as a leading Jacobite in 1727. Throughout this period, he was supported by the sterling endeavours of James Carnegie, a Roman Catholic priest as well connected to the ducal houses of Gordon and Hamilton as to the Earl of Mar. Based in Edinburgh, Carnegie collated military and political intelligence which was passed on through the Scots College in Paris to the courts in exile. Carnegie also acted as a postmaster for correspondence between prominent Scottish Jacobites at home and abroad. After the Union, Carnwath had enjoyed moderate success both in securing the return of Scottish Tories and in his guerrilla campaigning with British parliamentary procedures at

Westminster. In 1713, Carnwath was a leading co-ordinator of a motion to initiate proceedings to terminate the Treaty of Union, which was only lost narrowly in the House of Lords by four votes exercised through proxies. Although his parliamentary career in London was eclipsed by the Hanoverian succession, he continued to preserve a measure of coherent organization for Scottish Jacobitism despite the petering out of the Fifteen, the failure of the minor risings in 1708 and 1719, the failure of the Swedish Plot to get off the ground in 1717 and the aborting of a planned rising in 1723. Carnwath played a prominent role in convincing James VIII & III in 1720 to establish a Commission of Trustees in Scotland to promote the affairs of the exiled Stuarts. As secretary to this rather shadowy commission, he was primarily involved in reporting on internal politics rather than preparing for risings, plotting the removal of the government or capitalizing on continuing unrest with Union. The commission became embroiled in the factions surrounding the rise and fall of the secretaries of state attending the courts in exile. More damaging, as a disillusioned Lockhart diagnosed, was the failure of James VIII & III to assert his authority over factions in civil and ecclesiastical affairs.

While Lockhart of Carnwath operated primarily south of the Tay, the organizational framework for Scottish Jacobitism was also furthered by Patrick Lyon of Auchterhouse in the northeast, Colin Campbell of Glendaruel and later John Gordon of Glenbucket in the Highlands. Campbell of Glendaruel, at the behest of the Earl of Mar, discomfited and perplexed members of the judiciary administering Scotland in the wake of the Union. He did so by going round the Highlands between September 1714 and February 1715 gathering up signatures of chiefs and leading clan gentry to support the Hanoverian succession. At one level, this can be viewed as an attempt to secure loyalty payments for the clan elite. But, more plausibly, Glendaruel was wrong-footing the Scottish administration and simultaneously testing the waters for Mar's support among the clans. Following his removal from office as a Tory secretary of state for Scotland at the Hanoverian succession, Mar activated this clan support in the Fifteen. Glendaruel, who mobilized a contingent of Campbells for the Jacobite cause in 1715, was subsequently engaged in the minor rising of 1719, when he was firmly on the side of a coterie of French exiles favouring the Marquess of Tullibardine rather than the Spanish-backed Earl Marischal. Also involved in both risings was Gordon of Glenbucket, who had fought as a youth in the first rising of 1689–91. But his Jacobite engagement became rather more compromising than that of Glendaruel. For Glenbucket, a minor laird in Aberdeenshire and factor on the extensive estates of the Duke of Gordon in the Highlands and the northeast, was actively recruited as a double agent after release from imprisonment in Carlisle in 1716. Glenbucket duly provided the Hanoverian military command with regular intelligence reports in 1719, a practice also followed by the notorious Highland cattle dealer and racketeer Rob Roy MacGregor for John Campbell, 2nd Duke of Argyll, who commanded the Hanoverian forces in Scotland during the Fifteen, and his brother, Archibald Campbell, Earl of Islay (later 3rd Duke of Argyll), who became the undisputed political manager of Scotland after the Shawfield Riot of 1725. Islay passed on Rob Roy's undercover services to General Wade when he set about his programme to pacify the Highlands.

Two years after he had sold his Aberdeenshire estate, and one year after he had journeyed to Rome to ingratiate himself with James VIII & III, Glenbucket came back into Jacobite prominence in 1739. He instigated the formation of the Scottish Jacobite Association in response to the diplomatic opportunities opened up by the mounting international rivalries that led to the War of the Austrian Succession in 1740, when Britain was once again aligned against France, Sweden and Spain. The association's leading members were three lords, a clan chief and a transatlantic colonial undertaker. The lords were James Drummond, 6th Earl of Perth (and 3rd Duke of Perth in the Jacobite peerage; despite his father's attainder, he had taken on the running of his family estates in central Scotland by 1732); Charles Stuart, Lord Linton (later Earl of Traquhair), with estates in the shire of Peebles; and Simon, Lord Fraser of Lovat, who had an almost inexhaustible capacity for political intriguing, especially for linking prominent military commanders in Scotland to the courts in exile. Having used up his patronage from the Hanoverian regime, he, like Glenbucket, had reverted to Jacobitism. The chief was Donald Cameron, younger of Lochiel, whose clan was a mainstay of Jacobite risings since the Revolution. The colonial entrepreneur was Sir James Campbell of Auchinbreck, an Argyllshire laird promoting settlement in North Carolina along the Cape Fear River.

Within two years, largely under the auspices of Perth's brother and eventual successor, John Drummond, the association had negotiated successfully with Louis xv's ministers, pledging to raise 20,000 clansmen to bring about a Stuart restoration in return for support from the French king's Irish Brigade. By 1744, the Royal Scots were formed in France under the command of John Drummond, with regimental recruitment being carried out surreptitiously in Scotland. During the Forty-Five, this regiment became the backbone of the French expeditionary forces. Although the association eventually prepared the ground for the Forty-Five, as its energetic secretary, John Murray of Broughton, subsequently disclosed, liaison with the court in Rome through unreliable agents strained political credibility and severely hampered preparations. Francis Sempill, 2nd Lord Sempill in the Jacobite peerage, a Franco-Scot based in Paris, was prone to drunken conviviality that exaggerated English support for the exiled Stuarts. But the most devious agent was William Drummond of Balhaldy, the son and heir to the chief of Clan Gregor, whose duplicity in Paris and Rome was immortalized by Robert Louis Stevenson in *Kidnapped* and its sequel *Catriona*. By 1741, the Jacobite leadership in Scotland was afraid to initiate a propaganda campaign in the certainty that plans for a rising would be leaked to the British government. As agents continued to compile reports exaggerating the support for the Jacobite cause within the three kingdoms, the association waited for newspapers to authenticate reports of a projected French invasion in 1743.

Scottish Jacobites were far from a state of readiness in the run-up to the Forty-Five, notwithstanding that Prince Charles Edward Stuart had accepted a summons to the French court at the outset of 1744. Although Louis xv pulled back from a planned invasion of England in March, the prince was not deterred. Nor was he put off by the arrival in Paris that August of John Murray of Broughton, who was adamant that Scottish support for another rising was conditional on Charles bringing not only ample supplies of arms and munitions but significant French support in men and money. Prince Charles eventually landed on the isle of Eriskay in the Western Isles in summer of 1745 on a vessel chartered from Anthony Walsh, an Irish transatlantic trader based at the port of Nantes in France. He brought only seven followers, a shipload of arms and 4,000 French gold coins. He thereby set aside prophetic warnings from the association that unless he could bring 6,000 regular troops, arms for 10,000 more and 30,000 French gold pieces, it would mean ruin to himself, his supporters and the Jacobite cause.

One of Prince Charles Edward's companions to Scotland was George Kelly, an Irish nonjuror who had served intermittently as a courier for the English Jacobites to the courts in exile from 1718, a service interrupted by almost a decade in imprisonment for his involvement in the Atterbury Plot. Kelly became the principal adviser to Prince Charles after his eventual flight to France with other prominent Jacobites in the wake of Culloden. Kelly firmed up the prince's resolve that further Jacobite incursions into the three kingdoms should focus on England. Kelly was supported by the military leadership of the Irish Brigade in French service, which had decisively defeated Cumberland at Fontenoy in May 1745 and again at Laffeldt in July 1747. But he did not enjoy the support of other Irish companions of Prince Charles, notably John William O'Sullivan, the incompetent quartermaster for the Jacobite forces in the Forty-Five. Kelly was also avidly opposed by the remnants of the now defunct Jacobite Association, particularly by Donald Cameron of Lochiel, Lord Sempill and Drummond of Balhaldy. Prince Charles had sought to assuage his switch away from a Scottish theatre by suggesting that Scottish exiles in French service, such as Lochiel, should emulate the Irish and form a Scottish brigade and perhaps even another in Spain. Rather than accept the new focus on England, based largely on unsubstantiated reports of widespread support for another rising in and around London, Lochiel argued that the prince had a duty of care to prevent further devastation in the Highlands. He should launch another invasion from France in which ten regiments would come to the aid of the clans. Lochiel perceptively argued against following the Irish example, which would prioritize fighting for France on the Continent or overseas above Scottish commitments to a Stuart restoration. When Lochiel, Sempill and Balhaldy duly pressed their case in Rome, they received a sympathetic hearing from James VIII & III, which strained an already tense relationship with his son.

Stuart prospects for a restoration took a dramatic downturn in 1748. The decision by Prince Henry Benedict, who had mobilized funds for the Forty-Five in Genoa, to pursue a career as a Roman Catholic cardinal with the blessing of James VIII & III occasioned a deep rift not only between Prince Charles and his brother, but with his father. While the deaths of Lochiel and Sempill later that year lessened concerted Scottish opposition to Kelly, Charles was steadily losing the support of Louis XV's ministers, if not the king himself, for his apparent willingness to trade French for Spanish support. In compliance with the treaties drawn up at Aix-la-Chapelle in October to conclude the War of the Austrian Succession, Louis XV was obliged to expel Prince Charles from France. Although he was not cast adrift on the Continent, the prince became an itinerant supplicant for diplomatic backing and patronage over the next five years. In travels from the Mediterranean to the Baltic, he occasionally appeared incognito in Paris, Berlin and London. His brief visit to London in September 1750 was marked by his abjuring of Roman Catholicism and his acceptance into the Anglican communion, a conversion which enhanced his appeal to English Jacobites, who still preferred drunken revelries at English racetracks over actual commitment in the field or the streets. This preference again became apparent in the failure of the Elibank Plot of 1753, although the arrival of Alexander Murray to join the prince's inner circle in 1751 had diluted but not displaced Kelly's controlling influence. His conversion to Anglicanism having estranged his brother, his father and the papacy, Charles could now be castigated accurately as a rash adventurer with no meaningful prospect of ever being crowned Charles III.

## The Covert Dimension

Ostensibly, the organization of Scottish Jacobitism was beset by factional problems. But there was a sustained and purposeful covert dimension that borrowed and adapted from the later Covenanters as a Scottish movement of protest in the late seventeenth century. The Covenanters, as militant Presbyterians, deployed a cellular structure rooted in federative associations. Accordingly, their cause was sustained not by formal agencies or assemblies, but by discrete praying societies meeting in houses and halls and open field conventicles, which enabled of the Covenanters to stage episodic risings involving the mobilization between 4,000 and 14,000 combatants: figures like the numbers who were out for the Jacobites in the three major risings. Conventicles in houses were first identified among Jacobites in London during the 1690s, while the most notable field conventicle was that held over four days in May 1731. Mr John MacLachlan, nonjuring clergyman in Appin, preached in a field at North Ballachulish from Friday, 16 to Monday, 19 April. As well as preaching to over five hundred people drawn from the MacLachlans of Ardgour, the Camerons of Lochaber, the MacDonalds of Glencoe and the Stewarts of Appin, he administered the sacrament of communion to over 240 and examined another hundred persons. This was allegedly the largest meeting of Jacobites in the Highlands since the Fifteen. They took the sacrament to affirm they held steadfast to the exiled James VIII & III. At Culloden, fifteen years to the day after his field preaching in North Ballachulish, MacLachlan again administered communion, using oatcakes and whisky rather than bread and wine, to many of the same clansmen who were to confront the superior military forces of a vengeful British Army. In giving communion, MacLachlan used a chalice and paten made in Edinburgh at the behest of a local laird, Alexander Stewart of Ballachulish, that was presented to the parish of Appin in 1723. Such landed patronage marks a clear difference between the Jacobites and the Covenanters, who were noted for their social insubordination in the late seventeenth century. Patronage from landed families north and south of the Tay was not always consistent and continuous. But even if they only flirted with the cause of the exiled Stuarts, their covert backing enabled Jacobites to circumvent the oaths of allegiance and abjuration deemed mandatory to hold office and thereby penetrate government posts, such as justices of peace and commissioners of supply in the shires, the magistracy in the towns and even into the postal service. Covert engagement with shipping masters also enabled Jacobites to escape into exile in the Netherlands or via Norway when risings failed.

The distinctiveness of Scottish against English or Irish Jacobitism can ultimately be measured by its capacity and readiness to form alternative governments, nationally and locally, in these major risings. At the Fifteen, the Jacobites took control of the towns of Perth, Dundee, Montrose, Aberdeen and Inverness and their respective rural hinterlands from the outset of the rising. In the Forty-Five, only Aberdeen and its hinterland readily came under Jacobite control. More tantalizingly, however, the rising did secure Edinburgh; an army of provisional government was briefly installed at Holyroodhouse. All areas of Scotland, Whig as well as Jacobite, duly expected to be taxed. As in the Fifteen, so in the Forty-Five, the Jacobites appropriated the collection of the quarterly land tax, the cess. This was accomplished readily in the towns and shires of Aberdeen and Inverness from the outset of the rising in September 1715. William Mackintosh of Borlum, as baillie for the Highland estates of the ducal house of Gordon, had led a protest in August 1697, by the chiefs and leading gentry of the Clan Chattan confederation, against the Scottish Privy Council levying a tax on coal and candles to maintain military forces, an unwelcome coercive presence which they deemed arbitrary as it lacked parliamentary warrant. As the brigadier general commanding the Jacobite forces heading into England in October 1715, Borlum demanded and received six months' cess in advance from the Border towns of Kelso and Jedburgh. The use of military force to raise taxes was more pronounced in the Forty-Five. Having secured their control over Edinburgh in September, uplifting cess was accomplished without recourse to compulsion in Midlothian and East Lothian in October, as was already the situation in Perthshire, where Jacobite collectors uplifted taxes for all four terms in 1744 as well as 1745, but only two in 1746. In Renfrewshire, where the principal tax collector had declared for the Jacobites, landowners and tenants withheld their payments of cess and only agreed, despite threat of force on the Hanoverian side, to resume payments once the Jacobite Army was retreating north of the Tay in February 1746. By this juncture, force was being used routinely to raise the Jacobite cess in the shires of Aberdeen, Banff and Kincardine.

The levying of cess in the major risings indicates an understated element of Jacobite commitment in Scotland. James VIII & III had viewed malt taxes imposed on Scotland in 1713 and 1725 as unwarrantable impositions. In 1743, in anticipation of a French invasion of Scotland, he called for tax collectors to retain all and any cess raised for the Hanoverian regime until it could be delivered to accredited Jacobite officials. But taxation as a material consideration was less integral to the Jacobite cause than dynastic, confessional and patriotic commitments.

## Commitments and Priorities:
## Dynastic, Confessional and Patriotic

The dynastic appeal of Jacobitism was rooted in adherence to the hereditary principle of kinship. Scottish affirmations of support for James VII & II also had particularly proactive roots, notwithstanding his imposition of summary justice on radical Presbyterians or Covenanters who contested his right to be king. Jacobitism can be dated to the arrival of James in Edinburgh as Duke of Albany and York in 1680. Apart from re-establishing a royal court at Holyrood, he created a formidable constituency in Scotland by deepening and broadening political, religious and commercial horizons. He promoted religious toleration for his fellow Roman Catholics and still retained the adherence of the bishops and other Episcopalian members of the Protestant establishment. He gained enduring support from the clans in the Highlands and Islands by reversing decades of oppression for purported lawlessness in favour of conciliation. He brought clan chiefs and gentry into peacekeeping initiatives to contain banditry and feuding. James was the only Stuart monarch since the Union of the Crowns in 1603 not to promote political incorporation with England. Instead, he reaffirmed Scottish trading priorities with the Dutch Republic and France and sponsored colonial undertakings in America, initially in South Carolina and then in New Jersey.

Notwithstanding the Revolution, the royal house of Stuart was the rightful trustee of Scotland in the same way that Highland chiefs and Lowland heads of families were the customary protectors of their kindreds' patrimonies. Dynastic legitimacy was seen as the source of justice, the basis of government. But the lawful exercise of government and the maintenance of justice in Scotland were imperilled by the sundering of genealogical continuity, first by William of Orange in 1689 and then by the Hanoverian succession in 1714. It was primarily through vernacular poetry, both in Gaelic and in Scots, that Jacobitism was seen as a corrective to political, social and commercial deviations from custom. Jacobitism represented the maintenance of a divinely warranted tradition. However, vernacular poets were essentially upholding the rightful trusteeship of the Stuarts, not their divine right as monarchs to suspend or dispense with laws or custom.

The dynastic appeal of Jacobitism in Scotland was given a cutting edge by the vernacular practice of political and social criticism that was absent in Irish dream poetry. But the optimistic equation that the rightful triumph of Jacobitism would secure social justice and, in turn, would lead to religious toleration and political independence gave way to an unredeemed fatalism with the failure of the Forty-Five. For Alasdair MacMhaighstir Alasdair (Alexander MacDonald), who had served in the rising as an officer in the Clan Ranald regiment, its failure and the exile of Prince Charles Edward Stuart undermined the whole fabric of society:

> Chaill sinn ar stiùir 's ar buill-bheairte
> Dh'fhalbh uainn ar n-acair-bàis,
> Chaill sinn ar *compass* us ar cairean,
> Ar reul-iùil, 's ar beachd ga là.[1]

[We've lost our tiller and our rigging, our Sheet-anchor's torn away, we've lost our charts, our compass with them, our pole-star, our daily guide.]

Although Alasdair's staunch commitment to the cause of the exiled Stuart had led him to turn Roman Catholic, his father, Maighstear Alasdair, was an Episcopalian priest opposed to the altered establishment of the Church of Scotland at the Revolution.

In 1690, Presbyterianism (government by church courts) had been re-established at the expense of Episcopalianism (government by bishops). Nevertheless, Episcopalian priests, especially in large rural parishes, resisted their replacement by Presbyterian ministers. Maighstear Alasdair (MacDonald), with the support of his parishioners, held out for a record 27 years in Ardnamurchan. Where Presbyterians supported a contractual political policy, both Episcopalians and Catholics were

traditional supporters of an organic body politic. Although the exiled
Stuarts consistently promised to uphold a Protestant establishment
maintained with parliamentary approval in both Scotland and England,
the use of his prerogative powers by James VII & II to set aside penal
laws against Roman Catholics was instrumental in his removal from the
British throne. His son, James VIII & III, remained a staunch Catholic
and refused overtures from his half-sister, Queen Anne, to declare himself a Protestant to pave the way for his own succession instead of the
Hanoverians on her death. Prince Charles only declared pragmatically
in favour of Protestantism after the Forty-Five was lost. Such persistent if not always pious adherence to Catholicism certainly acted as a
deterrent to Scottish as well as English politicians prepared to flirt with
but not commit to Jacobitism. However, the exiled house's refusal to
sacrifice their faith for political advantage stiffened the resolve of not
only Catholics but Episcopalians in Scotland not to be reconciled to the
Presbyterian establishment in the Kirk.

In Scotland, even more so than in England and in direct contrast
to the situation in Ireland, adherence to Roman Catholicism was a
minority pursuit among Jacobites. The Scots colleges for training future
Catholic missionaries in Rome and Paris, and to a lesser extent in Douai
and Valladolid, had extensive networks linking Scottish Catholic families
to clerical and political patrons in Italy, France and Spain. From 1623,
oversight of all regular and secular clergy, other than the Jesuits, on
the Scottish mission was exercised spiritually, if not always financially,
by Propaganda Fide (Sacred College of Propaganda) at Rome. The
Jesuits had remained reluctant to co-operate with other missionaries,
particularly the secular clergy, whom they deemed less well equipped
intellectually, administratively and materially to endure a life of personal privation and constant movement to spread the faith. Catholicism
was given a unifying focus and the Scottish mission a more cohesive
organization following the appointment of Thomas Nicholson as vicar-
apostolic in 1697. James Gordon joined him as coadjutor bishop in 1705.
Two years later, the bishops on the Scottish mission, the overseas colleges, prominent laity, and their associates in the exiled Jacobite court
refused to contemplate clerical union with England or promote shared
British missions. Instead, the bishops established training colleges for

priests that made the Highlands markedly less dependent on Irish missionaries – notably, the Franciscans, Vincentians and Dominicans – who had worked there intermittently since 1619 and cut the costs of sending trainee priests to the Scots colleges on the Continent. Hugh MacDonald from Morar, the first native bishop trained in Scotland since the Reformation in the mid-sixteenth century, was given charge of the newly created Highland mission in 1731. Priests reporting back to Propaganda became ever hopeful of winning over Episcopalians in Jacobite heartlands throughout the Highlands.

Nonetheless, missionary work was severely hampered by internal rivalries between Lowland and Highland districts that mirrored the tensions between the Scots colleges at Rome, Douai and Valladolid with Paris. Only Paris was not controlled by the Jesuits. These domestic and international rivalries led to heretical charges of Jansenism against the Lowland district and the college at Paris. No less pressing from the point of view of the clerical instigators of dissent from the Highland district was the discriminatory division of limited funding. That for the Scottish mission was loaded in favour of the Lowland district, where the priests tended to serve in the households of landed society rather than travel among communities dispersed in the isles, glens and straths. The acrimony engendered by this debilitating dispute all but emasculated the Scottish mission and its capacity to provide reliable intelligence for Jacobite aspirations in the run-up to the Forty-Five.

The confessional allegiance of Scottish Jacobites, especially in the heartlands of the Highlands and the northeast, was overwhelmingly Protestant and Episcopalian. A minority of Episcopalians, particularly career-minded politicians and merchants engaged in the colonial trade, were prepared to seek accommodation – first with William of Orange, then Queen Anne and the Hanoverians – to secure religious toleration. These Episcopalians, who became known as the jurors, avoided direct association with Jacobitism and effectively became outposts of the Anglican Church of England. The refusal of most Episcopalians to abjure the royal house of Stuart led them to reject an accommodation with the Presbyterian establishment in 1695 and toleration from the British government in 1712. As a result, they, no less than the Roman Catholic community, were subject to penal laws. The general assembly of the Presbyterian Kirk tended to discriminate against them discreetly rather than fulminate against them publicly, given the Episcopal sensibilities of the Anglican establishment in England. However, divisions between jurors and nonjurors were not inflexibly sectarian, particularly in selecting liturgical readings from Anglican and Scottish prayer books, a trait evident in Edinburgh, Dundee and Aberdeen. In Aberdeen town, notwithstanding penal laws restricting nonjuring clergy from communicating with more than five associates from 1719, nonjuring laity pragmatically took oaths abjuring Jacobitism for political preferment as civil magistrates during the 1720s. Jurors in Aberdeenshire were as remiss as nonjurors either in omitting or in ignoring the legislative requirement for prayers for the incumbent British royal family, especially after the Hanoverian succession in 1714. Rarely if ever did jurors go so far as to pray for the Jacobite court in exile, however. Juring and nonjuring clergy assisted each other in Glasgow.

Nonjuring, which was grounded in a spirit of obedience and submission to rightful royal authority, became the sacramental cement of Scottish Jacobitism. Nevertheless, the political allegiance of many clergy to Jacobitism was undertaken reluctantly and ritually rather than enthusiastically. They had come to see the loss of establishment status at the Revolution as a gateway to liturgical liberation. They not only desired to distinguish themselves doctrinally from the Presbyterians, but were averse to becoming adjuncts of Anglicanism. This led some to move in the direction of Flemish mysticism, others towards flirtation with Coptic Christianity and Greek and Russian Orthodoxy. Alexander Campbell, along with Thomas Gadderar, his successor as nonjuring bishop of Aberdeen, were to the fore in a group of Scottish and English nonjurors in London who began a rapprochement with Greek and Russian Orthodoxy from 1716. Despite backing from Peter the Great of Russia, there was limited unity among the English nonjurors. Before negotiations had collapsed by 1728, Scottish endeavours had been increasingly directed to returning their English colleagues to what they deemed as the usages of the Primitive Church. Although the nonjurors had more considerable presence in Scotland than in England, both communities had already split over the usages, primarily the mixing of water with wine in the communion chalice.

In the aftermath of the split on the usages, Bishop Campbell came to view the Scottish bishops as being in league with their Anglican counterparts to make the Scottish Episcopal Church entirely dependent on the Church of England. The persistent failure of the exiled Stuarts to appoint to Scottish sees had led to the formation of the College of Bishops, which perpetuated itself from 1720 by consecrating bishops to ad hoc territories rather than to established dioceses. The college's resolve from 1731 to override elections – whether territorial or diocesan – that favoured 'usagers' for episcopal vacancies was a further cause of dissent in Scotland. Nonjurors in both Scotland and England subsequently sought to regroup in 1744 by subscribing to new spiritual paths in *The Ancient Liturgy of the Church of Jerusalem* that sacramentally united them as the true apostolic heirs to the primitive purity of the Universal Catholic Church. Essentially this was the work of Bishop Thomas Rattray of Brechin, who broke ranks with the College of Bishops on such issues as the appointment of usagers and diocesan elections. However, new religious directions moved some nonjurors towards pietism that inhibited political action. Among the subscribers to the spiritual path published in 1744 there were few prepared to risk all for political deliverance in the Forty-Five.

Notwithstanding the creation of the College of Bishops in 1720, nonjuring Episcopalianism was further beset by organizational and financial difficulties. Nonjuring bishops increasingly lost their parochial links as episcopal responsibilities were shared across several dioceses. Lacking the state support given to Presbyterianism and the external funding available to Roman Catholics from the College of Propaganda in Rome, nonjuring priests had to rely increasingly on voluntary offerings from their congregations. Nonetheless, Presbyterians encountered significant difficulties, legal and physical, in consolidating their establishment status in the Jacobite heartlands north of the Tay. Magistrates and juries were considerably more sympathetic to nonjuring than in the Presbyterian strongholds south of the Tay. The general assembly of the Kirk encouraged presbyteries, as district courts, to bring civil actions to remove nonjuring Episcopalians from parishes within their bounds. Exemplary evictions of nonjuring priests were notably encouraged in the aftermath of the Treaty of Union in 1707. In the wake of the Fifteen, Presbyterian ministers attempting to take over parochial charges from nonjurors in the shires of Angus and Kincardine were subjected to rabbling and even organized disturbances with the approval of the landed elite to make their position untenable. Women among the landed elite were notable promoters of disaffection, especially if their husbands and sons were forfeited or exiled for Jacobitism. In rural Aberdeenshire at the outset of 1718, seven nonjuring priests faced fines and bans from ministering in their former parishes. But their fines, much to the chagrin of the Crown Solicitor in Scotland, Robert Dundas, were never debilitating. Bans were localized rather than blanket prohibitions from preaching and administering the sacraments. Such selective prosecutions tended to be sporadic rather than sustained. After the Forty-Five, however, the wholesale eviction of nonjuring priests as well as the razing of their meeting houses became prime objectives for the Hanoverian forces.

There was a manifest compatibility and, indeed, synergy between dynastic and confessional commitments to Jacobitism. Commitment to a hierarchical church – Roman Catholic or Episcopalian – enhanced commitment to a hierarchical, organic state over which a paternalistic monarch ruled as head of the body politic. However, the third element of Jacobite commitment – unique to Scotland – was less rooted in tradition, less deferential to royal authority and potentially more disruptive for Scottish liaison with the courts in exile. Patriotism questioned the role of monarchy as the principal focus and inspiration for national identity and even led to the promotion of constitutional limitations on a Stuart restoration. As well as introducing a contractual element into Jacobitism, patriotism was sustained within Scotland after 1707 by anti-unionism provoked by the serial mismanagement of Scottish affairs from London. Scottish Jacobitism required not only new impetus but new direction from the making of the Treaty of Union. Before 1707, Jacobitism had sought to amend the political direction of Scotland. After 1707, this objective was submerged in the struggle to reassert and retain the polit-ical identity of Scotland. A new generation of vernacular poets, led by Allan Ramsay and his literary associates in the Easy Club (established in Edinburgh in 1712), articulated popular antipathy to the Union and saw in Jacobitism an appropriate vehicle to end Scottish political sub-jugation. Patriotic no less than dynastic or confessional commitment was becoming the driving force for Scottish Jacobitism in the Fifteen and the Forty-Five.

Patriotic commitment was part of the continuous process of redefinition of Jacobitism in Scotland. This process, which was not always to the taste of the exiled house of Stuart, was based on the concept of *patria* that was founded on humanist teaching, specifically neo-Stoicism as received in Marischal College, Aberdeen, in the wake of the regal union after James VI of Scotland became James I of England and established the Stuarts as a British dynasty. The identity of the Scottish people was expressed through the momentous achievements of scholars, soldiers and adventurers no less than monarchs, an identity that was energized by the epic heroism of the likes of William Wallace, the leader of the Scottish community of the realm during the Wars of Independence from England in the late thirteenth and early fourteenth centuries. Two authors with strong family connections to the Jacobite heartlands, Patrick Abercromby in his two-volume *The Martial Achievement of the Scottish Nation* (1711–15) and George MacKenzie in his three-volume *The Lives and Characters of the Most Eminent Writers of the Scottish Nation* (1708–22), articulated the concept of the *patria* in the aftermath of the parliamentary union to signal that territorial nationhood should take precedence over dynastic statehood. Strong monarchy was to be commended for liberating Scotland from the dominance of baronial interests, but the nation was now considered as having moved beyond the provenance of the political elite to a shared cultural, literary and territorial heritage of its people.

The concept of the *patria* has further political significance in focusing the debate within Scottish Jacobitism on constitutional aspects that promoted limitations but not necessarily binding contractual restrictions on the Stuarts on their return from exile. These limitations can be traced back to James Graham, 1st Marquess of Montrose and hero of the Royalist campaigns in Scotland for Charles I during the 1640s. Montrose, who had initially supported the binding restrictions on monarchy imposed by the Covenanting movement in Scotland, came to advocate the maintenance of a constitutional equilibrium in which Parliament would be a safeguard, not a permanent check on monarchy. A similar sentiment was expressed by James, Duke of Hamilton (then

Earl of Arran) during his forlorn endeavours to prevent the replacement of James VII & II by William of Orange in January 1689. At the outset of Queen Anne's reign, when Hamilton was attempting to hold together the confederated opposition to incorporating union, Andrew Fletcher of Saltoun emerged as the forthright spokesman of constitutional reformers. Although he wished to return to Covenanting limitations on monarchy in affairs of state, Saltoun drew support from prominent Jacobites such as Charles, Earl of Errol and William, the Earl Marischal. Indeed, so strong was this association that Fletcher of Saltoun was interned with the same earls and other leading Jacobites once the attempted invasion of Scotland ordered by Louis XIV in 1708 was aborted.

A patriotic sense of constitutional equilibrium was integral to the thinking of Alexander, Lord Forbes of Pitsligo, a leading Jacobite intellectual, committed nonjuror, occasional courtier and active participant in the Fifteen and the Forty-Five. Between the risings, Pitsligo realized that some intellectual attempt had to be made to come to terms with the Hanoverians as de facto monarchs pending the restoration of the *de jure* Stuarts. Indeed, even the court in exile was dropping hints by 1740 that James VIII & III was prepared to curtail his prerogative powers. Sources close to the house of Argyll appear to have elicited an overture to John Campbell, the 2nd Duke, who was briefly flirting with Jacobitism, that the exiled king was fully resolved 'to make the Law the rule of my Government and absolutely disclaim any pretensions to a dispensing power'.[2]

Notwithstanding that all risings ended in failure, popular antipathy to the Treaty of Union saw in Jacobitism an appropriate vehicle to reassert Scottish patriotism. Antipathy towards the Union was compounded by mismanagement of Scottish affairs by successive British ministries after 1707. The scrapping of the Scottish Privy Council to curtail sources of patronage during the first elections to the Parliament of Great Britain in 1708 was a monumental blunder. At a stroke, executive government was deprived of its central intelligence agency in Scotland, an agency never satisfactorily replaced or compensated by the occasional placement of secretaries of state and other leading Scottish politicians in the emergent cabinet council in London. The pre-emptive tactic of apprehending suspect Jacobites among the landed elite certainly contributed to the termination of the intended diversionary rising of 1708. However, the removal of over twenty nobles, clan chiefs and other landed gentry to London, and the associated foisting of the ferocious and ill-defined English law of treason on Scotland, were viewed among the foremost grievances Scotland was obliged to endure in the wake of Union. The crass incompetence of the British government was further highlighted by the precipitate measures to encourage loyalty in 1715, which required around fifty leading landowners to disown their suspect Jacobitism on pain of forfeiture. This measure, subsequently given the misnomer 'the Clan Act', assisted recruitment for the Fifteen.

Constrictions on patronage post-Union limited the prospects for winning over wavering Jacobites. Placements as a Member of Parliament, posts in central and local government and the award of development grants for textile manufactures and fisheries were usually at the expense of hitherto loyal Whigs who, in turn, could use the bargaining counter of Jacobitism to maintain their own preferment. Although regulated access to the British Empire after 1707 opened up prospects of increased places of profit in civil and military government overseas, Scottish participation in colonial service was more occasional than persistent during the Jacobite era. Development funds, channelled from 1727 through the Board of Trustees for Fisheries and Manufactures in association with the Royal Bank of Scotland, were primarily forthcoming because of the fear of Jacobitism. Indeed, the Bank of Scotland, established in 1695, was not trusted as the conduit for these funds because of its directors' association with Jacobitism. Sheep farming districts in the Jacobite heartlands of the Highlands and the northeast were excluded from access to woollen bounties. However, the provision of drawbacks for linen exports in the early 1740s promoted the formation of copartneries as British endeavours and gave Scottish colonial adventurers a vested interest in maintaining the Union and the Hanoverian succession. Nevertheless, central government was chronically unprepared at the outset of the Fifteen and the Forty-Five when the fortifying of defences, mobilizing of support and provisioning of troops were left primarily to prominent Whig families who usually took their lead from the house of Argyll, headed by the chiefs of Clan Campbell.

## Political Divisions and Religious Differences

Although the house of Argyll constituted the premier Whig grandees in Scotland, John Campbell, the 2nd Duke, was not given full recognition for his successful command of the Hanoverian forces in the Fifteen. His brother Archibald, Earl of Islay (later 3rd Duke of Argyll) was kept out of the initial Whig ministries or from the management of Scottish affairs until 1725. His much-vaunted political management of Scotland was sidelined from 1743 and was only reasserted in the aftermath of Culloden. Argyll and then Islay were gradually alienated from Walpole as prime minister, Argyll breaking with him in 1738 while Islay helped to engineer his fall from office in 1742. They did so by colluding with the Patriot party, not the Jacobites. The Patriot party differed in important respects from the Jacobites in Scotland. First, they could organize openly, with James Erskine, Lord Grange, being retained as the Patriots' principal agent from 1734. Second, the Patriots liaised constructively with their counterparts in England, mainly through John Dalrymple, Earl of Stair, an army general and a British diplomat who served with distinction in Paris from 1715 to 1720, where he exposed several Jacobite plots and turned Grange's brother, John, Earl of Mar, into a double agent. Third, the Patriots looked primarily across the Atlantic rather than to continental Europe. Their leading polemicist was Sir William Keith, initially a Jacobite sympathizer and former governor of Pennsylvania who retained family ties to Aberdeenshire. Keith stressed that the British nature of empire was predicated on equality rather than English dominance. Having become an American spokesman for the party in the 1730s, Keith later relocated to London. The Patriots were comprehensively outmanoeuvred in Scotland at the general election of 1734 by the Whig interest of Argyll and Islay. But when this interest made common cause with the Patriot party by the general election of 1741, they became sufficiently powerful to bring down Walpole the following year.

Notwithstanding the house of Argyll's periodic stranglehold on political management under the Whig ascendancy, the Campbell chiefs could not rely on unstinting opposition to Jacobitism within their own clan. In the six fiscal divisions of the shire, the Campbells of Argyll could only draw on Mid-Argyll and Kintyre to provide wholesale military backing to oppose all three major Jacobite risings. The Campbells of Glenorchy (under the earls of Breadalbane) had a strong presence in Lorne as well as in the Perthshire Highlands. This branch of the clan had remained neutral in 1689–91, then mobilized for the Jacobites at the Fifteen and only became active Whigs at the Forty-Five. The Campbells of Cawdor, who were present in strength in Lorne, Cowal, Islay and Mull as well as in Nairnshire, moved from being Whig supporters at the Revolution to being divided in their allegiances at both the Fifteen and the Forty-Five. A notional estimate of the armed strength of the Highland clans for the Whig ministry in the wake of the Fifteen asserted that the ducal house of Argyll had 10,000 fighting men at their disposal out of a total force of 24,100. However, when the Jacobite clans living under the feudal superiority of the ducal house were stripped out along with the Campbells sympathetic to Jacobitism, the Campbells of Argyll were reduced to 3,500 fighting men who had been opposed by 2,200 from the Campbell branches in 1715.[3]

However patchy, Campbell commitment first to William of Orange and then to the Hanoverian succession under the ducal house of Argyll was considerably more consistent than that of the ducal houses of Hamilton, Gordon and Atholl to Jacobitism. James, Duke of Hamilton's inept political leadership of the confederated opposition, compounded by his own Jacobite intriguing, facilitated the passage of the Treaty of Union through the Scottish Estates in 1706–7. Arrested in anticipation of a French invasion, Hamilton was soon released on promising to support the Whigs in the first British general election in 1708. Abandoning the Whigs to support the incoming Tory ministry in 1710, he was made a British peer as Duke of Brandon. But as he was not an English peer, he was denied an automatic seat in the House of Lords and banned from standing as a Scottish elective peer. In 1712, he was due to be despatched to Paris as Queen Anne's ambassador to the French court, an appointment that alarmed Whigs that he was being sent to pave the way for the succession of James VIII & III. These fears were pre-empted when a family dispute over the extensive English inheritance of his wife, Elizabeth Gerrard, led to his fatal wounding in a duel in Hyde Park, London. There was no further involvement of his ducal house in Jacobitism.

George Gordon, 1st Duke of Gordon, continued his family's tradition of staunch Roman Catholicism. He declared for the Jacobites at the Revolution but sided with the papacy rather than James VII & II over the issue of Gallicanism. George held Edinburgh Castle for the Jacobites in 1689 but made no other contribution of distinction to the first major rising. He was to return to Edinburgh Castle as a prisoner rather than as governor at the outset of the Fifteen. He was succeeded by his son Alexander as second duke in 1716. Alexander, then Marquess of Huntly, made no effort to oppose the Union in 1707, although he was detained as a strong Jacobite supporter in 1708. In the interim, his commitment to the cause was severely tested by his marriage to Henrietta Mordaunt, a daughter of the Earl of Peterborough and Monmouth. She was resolutely Whig and Anglican, favouring jurors over nonjurors on the widespread Gordon estates in the Jacobite heartlands. Alexander Gordon did oppose the Hanoverian succession and raised 500 horse and 1,200 foot for the Jacobites in the Fifteen. But his contribution at Sheriffmuir was undistinguished. He was negotiating for a cessation of hostilities with John, Duke of Argyll by the time James VIII & III belatedly arrived in Scotland. Although he was duly imprisoned in Edinburgh Castle for six months after his formal surrender, he was not, as anticipated, brought to trial at Carlisle. Instead, as 2nd Duke of Gordon, he was absolved by a parliamentary Act of Grace in 1717 and went on to pledge loyalty to the Whig government and to reconcile the northeast to the Hanoverians, a task carried on enthusiastically by his widow from 1728. Notwithstanding the best endeavours of the dowager duchess, the ducal family was markedly divided at the Forty-Five. Cosmo, the 3rd Duke of Gordon, took no active part for either side, but his brother Adam held a commission in the Hanoverian forces, while another brother, Ludovic, was a forcible Jacobite commander in the northeast.

The complexities of fundamental divisions between Whigs and Jacobites were laid bare by divergent opinions within the ducal house of Atholl. John Murray, the first duke, had hedged his bets in 1689, personally supporting William of Orange but not preventing the recruitment of his tenantry for the cause of James VII & II. A noted, if lukewarm, opponent of the Treaty of Union in 1707, he was reconciled with the Hanoverian succession by the Fifteen. However, his eldest son, William, Marquess of Tullibardine, a former officer in the Royal Navy, commanded the Atholl Brigade for the Jacobites. Although exiled, attainted and debarred from the succession of the dukedom, he was joint commander in Scotland of the abortive Spanish expedition in 1719. He was again to return from exile in the entourage of Prince Charles Edward Stuart in the Forty-Five. His brother James, an officer in the British Army, had succeeded as second duke in 1724. Although James played no active part in the Fifteen, he was in the entourage of William, Duke of Cumberland fighting against the Jacobites in the Forty-Five. Two younger brothers, Charles and George, also officers in the British Army, switched sides to command regiments in the Atholl Brigade in 1715. Charles died in 1720 after a period of imprisonment in London. George returned from continental exile to participate in the minor rising of 1719. Notwithstanding his pardon in 1724, Lord George Murray rejoined the cause as the most accomplished Jacobite commander in the Forty-Five. He was opposed by his half-brother, Lord John Murray, who helped to raise a clan regiment (the 43rd Highlanders) for the Hanoverian forces. Lord George's eldest son, John, the future third duke, served in this regiment as a captain.

Family divisions occasioned by ideological and pragmatic differences between Jacobites and Whigs were compounded by the prioritizing of commitments among Jacobites. Dynastic, confessional and patriotic commitments were not rigidly adhered to. These commitments can be regarded as not always consistent, first, from how far eighteen leading Jacobite clan contingents fulfilled their notional fighting strengths in the Fifteen and the Forty-Five and, second, from case studies of the actual engagement of the fifty leading clans, both Jacobite and Whig, in the three major risings. Only five out of the eighteen clan contingents matched the general reckoning of their fighting strength in both the Fifteen and the Forty-Five, although two in the latter exceeded their estimated strength: the MacDonalds of Glengarry and their associates among the Grants of Glenmoriston and Glenurquhart mobilized 800 against a general reckoning of 450 and the Stewarts of Appin rose from 250 to 300. The Camerons of Lochiel, who failed by a hundred to match their general reckoning of seven hundred in the

Fifteen, mobilized nine hundred from Lochaber, making them the largest contingent at the Forty-Five. Three other clans, with a general reckoning of seven hundred men or above, had a more mixed record. The MacKenzies of Seaforth, with the highest general reckoning of 2,000 men, raised no more than 1,500 for the Fifteen and only five hundred in the Forty-Five, when the clan was divided in its commitment to Jacobitism. The Frasers of Lovat raised five hundred men out of a general reckoning of seven hundred in both major risings; the clan was divided in the Fifteen, though firmly Jacobite at the Forty-Five. The MacLeods of Dunvegan, whose territories ranged from Glenelg and Skye to Harris, were assigned an identical reckoning but no numbers for the Fifteen, when they were active Jacobites, and only two hundred for the Forty-Five, when they were divided in their loyalties between Jacobites and Whigs.[4]

The evidence for fluidity in commitment is more detailed from case studies of the fifty leading clans. As evident from the table below on the political affiliation of these clans in the three major risings, Jacobites always constituted a significant majority, but clan support declined, as it did for the Whigs. Switching of sides during campaigning was a rarity, though there was a greater drifting away among Jacobite clans towards division, much more so than towards neutrality. Clans were more inclined to remain neutral and latterly to division than to support the Whigs.

*Political Affiliations of the Clans*

|  | 1689–91 | 1715–16 | 1745–6 |
| --- | --- | --- | --- |
| Jacobite | 28 | 26 | 18 |
| Switched | 1 | 0 | 1 |
| Whig | 9 | 8 | 7 |
| Divided | 2 | 5 | 12 |
| Neutral | 10 | 11 | 12 |

However, as evident from the second table on political continuity, the minority Whig numbers held up better than the majority supporting Jacobitism. There was only one clan, the Sinclairs in Caithness and Orkney, which consistently remained neutral, although this was a pragmatic decision. The clan was Jacobite inclined but was surrounded by Whig neighbours. Similar pragmatism led to the only switch in allegiance in the first major rising, when the MacAllisters in Kintyre and Bute, who were also surrounded by Whig neighbours, left the Jacobite ranks to join them. They remained neutral in the Fifteen and Forty-Five. The one switch in the latter rising was among the Clan Chattan, who had been neutral in 1689–91 and Jacobite in 1715–16. Their chief, William Mackintosh of Mackintosh, had been commissioned to raise an Independent Company by the Whig government. Only a handful of the six hundred clansmen he recruited did not desert when his wife, Lady Anne Mackintosh, declared for the Jacobites. The number of divided clans rose for every rising. However, only two, the Grants and the Atholl men (Stewarts, Murrays and Fergussons), were consistently divided: the former between their settlements in Speyside, which were Whig, and those in Glenmoriston and Glenurquhart, which were Jacobite; the latter reflected the divisions in the ducal house of Atholl.

*Political Continuity among the Clans*

|           | 1689–91 | 1715–16 | 1745–6 |
|-----------|---------|---------|--------|
| Jacobite  | 28      | 18      | 13     |
| Whig      | 9       | 7       | 5      |
| Divided   | 2       | 2       | 2      |
| Neutral   | 10      | 3       | 1      |

Both the Grants and the Atholl men were also divided in terms of their confessional allegiances: the Grants having Roman Catholics, nonjuring Episcopalians and Presbyterians among their numbers, while the Atholl men were split between nonjurors and Presbyterians. Religious division among clans was not necessarily a straightforward identification of nonjurors and Catholics with Jacobites and Presbyterians with Whigs. As evident from the table here, no exclusively Presbyterian clan favoured Jacobitism, which was primarily but inconsistently supported by nonjurors in all three major risings, with Catholic clans always in a minority. Jacobitism also attracted significant but declining support from clans with mixed denominations of nonjurors, Roman Catholics and even Presbyterians.

*Religious Affiliations and Jacobitism*[5]

|                          | 1689–91 | 1715–16 | 1745–6 |
|--------------------------|---------|---------|--------|
| Jacobite clans           | 28      | 26      | 18     |
| Nonjuring Episcopalians  | 14      | 15      | 11     |
| Roman Catholics          | 6       | 6       | 4      |
| Presbyterians            | 0       | 0       | 0      |
| Mixed denominations      | 8       | 5       | 3      |

Confessional commitment, particularly when political priorities cut across denominational ties, was less vital to Jacobitism than dynastic or patriotic endeavours to restore the Stuarts and Scottish independence. William MacKenzie, 5th Earl of Seaforth, a Roman Catholic, led out his predominantly nonjuring clan in the Fifteen when Angus MacDonald of Glengarry, a nonjuror, led his Catholic clansmen at Sheriffmuir. Coll MacDonald of Keppoch, who fell at Culloden, was likewise a non-juring chief of a Catholic clan. Some Presbyterian ministers, such as the Reverend John Cameron in Lochaber, supported the Jacobite cause in the Forty-Five when Francis Farquharson of Monaltrie, a Presbyterian, led out his clan in support of Prince Charles Edward Stuart. A few idio-syncratic Presbyterians in the Lowlands, such as Lord Boyd of Kilmarnock, also came out for Jacobitism.

Although dynastic and patriotic commitments took practical prece-dence over the confessional, there were also divisions in the Jacobite ranks about which should have priority. Archibald Burnet of Carlops from the shire of Peebles was captured at Preston in November 1715 and imprisoned, pending trial, in Carlisle. On 10 January 1716, he wrote to his publisher in Paris affirming that by natural and divine right the exiled Stuarts were the legitimate monarchs of Scotland, England and Ireland. The Hanoverian George I, like William of Orange before him, was a usurper dependent on a standing army and foreign alliances who had no call on the affections of the British nation. His dynastic call to restore their rightful king and constitution swept aside at the Revolution was a British endeavour that had no place for Scottish patriotism. Carlops was duly tried and condemned not just to be hanged, but to be drawn and quartered, an excruciatingly painful if exceptional form of execution. His dynastic priorities were echoed by the Aberdeen poet William Meston, who was removed from his academic post as regent at Marischal College after the Fifteen. Meston was at least more cognisant of Scottish patriotism than Alasdair MacMhaighstir Alasdair, and the other leading Gaelic poet who was also a commander in the Forty-Five, John Roy Stewart from Badenoch. However, the veteran Jacobite and clan chief Alexander Robertson of Strowan, who featured in all three major risings, came to realize in his Latin verse that patriotic no less than dynastic commitment had become the driving force for Scottish Jacobitism after 1707.

Patriotic priorities for constitutional limitations on monarchy and the restoration of Scottish independence were prominent in Jacobite preparations for what became the minor rising of 1708. Although they were received with no more than lukewarm enthusiasm at the court in Saint-Germain, these priorities were given a measure of recognition in the Jacobite manifestos for the subsequent major risings in 1715 and 1745. Proclamations issued on behalf of the exiled house of Stuart at the commencement of both risings promised the revocation of the Treaty of Union and the summoning of the Scottish Estates to settle civil and religious affairs. However, James VIII & III arrived too late in Scotland to effect the anticipated summoning of a parliament at the outset of 1716. He certainly regretted that he was obliged to depart Scotland without securing safety, welfare and justice for his followers and his cause. Such regrets did not unduly concern his son, Prince Charles, who singularly failed to call a parliament after he seized control of Edinburgh in September 1745. His peremptory move into England made this prospect unobtainable. Differing dynastic and patriotic priorities led to strategic tensions and inconsistencies that were particularly evident during the Fifteen and the Forty-Five, when first the Earl of Mar and then Prince Charles failed to consolidate in Scotland before countenancing expeditions to England. In both major risings this led to a collective loss of political will to sustain Scottish campaigning after respective military reversals at Sheriffmuir on 13 November 1715 and at Culloden on 16 April 1746.

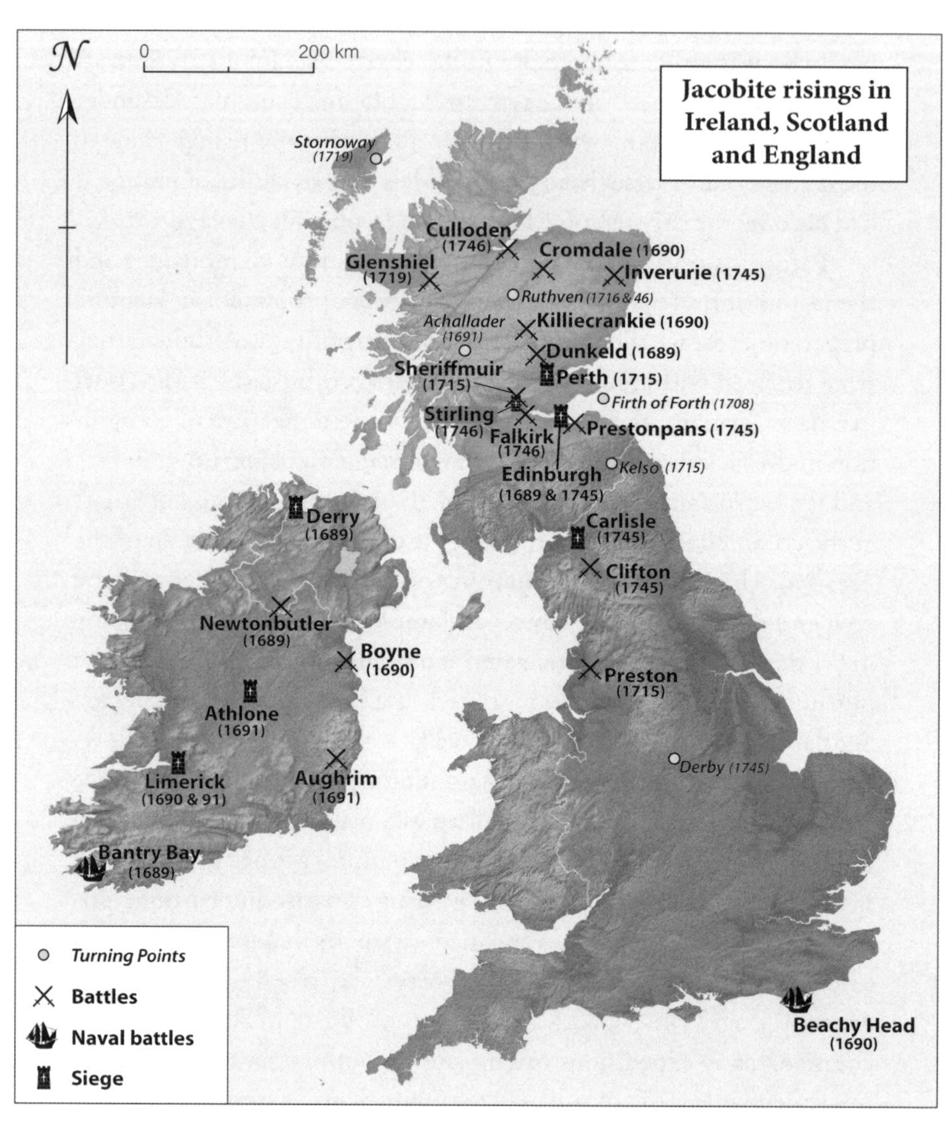

N
0          200 km
Jacobite risings in Ireland, Scotland and England
Stornoway (1719)
Culloden (1746)
Cromdale (1690)
Glenshiel (1719)
Inverurie (1745)
Ruthven (1716 & 46)
Achallader (1691)
Killiecrankie (1690)
Dunkeld (1689)
Sheriffmuir (1715)
Perth (1715)
Firth of Forth (1708)
Stirling (1746)
Falkirk (1746)
Prestonpans (1745)
Edinburgh (1689 & 1745)
Kelso (1715)
Derry (1689)
Carlisle (1745)
Clifton (1745)
Newtonbutler (1689)
Boyne (1690)
Athlone (1691)
Preston (1715)
Limerick (1690 & 91)
Aughrim (1691)
Derby (1745)
Bantry Bay (1689)
Beachy Head (1690)
Turning Points
Battles
Naval battles
Siege

# 3

# Risings and Reprisals

Public expressions of Jacobitism can be most readily associated with overt risings rather than covert plots. The risings affected all three kingdoms, with Ireland being to the fore in the first, 1689–91, in the wake of the Revolution and Scotland in the other two major risings in the Fifteen (1715–16) and the Forty-Five (1745–6) as well as the minor risings in 1708 and 1719. Although not noted for its Jacobite activism, England was the ultimate goal in all risings to ensure the British restoration of the exiled Stuarts. All Jacobite campaigns were afflicted by varying measures of ill-luck, crass incompetence, organizational problems, ideological differences and, above all, strategic inconsistencies. The failure of each Jacobite rising was marked by government reprisals of escalating barbaric degrees, particularly but not exclusively at the expense of the clans. Highland chiefs and leading clan gentry, like landlords, merchants and members of the professions in the Lowlands, Ireland and England, faced forfeiture and execution if they failed to escape overseas. Although less likely to be executed, their followers and associates, like tenants, artisans and labourers elsewhere in the three kingdoms, faced compulsory penal servitude in British colonies. Transportation ships were at the mercy of pirates and privateers on the open seas.

## The Risings

In England the 'Glorious' Revolution was accomplished with a relative lack of bloodshed, in marked contrast to the situation in Ireland

and Scotland. The Revolution was instigated in England by the arrival of William of Orange and his Dutch forces at Torbay in Devon in November 1688. His arrival was heralded by popular insurgences with mobs not just in London, but in the West Country, East Anglia, the Midlands and the North, mounting sectarian attacks on Roman Catholics, their property and their places of worship. These attacks were subsequently broadened to assaults on government agencies and officials deemed integral to the authoritarian kingship of James II. After the king abandoned England for France and ordered his army to disband in December, the underpaid and underfed troops engaged in local riots that were joined in London and Lancashire by Catholic counter-protestors. But there was no formal rising before or after Parliament resolved that James had abdicated and his throne was offered and accepted by William and Mary in February 1689.

Ireland, in contrast, became a major theatre not just for civil war between the supporters of William of Orange and of James VII & II, but for the Nine Years War between the Dutch-led League of Augsburg and France under Louis XIV. Immense forces, up to 35,000 men, were mobilized by both sides in a hotly contested campaign which commenced with the unsuccessful Jacobite siege of Derry in April 1689 and drew to a conclusion with the inconclusive siege of Limerick by William's army from August 1691. In the interim, William's army had won two battles of significance, the first at the Boyne, near Drogheda in County Louth on 1 July 1690. William and James both took personal command of their troops. Defeat led James to leave Ireland for France and considerably weakened the Jacobite control of Ireland which James had consolidated by his arrival in Kinsale in March 1689. Reversal of the Boyne seemed feasible when an Anglo-Dutch fleet was emphatically defeated by a French fleet off Beachy Head in Sussex on 10 July. However, prospects of French reinforcement being sent to Ireland were negated when Prince Eugene of Savoy joined the Augsburg League, thereby requiring France to divert troops to its exposed southern frontier.

The second battle, more decisive than the Boyne, was that at Aughrim in County Galway on 12 July 1691. William's forces, under the Dutch commander Godert de Ginkel, smashed the Jacobites led by the French general Charles Chalmot de Saint-Ruhe in what was certainly the bloodiest battle in all the major risings. Around 7,000 men were lost on both sides: 3,000 of the Williamites and 4,000 Jacobites. Another 4,000 Jacobites deserted from combat. In the aftermath of the battle there were killings in cold blood (perhaps up to 2,000 Jacobites) by the victorious forces. While Ginkel arranged for the burial of his own forces killed in action, fallen Jacobites were left unburied with their remains scattered over the battlefield for several years. The Jacobites were not vanquished, however, and regrouped at Limerick under Patrick Sarsfield, 1st Earl of Lucan. After six weeks, the besieged forces were able to negotiate a peace on 3 October. The Treaty of Limerick, which brought the siege and the Irish theatre of the Nine Years War to an end, enabled Sarsfield to sail for France in late December with 12,000 Irish Jacobites – an episode famed as 'The Flight of the Wild Geese'. This led to the formation of the Irish brigades, first in the service of France and then of Spain, which attracted reinforcements of around 1,000 per annum until the 1740s.

There were more immediate ramifications for the Jacobite campaign in Scotland from the Irish theatre of the Nine Years War. The Boyne ended all hopes of substantial reinforcements coming across the North Channel. By Aughrim, most of the Scottish-Dutch forces had crossed over that channel to fight in Ireland. Nevertheless, Scotland remained an ancillary theatre for Jacobite activity from 1689 to 1691, with its own distinctive rising.

The Revolution was vigorously challenged in Scotland with the clans to the fore as supporters of James VII & II. Led by John Graham, Viscount Dundee, 2,700 Jacobites defeated numerically superior forces drawn mainly from Scots in Dutch service, who were led by a Highlander, Hugh Mackay of Scourie, at Killiecrankie in Perthshire on 27 July 1689. Dundee was killed towards the close of battle. Command passed to two officers, Major-General Thomas Buchan and Brigadier Alexander Canon, despatched by James VII & II from Ireland. They proved incapable of harmonious management of the clans. Although numbers had swelled to around 5,000, their forces depleted markedly when the Jacobites failed to break out of the Highlands, being held at Dunkeld in Perthshire on 21 August by considerably fewer numbers of Cameronians and militant Covenanters drawn from the Presbyterian

United Societies. An inferior number of Scottish-Dutch forces turned back the Jacobites at Cromdale in Aberdeenshire on 30 April 1690. Thereafter, the campaign petered out. Jacobites in Scotland remained in arms throughout 1691, but they were vulnerable to reprisals.

In 1708, bad judgement trumped bad luck. The French-backed invasion was delayed because James VIII & III caught measles. The invasion fleet with 6,000 troops eventually arrived in the Firth of Forth, but the appearance of superior forces of the Royal Navy prevented the establishment of a beachhead. On being forced back to France around the north of Scotland and Ireland, the faulty navigation of the naval commander, Claude, Comte de Forbin, caused virtually the whole fleet to flounder. While the rising was being lost at sea, Jacobites in Scotland had barely begun to mobilize. There were some stirrings in Stirlingshire but none of note in the Highlands or the northeast. Scottish courts remained reluctant to convict Jacobite activists who had never been required to fight. Over sixty leading Jacobites had been arrested and imprisoned in Edinburgh in anticipation of the rising. Twenty-two reputed ringleaders were transferred to London in its wake. None was prosecuted.

John, Earl of Mar, who had steered the Union through the Scottish Parliament, was removed from office as secretary of state for Scotland at the Hanoverian succession. He was able to play on the Scottish Jacobites' need for a leader at the Fifteen. The most prominent European commander with Jacobite connections was James Fitz James, Duke of Berwick, the illegitimate son of James VII & II. Berwick, a veteran of the Nine Years War and the War of the Spanish Succession, had acquired the dukedoms of Liria in Spain and Fitzjames in France. He was refused leave from French service by Regent Orléans. The best British alternative, the Duke of Ormonde, was indisposed. Mar failed to channel widespread discontent with the Union into a successful patriotic rising. By a disastrous combination of chronic indecision and tactical illiteracy, he threw away the overwhelming superiority of the Jacobites over the Whigs. Having mobilized around 16,700 men and captured both Inverness and Perth by the end of September, Mar dallied for over a month rather than press home his military advantage over the 4,000 Whig forces commanded by John, Duke of Argyll. While in Perth, no attempt was made to secure adequate provisions, repair arms or erect fortifications.

No determined effort was made to lay siege to Stirling, the garrison at the crossroads of Scotland, or to engage openly the Whig troops, who were in no position to absorb or replace any casualties of scale.

Mar then condoned a British dynastic over a Scottish patriotic strategy. Rather than consolidate in the central Lowlands by moving from Perth on Edinburgh, Mar sent a detachment of 2,500 across the Firth of Forth under the command of William Mackintosh of Borlum, 1,500 of whom, predominantly Highlanders, met up with troops from Teviotdale, other parts of the Scottish Borders, Dumfriesshire and Galloway. They joined a contingent of English Borderers, mainly from Northumberland. Instead of effecting a pincer movement on Edinburgh, the Northumberland gentry under Thomas Forster MP and James, Earl of Derwentwater insisted upon marching into England: a course to which the Highland contingent violently objected at Kelso. Nevertheless, as the defences of Newcastle had already been reinforced, Borlum acquiesced on a western incursion into England which ended in emphatic defeat at Preston on 13 November 1715, the same day Mar failed to win at Sheriffmuir near Dunblane. Five hundred Scottish Jacobites had refused to cross into England; three hundred were captured in the vicinity of Glasgow on their return home.

Although Mar's forces on the march in Scotland still outnumbered those of the Whigs by a ratio of more than two to one, Argyll had been allowed to choose the battlefield of Sheriffmuir. There were poor communications and no co-ordination between right and left wings of the 10,000 Jacobite troops of horse and foot. The right wing overpowered their Whig opponents, but the left wing gave way, lost their artillery and eventually took flight. The right wing could have retrieved the situation but chose not to press home their numerical advantage and let Argyll's jaded forces make an orderly retreat unmolested. Robert Freebairn, the printer who had arrived from Edinburgh to aid Mar issue manifestos from Perth calling for a British restoration of the exiled Stuarts and the dissolution of the Union, promptly claimed that the Jacobite forces had carried the day. Notwithstanding Whig claims to the contrary, the Jacobites had suffered fewer casualties and had fewer of their troops taken prisoner. But the battle was no more than a draw, which became a decisive reversal once Mar surrendered the initiative and retired to

Perth to await the belated arrival of James VIII & III in December. This led to no tangible results other than a dispiriting six-week conducted tour of Jacobite strongholds in the northeast prior to James's departure to France.

In 1719, Berwick was once again unavailable and the prospects of Ormonde leading the main invasion of England were wrecked when the Spanish fleet was blown off course. The command of the expeditionary forces sent in April to the Western Isles, reflecting divisions among Jacobite exiles, was disputed by William, Marquess of Tullibardine, and George, the Earl Marischal. Protracted delay in Stornoway meant that the Whig forces had already mobilized under General Joseph Wightman by the time Tullibardine was attempting to rally the clans on the mainland. No more than 1,500 clansmen answered his call to fight with a Spanish detachment drawn from the Galician Regiment. Wightman, with marginally fewer but more committed troops, won a decisive victory on 10 June on the slopes at Glenshiel in Wester Ross, again helped by the Jacobite tendency to score own goals. Once the Royal Navy had blown up the main Jacobite arsenal at Eilean Donan Castle on 10 May, the Spanish troops destroyed the ancillary arsenal at Loch Duich to prevent its confiscation.

During his clandestine visits to Scotland as a French agent at the Union, Colonel Nathaniel Hooke wrote the Jacobite playbook for military incursions from Scotland into England. In doing so, he updated the successful strategy implemented by the Scottish Covenanters to win the Bishops' Wars against Charles I in 1640. Instead of mounting an overland assault through England, Covenanting forces captured Newcastle, cut off the coal supply to London and provoked a financial crisis. Updated, this strategy had the additional merit of destabilizing stocks and shares, and forcing a run on sterling, which would severely compromise the capacity of the British government to pay its allies in the War of the Austrian Succession as well as pay for the relocation of British and allied troops to England from the Continent. Jacobites in Scotland would be in a strong negotiating position to reclaim Scottish independence and leave options open for a British restoration of the Stuarts. It was not feasible to implement this patriotic strategy during the minor risings of 1708 and 1719, but it certainly was during the major risings of the Fifteen and the

Forty-Five. However, Mar permitted the English Jacobite contingent from Northumberland under Forster and Derwentwater not to move east on Newcastle but instead to push westwards and then overland to London in the unfulfilled hope of attracting support from the considerable Roman Catholic community in Lancashire. Prince Charles, firmly committed to a British dynastic strategy, replicated this westward route in the Forty-Five when he pushed on from Edinburgh into England. Newcastle would have been a more difficult military target as George Wade, now promoted to field marshal, was preparing its defences. The only recruits gained by going west were the Manchester Regiment.

The Forty-Five was presaged by another storm wreaking havoc with an invasion fleet, on this occasion from France in 1744. The conclusion of this major rising was hastened by another naval misfortune when the Swedish fleet preparing to reinforce the Jacobites in Scotland was trapped in ice at Gothenburg. Although the Jacobites did have a military commander with a dash of brilliance in the Forty-Five, Lord George Murray was constantly undermined by a fatal personality clash with the charismatic but strategically inept Charles Edward Stuart. The prince's only previous military experience was the concluding six days of the four-month siege of Gaeta, near Naples, in August 1734, when he was not quite fourteen years of age. Mentored by the Duke of Berwick, they took cover in the trenches from overhead artillery discharges as combined Spanish and French forces dislodged those of Austria. Notwithstanding his lack of a previous command in the field, Prince Charles preferred to issue orders to which he expected unquestioning obedience instead of working through a council of war and giving discretionary powers to his field commanders. More so than Mar in the Fifteen, he was committed to a British dynastic over a Scottish patriotic strategy.

Within one month of raising his standard at Glenfinnan in August, Edinburgh was taken and the establishment of a provisional government in the Scottish capital was covered with benign neutrality by the thrice-weekly *Caledonian Mercury*. Whigs were also annoyed by the coverage of the taking and retention of Edinburgh by the monthly *Scots Magazine*. Their spirits were revived by news that Field Marshal Wade – with 18,000 men, including a Dutch battalion – was fortifying

Newcastle while the Jacobites still remained in Edinburgh. At the same time, reports from the British Admiralty affirmed that there were no preparations in the French ports of Brest and Dunkirk for an invasion across the Channel. Confidence that Jacobite endeavours would wither away was furthered by an effective but not comprehensive blockade of Scottish ports by the Royal Navy, assisted by the freelance endeavours of English privateers to seize ships carrying money or specie in silver and gold, arms and ammunition that had sailed from continental and North American ports to aid the Jacobite cause. Nevertheless, the Admiralty deemed it prudent to protect London by reinforcing dockyards and magazines on the Thames and Medway well into December. By this juncture, it was evident that the initial success of Prince Charles and his predominantly Highland army had flattered to deceive.

On 21 September 1745, 2,580 Jacobite troops had defeated a similarly sized force of Whig soldiers under Sir John Cope at Prestonpans in East Lothian. Their numbers were enhanced to 6,000 by Prince Charles taking Edinburgh. Most of these troops then marched as far south as Derby, avoiding pitched battles in taking Carlisle, Manchester and Preston. But, having spent no more than five weeks in Edinburgh, Prince Charles had failed to consolidate in Scotland before invading England – a decision carried by only one vote in his council of war split along dynastic and patriotic lines. This allowed Whig forces to regroup on a British basis, permitted civil war to flourish in Scotland, and prevented the establishment of any secure bridgehead for foreign intervention. The manifest lack of foreign support undermined the confidence of English Jacobites and led the Welsh Tory Sir Watkins Williams-Wynn, MP for Denbighshire and largest landowner in North Wales, to renege on his past flirtations with Jacobitism that promised an armed force for Prince Charles. The wholesale adoption of Highland garb by the Scottish Jacobites led to the complete failure to identify with the prince's army in England. English matrons allegedly believed that Donald Cameron of Lochiel ate babies – the only foundation for this rumour being the vampire kiss his grandfather Ewan had given to an English officer to avoid capture during the Cromwellian invasion of Scotland in the 1650s.

By the time Prince Charles reached Derby at the outset of December, Jacobite lines of communication had been overextended. Provisioning was extremely difficult. Both at the front and the rear the Jacobite Army was faced with superior English forces under the respective commands of William, Duke of Cumberland, now recalled from the Continent, and Field Marshal Wade. The Brigade of Guards stood between the prince and London. Clansmen whose livelihoods depended on the black cattle trade were particularly discomfited to encounter a virulent cattle distemper that had spread from the Continent and was reportedly transmissible to humans. Ultimately, the decision to retire was the result of Scottish pressure in a council of war now carried by the patriots. According to the campaign journal kept by David Wemyss, Lord Elcho, the reassertion of patriotic over dynastic commitments was articulated by Lord George Murray: '4,500 Scots had never thought of putting a King upon the English throne by themselves . . . they should go back and join their friends in Scotland and live and die with them.'[1]

Although forced to retreat from England against the inclination of Prince Charles, morale was still high because of the successful rearguard action fought by Lord George Murray and the arrival at Montrose in late November of reinforcements from France under the command of Lord John Drummond, the titular 4th Duke of Perth. These were the Royal Ecossais recruited clandestinely from Scotland in 1743–4, supplemented by a contingent from the Irish Brigade. Significant mobilization, mainly in the northeast and other Lowland districts north of the Tay on the return of the army from England, boosted forces to 8,000 at the battle of Falkirk on 17 January 1746, where the Jacobites defeated a similar number under General Henry Hawley as emphatically as they had General Cope at Prestonpans. Clan forces raised for the British government under the command of John Campbell, 4th Earl of Loudon, had been defeated at Inverurie in Aberdeenshire on 23 December 1745 in a skirmish involving just over a thousand on either side. They were further harried in the north of Scotland once the Gordons, Mackenzies and Frasers mobilized belatedly for Prince Charles and took Inverness on 17 February. At the same time, reinvigorated clan forces neutralized the other garrison founded or refurbished by the then General Wade at Inversnaid on Loch Lomond, Forts William and Augustus in the Great Glen, and the barracks at Bernera in Glenelg and Ruthven in Badenoch. The failure of the main Jacobite forces to take Stirling exposed their ramshackle command structure, as did the splitting of their forces to move north either by the way of Aberdeen or by Atholl before regrouping and retreating in diminished numbers to Inverness. Provisioning of the troops and supplies of munitions had been woefully neglected. No meaningful attempt was made to defend against the advance of Cumberland beyond the River Spey. Underfed troops were unable to complete a night march on Nairn ordered by Prince Charles that was aborted by Lord George on 15 April. Mutiny was threatening within Jacobite ranks.

No more than 5,000 in an army of just under 7,000 could fight the next day at Culloden. The tactical ineptitude of Prince Charles and his chief adviser, the negligent Irish quartermaster Colonel William O'Sullivan, was amply demonstrated by their choice of Culloden for a pitched battle on flat but boggy ground rather than on the adjacent slopes. Chronic vacillation on the part of the prince exposed his army to a demoralizing, one-hour cannonade of grapeshot without reply. The Jacobites had no ammunition to match the calibre of their now redundant artillery. Having conceded height advantage, the clans who formed the Jacobite frontline were obliged to charge towards superior forces of around 9,000 men equipped with workable artillery, well drilled in rapid fire musketry and in using bayonets to maximize casualties. At Cumberland's behest, the resulting carnage was perpetuated long after the battle.

After an emphatically brutal defeat at Culloden, the Jacobite leadership lost the political will to sustain patriotic campaigning. At Ruthven in Badenoch on 20 April, there was a general disbandment of around 5,000 forces drawn mainly from the north, west and central Highlands as well as survivors from Culloden. This was not an amicable parting of the ways for Prince Charles and Lord George Murray, who escaped separately overseas. For their followers who were not executed or banished, open season was declared on their lives, their livestock and their property.

## Reprisals

Ireland, as the major theatre for the first Jacobite rising, was subjected to a series of atrocities by both sides, perhaps instigated by Scottish Protestants once the siege of Derry was lifted in August 1689. But they were sustained by rapparees acting as a guerrilla force for the Jacobites, when their predatory instincts frequently took priority over their political allegiance, much to the chagrin of the Irish Gaelic poets. Rapparee predations were a convenient excuse for the Williamite forces to inflict indiscriminate reprisals on local populations. Lack of prompt payment and supplies among Jacobite forces encouraged desperate soldiers to become rapparees, as did some English and other deserters from the Williamites. However, these local atrocities, though brutal and callous, were sporadic and spontaneous rather than systematic retribution. The Treaty of Limerick did not end rapparee activity as many demobbed soldiers – perhaps as many as 2,000 – joined their ranks rather than return to the land as farmers and labourers. Although the treaty forestalled extensive land confiscations, it consolidated the intrusion of British Protestants into Irish Catholic estates since the later sixteenth century in the four provinces of Munster, Ulster, Leinster and Connaught. Only about one-seventh of all estates in Ireland were now held by Catholics. The departure of the Wild Geese outstripped the expulsion of Jacobites from Scotland and England in the other two major risings. The predominantly English Protestant supremacy secured by the treaty soon rolled back on any relaxation of the penal laws, which were renewed vigorously against Catholics from 1695.

The lack of a formal Jacobite rising meant England was spared wholesale forfeitures, executions and expulsions between 1688 and 1691. The first noted reprisals in London occurred with the exposure of the Assassination Plot of 1696. Nine of the ringleaders (five Catholics and four Protestants) were arrested. Trials began in March and executions in April 1696. The last to be executed, by beheading on 28 January 1697, was Sir John Fenwick. The former military commander, who had been in Dutch service with William of Orange as well as a major-general in the service of James VII & II before the Revolution, was attainted – that is, forfeited by Act of Parliament rather than by trial in the criminal courts. Six others were also apprehended but neither brought to trial nor attainted. One was eventually released, but the other five were incarcerated for life without ever having their day in court. The last to survive was John Bernardi, who had served under Fenwick in both the Dutch Republic and England. He died in Newgate Prison in London on 20 September 1736, forty years after his arrest. No punitive action was taken against around ten Scots and over thirty Irish Jacobites who were under surveillance or apprehended temporarily. Another English Jacobite who served an extensive term in prison was Neville Pain, a Jesuit priest apprehended in Scotland on suspicion of spying in December 1690. Despite repeated torture in Edinburgh Castle, he made no confession but was nonetheless detained without trial for over ten years. While prolonged detention without trial was a distinctive feature of English Jacobitism during and after the first major rising, English Jacobites caught up in the Fifteen and later in the Forty-Five were subjected to the same reprisals as their Scottish associates. Indeed, it can be readily ascertained from judicial proceedings against Jacobites that the English suffered proportionally no less than the Lowland Scots.

In Scotland, the three major Jacobite risings were marked by escalating reprisals, particularly against the Highland clans. The first atrocity against Jacobites was perpetrated by Edward Pottinger, an Ulster commander of a squadron in the Royal Navy patrolling the western seaboard against French privateers and monitoring activity in the North Channel. In May 1690, he ordered six hundred marines under Major James Ferguson on to the island of Eigg in the Inner Hebrides. They proceeded to massacre defenceless men, women and children affiliated to the Clanranald, a branch of the MacDonalds prominent in the Jacobite victory at Killiecrankie nine months earlier. In the aftermath of that battle, the only clan to go on the rampage was the MacDonalds of Keppoch, primarily to perpetuate their protracted feud with Lachlan Mackintosh of Torcastle, chief of Clan Chattan, over contested territories in Glenroy and Glenspean. Mackintosh and his clan were neutral in the rising. The MacDonalds of Keppoch, who had maintained a discreet distance from the other Jacobite clans from the outset of the campaign, were in a unique position. Coll MacDonald and his clan were outlawed both by the outgoing government of James VII for defeating government troops assisting the Clan Chattan in what became the last clan battle at Mulroy on 4 August 1688 and by the incoming Whig regime for supporting the Jacobite cause. The damage the MacDonalds of Keppoch inflicted on Strathnairn, Strathspey and in the town and hinterland of Inverness was more than matched by the destruction wreaked by the Whig forces under Mackay of Scourie.

In addition to Coll MacDonald of Keppoch, eleven chiefs or leading clansmen along with fourteen Lowland nobles and gentry were sentenced as Jacobites on 14 July 1690 to be forfeited and executed for treason by parliamentary enactment (effectively attainted). With Viscount Dundee already dead, all the rest failed to turn up to answer for their conduct before the Whig-dominated Scottish Estates. Moreover, the forfeitures were exemplary rather than perpetual and were gradually rescinded. The same circumstances were repeated on 2 July 1695, when three native-born Scots – the earls of Melfort and of Middleton as courtiers at Saint-Germain, and Sir Adam Blair of Carberry, occasional courtier and military commander – were attainted, forfeited and condemned to death in their absence for their continuing active engagement with France in the Nine Years War. In the interim, the MacDonalds of Glencoe were punished without warning.

Although the Jacobite Army had failed to break out of the Highlands after Killiecrankie, the continuance of the clans in a state of military preparedness well into 1691 served to heighten the frustrations of William of Orange and his Scottish government. When the MacDonalds of Glencoe – a small and isolated branch of the Clan Donald – failed to take William's offer of an indemnity by 1 January 1692, they were slaughtered. The infamous Massacre of Glencoe on 13 February 1692 was engineered by Sir James Dalrymple (later 1st Earl of Stair). A committed British unionist and joint secretary of state, he endeavoured to keep Scotland quiet in order not to distract William from the Nine Years War. The massacre of the clan – addicted to banditry and erroneously tarnished as popish – was intended to demonstrate Stair's fitness to be the sole secretary for Scotland. He manipulated the ambition and avarice of the military high command. Archibald Campbell, 10th Earl (later 1st Duke) of Argyll, readily agreed to deploy troops from the Argyll Regiment into Glencoe at the outset of February. William of

Orange conditionally authorized the massacre if the MacDonalds of Glencoe could be detached from neighbouring Jacobite clans. When news of the massacre leaked out, Stair was obliged to resign. But he, the military high command and King William were never held to account or obliged to make reparations.

In 1708, the ferocious and ill-defined English law of treason that made forfeitures permanent was foisted on Scotland in direct breach of the Treaty of Union. This measure made possible the show trials of Scottish Jacobites in English courts in York, Liverpool, Preston and Carlisle as well as London after the Fifteen and the Forty-Five. Moreover, after both risings, prominent Jacobites in Scotland and England were forfeited summarily by attainder rather than by due process of law. Despite siren voices within the British establishment calling for further exemplary measures along the lines of Glencoe, the greatest measure of leniency in any rising came after the Fifteen. This can be attributed, in part, to the need to establish the house of Hanover and, in part, to the remarkable escape record of leading Jacobites into exile, whether directly to the Continent or indirectly from imprisonment pending their trials and even their executions. Two Scottish lords, William Maxwell, 5th Earl of Nithsdale, and George Seton, 5th Earl of Winton, escaped from the Tower of London. In the night prior to Nithsdale's day of execution, his wife, Clarissa, came to the Tower with her maid, who was wearing a large cape and hood. Clarissa left with her husband disguised in the maid's outer garments. Winton hacksawed successfully through his prison bars several days before his intended execution. Two others captured at Preston escaped from Newgate, into which Jacobite prisoners had been packed and faced exorbitant maintenance charges. Thomas Forster, the MP for Northumberland, hid in the prison latrines while awaiting an opportunity to escape wearing a nightgown over his day clothes. Mackintosh of Borlum preferred the more direct route. The brigadier forcibly broke out from the prison's exercise yard with eight fellow inmates.

Primarily, leniency can be attributed to the widespread Jacobite affiliations of Scottish nobles and gentry. Because this Jacobite elite remained well connected to their Whig counterparts, there was a nationwide determination that landed families and their commercial associates should not be utterly ruined. Although occasional rioting was confined to Glasgow and Edinburgh, there was widespread public disquiet that 54 Scottish Jacobites were initially attainted for treason and a further 18 by 1717. Another contingent in excess of fifty prisoners in Edinburgh – drawn mainly from the landed elite, with a springling of merchants, professionals and artisans – were sent for trial to Carlisle in England. Suspected Jacobites were brought belatedly before sheriff courts in 1718. The Scottish juries tended to find their alleged guilt not proven. Simultaneously, judicial proceedings for forfeitures were partially obstructed by the Scottish courts allowing the process of sequestration, based on bad debts, to take precedence. Estates sequestered were often put under the charge of kin or agents of the person forfeited. But forfeiture enabled speculative interests, notably the York Buildings Company of London, to purchase Jacobite estates and to asset-strip timber and mineral rights.

Asset stripping was preceded by wanton destruction, a feature of the Fifteen no less than of the first major rising. The sacking of Strathearn, particularly the razing of the towns of Auchterarder, Blackford, Muthill and Crieff ten weeks after the inconclusive battle of Sheriffmuir on 13 November, was ordered and promptly regretted by the Jacobite high command. Nor should it be overlooked that the Whig forces under John, Duke of Argyll were under orders to plunder the estates of Lowland Jacobites in the four weeks before Sheriffmuir and wilfully plundered Jacobite estates in the Perthshire Highlands in the immediate aftermath of the battle. The only freelance profiteering was an unsolicited visit to Fife at the outset of 1716 by the roguish Rob Roy MacGregor, whose predatory proclivities, like those of the MacDonalds of Keppoch in 1689, led him and his followers to stand apart from the main Jacobite Army. Rob Roy was at Glenshiel in 1719 when the Jacobite defeat on 10 June led to selective reprisals being inflicted on clans in Wester Ross by General Joseph Wightman that served as a test-piece for state terrorism after the Forty-Five.

Parliamentary enactments for the disarming of the clans after the Fifteen and reissued in 1719 did not deter Jacobitism, being mainly observed by clans loyal to the Whig ascendancy. Among clans where chiefs and leading gentry had been forfeited, clan solidarity ensured that government attempts to sell their estates to other Scottish landowners or incoming adventurers were frustrated. Rents continued to be paid to chiefs and leading gentry exiled on the Continent. Two years after exemplary retribution in Wester Ross, attempts by government troops to lift rents in October 1721 were resisted violently. Donald Murchieson, chamberlain on the forfeited estates of the exiled William, 5th Earl of Seaforth, mobilized the MacKenzies and their local associates to ambush government troops, who were repelled with significant casualties at Ath-na-mullach in Kintail. After six years of civil disobedience, the forfeited estates in the Highlands were restored to chiefs and leading gentry in return for sureties for their own and their clans' peaceable conduct. Forfeitures proved no more of a deterrent to Jacobite activity than disarmament. Forfeitures were exacted against 12 of the 28 clans engaged in the first rising of 1689–91; all but 3 of the clans penalized were out in the Fifteen. Forfeitures were exacted against 16 of the 26 clans engaged in the Fifteen, and all but 3 of these clans were again active in the Forty-Five.

## Escalating Reprisals

Prince Charles Edward Stuart had been instrumental in ensuring that the Jacobite Army's highly mobile incursion into the English Midlands had remained orderly, civilized and restrained. Nevertheless, the march to Derby had persuaded the commanders of the superior British forces by land and sea that Jacobitism should be annihilated. Cumberland, hailed by Scottish Whigs as their deliverer from perpetual slavery and preserver of their religion, laws and liberties, was actively encouraged by the partisans of Hanover to make a final resolution of a damnable rebellion. By the time the rival armies manoeuvred for the showdown at Culloden, the Whig military command was describing their opponents no longer as rebels and disturbers of the peace of Great Britain but as cannibals. Prior to Culloden, Cumberland had commended the destruction of Jacobite clans. After Culloden, he moved in favour of the wholesale destruction of the livelihood and the lives not only of known Jacobites but of those suspected of being their associates. On 25 April, he instructed John, Earl of Loudoun, that on his troop manoeuvres in Glenelg and Ardnamurchan, 'you will constantly have in mind to distress whatever Country of Rebels You may pass through, & to seise or destroy all Persons You can find, who have been in the Rebellion, or their Abettors.'[2]

For their part, the Jacobite forces in the weeks before Culloden were notably apprehensive of the difficulties Cumberland was experiencing in holding his troops together in and around Aberdeen; likewise, by his licensing of summary justice by Whig clans in the western, central and southern Highlands. In particular, the Campbells of Argyll were condemned for their inhumanity and barbarity in burning houses, stripping women and children and exposing them to the severity of the weather in open fields, destroying cattle and stealing horses. Especially ominous was the recourse to state terrorism flagged up by naval bombardments and landings on the western seaboard, particularly in Morvern and Ardnamurchan. The aptly named *Terror* was among the ships principally engaged against estates that were owned but only nominally controlled by the house of Argyll. The officers involved in these reprisals by the Royal Navy later fabricated the extent to which Campbell contingents were engaged. So intent were the Whig forces on inflicting salutary and lasting punishment after Culloden that black propaganda against their Jacobite opponents was perpetrated deliberately throughout the British Empire. The *Virginia Gazette of Williamsburg*, which reported events two months after their occurrence, accompanied notice of Cumberland's victory with the reprint of the forged letter attributed to Lord George Murray ordering Jacobite troops to offer no quarter to the Whigs. The letter, which had not featured in the official account of the battle that reached London on 23 April, was first published as adverse publicity emerged about the severity of the repression after Culloden. Although the letter was repudiated by Lord George and other Jacobite commanders, public reaction to official news management became a test of loyalty to the British Empire and the Hanoverian monarchy. Houses from Aberdeen to London that did not burn white candles in their windows to celebrate victory became targets for mobs. Loyalists in Norfolk and other coastal towns in Virginia celebrated by burning a Jacobite effigy wrapped in tartan.

Jacobite forces were not blameless of charges of extortion, plunder and murder during the Forty-Five. But such violent incidents, which were compounded by excessive zeal in forcing out reluctant campaigners in the weeks prior to Culloden, were desultory not systematic. Whig expectations of Jacobite pillaging within Scotland were disabused by the orderly taking of Edinburgh in September 1745, by the mediation between Glasgow magistrates and Donald Cameron of Lochiel to provide supplies and provision in December, and by the civil conduct of Jacobite troops marching through the town of Falkirk prior to the battle on its muir in January 1746. The subsequent blowing up of St Ninian's Church near Stirling at the outset of February was an avoidable accident rather than the sectarian targeting of Presbyterian Whigs. The church had stored munitions. In the weeks prior to Culloden, Jacobite spokesmen complained that their lenient treatment of prisoners was not being reciprocated by Whig forces. Nevertheless, Whig troops were outraged by the treatment meted out to those of their number they found almost naked and eaten up with vermin in dark dungeons in Inverness after Culloden. These reports were issued to justify, not to explain, the severe treatment and little quarter for the Jacobite forces routed in the battle. In the eighteen months following Culloden, the Whig ascendancy issued periodic statements attesting to barbarous acts committed by Jacobite clans as far back as 1716 that had gone unpunished. By 1749, the ascendancy was belatedly collating denials of excessive brutality and other atrocities against Jacobite prisoners.

The immediate aftermath of the Forty-Five was marked by systematic state terrorism characterized by a genocidal intent that verged on ethnic cleansing. Burning, plundering and summary justice were ordered by Cumberland and the British high command, authenticated by the Whig ascendancy, and condoned by the Hanoverian monarchy. Cumberland was prepared to implement the Scotophobia prevalent within government circles. Scotophobia has been excused on the grounds of repeated rebellions from Scotland against the British state and the generally venal behaviour of Scottish politicians in seeking place and profit from successive British ministries since the Union of 1707. Such a defence can condone neither the state terrorism perpetrated in the immediate aftermath of Culloden nor the crass brutality of selecting clanship for eradication, for which wanton atrocities, unleashed brutality or devastating savagery are inadequate descriptions.

Reprisals intended to extirpate, cleanse and purge amounted to a campaign of genocidal intent marked by three distinct phases. The first was the wholescale slaughter of around 3,000 Jacobites not only at Culloden and in the days after the battle, but in the succeeding weeks prior to Cumberland's departure from Scotland at the outset of summer. The second was the selective terrorism directed against Jacobite districts by his successor, William Keppell, 2nd Earl of Albemarle, which followed on from the rumoured movements of Prince Charles Edward Stuart and slackened on his escape to France in September 1746. The third was the continuing and deliberate starvation of Jacobite and neighbouring districts through the wilful destruction of crops and livestock in glens and straths and of fishing boats on the coasts and lochs with the stated intention to effect either clearance or death. This last phase, though relaxed after Albemarle stepped down as commander-in-chief in Scotland during November, endured throughout the harvest season and restricted the remunerative droving of black cattle to market. The failure of harvests, loss of livestock and constriction of fishing had continuing repercussions well into 1747. Communities in the Jacobite heartlands of the Highlands and Islands, and the northeast of Scotland, were further terrorized by forced quarterings of soldiers and inquisitorial proceedings assisted by Presbyterian ministers to determine which landowners, tenants, labourers and servants had participated in the Forty-Five.

Cumberland and Albemarle were aided and abetted by ruthless English officers, such as Lieutenant Colonel Edward Cornwallis and Major James Wolfe, who both later served controversially in North America. They could also rely on the support of seemingly psychotic Lowlanders like Captain Caroline Scott and Major William Lockhart to run amok on land while Captain John Ferguson wreaked havoc by sea. Even such Highlanders as Captain George Munro of Culcairn and Captain Alexander Grant of Knockando engaged in state terrorism with a perverted will. A full flavour of the atrocities in the aftermath of the Forty-Five was collated in the voluminous work by Robert Forbes, *The Lyon in Mourning*.[3] Forbes, a nonjuring priest in Leith, had been apprehended at St Ninians near Stirling on his way to join up with the newly arrived Prince Charles Edward. He was imprisoned in Stirling Castle until February 1746 and subsequently in Edinburgh Castle until May.

Here he met many Jacobite activists, which made him decide to begin his account in the immediate aftermath of the Forty-Five. He had collated materials from witnesses, especially nonjuring priests, sufficient to fill eight volumes of at least two hundred pages each by 1762, when he became Episcopalian bishop for Ross and Caithness. He went on to complete a ninth volume by 1775 and start a tenth before his death on 18 November that year. While accounts of atrocities made up the substance of his work, he was also resolved to record every reported act of kindness performed by the victorious Hanoverian forces towards the vanquished Jacobites: not an overly demanding task.

Three episodes of state terrorism stand out. The first was the harrowing situation in Inverness immediately after Culloden when Jacobite prisoners were being summarily executed, notably when taken from incarceration in the principal Presbyterian charge in the town into its kirkyard. The second was the wanton assaults on the isle of Raasay in the Inner Hebrides before and after Culloden. No meaningful effort was made to spare men, women and children from repeated burning, looting and raping. The third was the fate of the three sons of Thomas Deacon, the nonjuring Bishop of Manchester, who had been recruited into the town's Jacobite regiment. All three were captured on the fall of Carlisle Castle to Cumberland following the retreat of the main Jacobite Army to Scotland. They were taken prisoner and brought to London for trial. Robert Deacon, a lieutenant in the regiment, died in prison awaiting trial. His elder brother, Thomas, a captain was hung, drawn and quartered at Tyburn – a gruesome ending that traumatized the youngest brother, Charles, an ensign who was subsequently transported to Jamaica. Prior to his public execution, Captain Thomas Deacon made an impassioned speech upholding Jacobitism as a rightful and lawful cause, castigating the regime of the Hanoverian usurper for its corruption and squandering of national resources, and commending the purity of nonjuring grounded in antiquity, universality and orthodox Christianity. This execution was one of the 24 inflicted upon the officers and men of the Manchester Regiment: a disproportionate 20 per cent of all Jacobite executions.

Soldiers who came from foreign service to participate in the Forty-Five were usually spared trial and execution if they were recognized as prisoners of war. But they were not automatically guaranteed such recognition. Colonel Henry Ker of Graden in Teviotdale was detained for two years after his capture at Culloden before being allowed to return to Spanish service.

Several factors on either side of the political divide determined that state terrorism was more noted for its genocidal intent than its achievement. Most of the regular Whig troops were unfamiliar with the varying Highland terrain. The sustaining of an underpaid army of occupation was hampered by logistical difficulties. Junior officers glorified in clearing out Jacobite neighbourhoods around the garrisons at Inverness, Ruthven, Bernera, Fort Augustus, Fort William and Inversnaid, where women offering succour to wounded or starving prisoners were in danger of being strip-searched and raped, and anyone found with arms was peremptorily put to death. Other officers had a comparatively more benevolent approach, notably Major General John Campbell of Mamore (the future 4th Duke of Argyll), his son, Captain John Campbell (later 5th Duke of Argyll), and especially John Campbell, Earl of Loudoun. These were the Whig commanders to whom the Jacobite clans were most inclined to surrender their arms. The distribution of at least half the sum equivalent to £40,000 despatched belatedly as military aid from France in the weeks before Culloden helped to relieve destitution. Merchants and other Jacobite sympathizers smuggled essential supplies through Fort William and Inverness. By late autumn 1746, overt relief for destitute women and children was also provided by quartermasters of garrisons.

State terrorism was condoned not only by chiefs of Whig clans but by chiefs whose clansmen had defied them to fight for Jacobitism. Before opting for ethnic cleansing, Cumberland had contemplated transporting all the Jacobite clans from Lochaber and the surrounding districts to the colonies. Further enquiries suggested this policy was not cost effective. Cumberland was encouraged to adopt the former option by the Whig clan chief, Donald Mackay, 3rd Lord Reay, who opined that it was easier to conquer than to civilize barbarous people. Commercial tensions between the clan elite and their followers were at the root of the defiance of chiefs in mobilizing for the Jacobite cause by MacKenzies in Easter and Wester Ross, MacLeods and MacDonalds in Skye, and

Mackintoshes and other members of the Clan Chattan in Strathnairn and Badenoch. Their respective chiefs promptly distanced themselves from errant clansmen after Culloden, as did non-combatant chiefs of the Stewarts of Appin, the Chisholms of Strathglass, the MacDonalds of Clanranald and, less successfully, the MacDonnells of Glengarry. Ludovic Grant of Strathspey had only sided with the Whig regime after Cumberland had crossed the border into Scotland. Immediately after Culloden, he rounded up for imprisonment and eventual transportation clansmen in Glenurquhart and Glenmoriston who had been early recruits for Prince Charles Edward.

Whig landlords and their factors deemed the situation desperate not so much when their Jacobite tenants had been killed, their widows harried and their houses burned, but when their rentals and other landed dues fell seriously in arrears. This was the case by 1747 in eight out of the ten townships from which the Stewarts of Appin paid teinds (tithes) to the earls of Breadalbane. Unsentimental Whig landlords, taking their lead from the house of Argyll in Mull, Tiree and Morvern in the 1730s, promoted the commercial reorientation of estate management; they introduced competitive bidding for leases to replace townships with multiple tenant farmers with single-tenant farms that reduced other tenants to labourers or assigned them to overcrowding crofting communities where agriculture had to be supplemented by fishing, quarrying and even recruitment into the British Army. While this process was suspended prior to the Forty-Five, it was renewed with vigour in its aftermath. Islay, now 3rd Duke of Argyll, carried out not so much displacement as wholescale clearance of disaffected tenantry in Morvern, a procedure soon followed by the Duchess of Gordon in Lochaber and the Duke of Montrose around Loch Lomond and the Trossachs.

These Montrose estates in the southern Highlands also testified to the problems of gaining redress for innocent victims of the burning of houses and plundering of livestock by government forces. In the aftermath of Culloden, troops under the command of a Major Forrester, who was reportedly uneasy and indeed reluctant to carry out indiscriminate reprisals, had removed over 2,000 cattle and horses as well as a significant number of sheep and goats. They were taken to Crieff by 14 June 1746 to allow innocent victims to claim full restoration of their livestock if not their property. Forrester was prepared to dispense with bureaucratic procedures which required an innocent victim to obtain a certificate from the Presbyterian minister of his or her parish that they had not been engaged in the Forty-Five, and likewise further certificates for the two witnesses helping to identify their livestock. However, even when innocence was proved, livestock could not always be redeemed. Government soldiers had killed and eaten all the kids and lambs along with some of the sheep. All the horses had already been sent to Perth for sale; some had been stolen by soldiers on their way to market and sold clandestinely and cheaply.

Redress was far from immediate even when injured parties took legal action against errant military. This was particularly evident in Aberdeen after what the magistrates viewed initially as an atrocious riot on the night of 1 August 1746 instigated and led by Captain Henry Morgan and sustained by Lieutenant Dudley Ackland, two other lieutenants and three ensigns. Officers and troops had been imbibing in taverns. They took offence at the failure of the town council to fully carry out instructions from their commanding officers that bells were to be rung and lights put in all windows to commemorate victory at Culloden. The magistrates, who had recently taken over from a Jacobite administration, were prepared to ring bells in public but not to instruct citizens to illuminate their houses. Morgan and his associates, having changed out of their uniforms, stirred up a riotous mob that went on the rampage throughout the night attacking the town council chambers and breaking windows in the warehouses of merchants and the abodes of citizens. The magistrates promptly appealed to Albemarle, the Scottish judiciary, the Convention of Royal Burghs, sympathetic nobles and the local MP, John Maule. They estimated damages at £230. Albemarle and the military high command were not initially receptive to reparations through a process of arbitration, the Scottish judiciary likewise. Both the military and the judiciary agreed eventually that this process could be devolved to two local gentry, George Middleton of Seaton, a former banker in London, and Patrick Duff of Premnay, the political manager for the Duke of Argyll in the northeast. After hearing evidence from the military, the magistrates and the citizens of Aberdeen, they issued a decree on 31 January 1747 which found that Captain Morgan had instigated the riot but obliged him to pay less than £60 towards reparations. Dudley and the five other officers were fined £1 in total. Reparations took six months to achieve and constituted just over 26 per cent of all damages.

Although denied any form of redress from state terrorism, the Jacobite clans had not been entirely passive victims. A few malevolent government officers, most notably Captain George Munro of Culcairn in Easter Ross, were assassinated in Lochaber, where the long-established bandit tradition of the district was augmented by displaced and harried clansmen led by such commissioned and non-commissioned officers as Captain John Roy Stewart and 'Sergeant Mor' Cameron. The association of banditry with social and political protest led to the persistence of guerrilla warfare in and around Rannoch until the 1750s. Conversely, the growth of banditry in the most mountainous districts of the southern and central Highlands enabled the British government to press home aspersions that all Jacobite clans were so tainted, and therefore they should continue to be subjected to punitive military pressures. As pointed out by John Farquharson of Invercauld, a chief sympathetic to the Whig ascendancy, the rigorous enforcement of another Disarming Act from the summer of 1746 exposed Whig as well as Jacobite clans to depredations by bandits.

A more widespread practice of civil disobedience was the payment of rents from forfeited estates to chiefs and clan gentry exiled on the Continent. This practice led to the show trial of James Stewart, a veteran of the Forty-Five who was sending rents to France and legally resisting the eviction of his clansmen by the government factor in Appin. Within six months of the murder of Colin Campbell of Glenure in May 1752 – most probably by another government agent, his nephew Mungo Campbell – Stewart was wrongly accused, tried and executed as an accessory. Stewart was a nonjuror, a member of the Episcopal community who were the principal victims of state terrorism, even though their harassment by penal laws was not so comprehensive as that of Jacobites in the Roman Catholic community. In the northeast as well as the Highlands and Islands, Episcopal and Catholic churches, chapels and meeting houses were destroyed and their priests imprisoned and banished.

Following adverse press publicity for the atrocities in the aftermath of Culloden, the British government moved away from extirpating to civilizing the clans. A legislative programme promoted from 1747 was marked by Acts disarming the clans and proscribing the wearing of tartan. These applied to all Highlanders, not just Jacobites. In the mistaken belief that the authority of chiefs was institutional rather than personal, the British government abolished heritable jurisdictions. Of far greater significance than regalities or baronies with criminal powers running local government throughout Scotland was the sustained, but not always thorough, purging of Jacobites and their sympathizers from the magistracy and town councils in the royal burghs and from commissioners of supply and justices of peace in the shires. The real intent of this abolition, however, was to reward chiefs and other land-owners who had opposed Jacobitism. Archibald, Duke of Argyll was empowered to distribute around £493,000 for jurisdictions that had largely become anachronistic. Not compensated were the forfeited, the exiled and the banished.

Even where the forfeited were occasionally pardoned, there was no clear pathway to recovering their landed estates, as evident from the experience of George Keith, Earl Marischal. Having compounded his forfeiture for participating in the Fifteen by further participating in the rising of 1719, by his service as a Jacobite envoy to Spain and France, and by his occasional stints at the courts in exile, the Earl Marischal had all but given up reclaiming his ancestral estates in the shires of Aberdeen and Kincardine by the Forty-Five. However, when Hanoverian Britain entered the Seven Years War as allies of Prussia, the Earl Marischal, by now a respected adviser to Frederick the Great, sought and was granted a pardon by George II in May 1759 while on a diplomatic mission to London. His pardon, subsequently confirmed by a parliamentary enactment, led to Marischal taking an oath of allegiance to the new Hanoverian monarch, George III, when he was again in London in June 1761. A further parliamentary enactment awarded him £3,618 with interest from 1725 on that portion (about half) of his estates which had been assigned to, but never fully paid up by, the speculative York Buildings Company, which had gone bankrupt in 1736. Although he attended the coronation of George III in September 1761, he was given no further assistance to reclaim the remainder of his ancestral estates, some of which he managed to purchase by 1763. However, in the following year, he sold them and gave up all claims to his remaining estates as he settled down to permanent residence, not temporary exile, in Prussia.

## Expulsion

Imprisoned Jacobites, whether captured in England or brought from Scotland to England, faced show trials after the Fifteen and especially after the Forty-Five. The prime issue to be determined in these trials was not of guilt but of destination. Rather than bring all prisoners to trial, lots were drawn to try one person from each cell with the remainder sharing the same fate. If an officer was tried and found guilty, he and all his cellmates were executed. If a lesser rank was tried and found guilty, he and all his cellmates were sentenced to penal servitude and banished to British colonies in North America and the Caribbean. Escapes from jail pending trial were particularly celebrated.

Although the lower ranks in both risings, even if convicted, were generally granted an amnesty and released, the impact of show trials is best summed up in the chorus to the Scottish folksong 'The Bonnie Banks of Loch Lomond', composed anonymously in 1746 and relating to the fate of two prisoners brought from Scotland for trial in Carlisle:

> O ye'll tak' the high road, and I'll tak' the low road
> And I'll be in Scotland afore ye
> But me and my true love will never meet again,
> On the bonnie, bonnie banks of Loch Lomond.[4]

The prisoner taking the low road was to be executed. While his spirit would soon be in Scotland, his lack of a bodily presence ruled out a tryst with his true love on the banks of Loch Lomond. The prisoner taking the high road faced transportation with no immediate prospect of a return to Scotland. Discounting those who had escaped into exile, most convicted Jacobites whose punitive sentences were carried out were expelled overseas. After the Fifteen, around 41 Jacobites were executed (all but 1 in England) and around 638 prisoners were transported to the

Americas. For every three who landed in North America, one went to the Caribbean, where prisoners indentured for seven years were effectively given a death sentence. After the Forty-Five, at least 120 prisoners were executed and 3,000 transported, but destinations are less easy to break down as Barbados was notionally the hub for the dispersal of prisoners to the colonies.

Shipping political prisoners to the colonies had a long pedigree, being regularized by Oliver Cromwell's conquest and occupation of Ireland and Scotland in the 1650s. After the restoration of the monarchy in 1660, the governments of Charles i and James vii in Scotland frequently condoned the transportation of dissident Covenanters to the Americas. Notwithstanding the incarceration of Jacobites in place of Covenanters in Dunottar Castle in Kincardineshire and on the Bass Rock off East Lothian, the transportation of political prisoners declined considerably from the Revolution until the Fifteen. A few transportation ships were taken over by the prisoners and sailed to ports such as Bordeaux on the French Atlantic coast. In practice, however, most prisoners were sold in the first port of call in the Americas, especially in colonies with a shortage of fit, skilled labour. Some affluent prisoners were able to bribe captains to let them go if their ships called in to Irish ports for provisions. Others were allowed to purchase their own indenture at the first colonial port in which their ship arrived. Those attached to commercial networks, or who already had kindred in American colonies, often had their indentures bought out on arrival. Some had their indentures bought for military purposes in Virginia and the Carolinas after the Fifteen and also in Georgia after the Forty-Five. Highlanders, in particular, were viewed as useful frontier fighters. Although most of the transported were denied the right to return to Britain on the expiry of their seven-year indenture, they were usually content to stay and make a new life for themselves in North American colonies.

However, not all Jacobites were transported following due legal process. On 31 March 1746, 125 Highlanders were induced to sign up or make their mark to indentures offering apprenticeships for seven years, each with a clause barring their return thereafter.[5] Their passage was to be arranged by Samuel Smith, a merchant in London, who assigned them to a shipmaster, John Handley, for their transportation to unspecified American colonies. However, this collective indenture was drawn up seventeen days before Culloden with no evidence that they had been brought to trial since their capture. Their guilt was presumed rather than established in a court of law. A more egregious and exotic example occurred when severely injured prisoners at Culloden ended up in Ethiopia.

A noted hazard for all ships carrying prisoners across the Atlantic was their capture by privateers and pirates. If the former, there was the prospect of their ransoming or their release into continental exile. If the latter, the safest option was often to join the pirates. Apart from loss of life, the worst option was to be sold into slavery in the Ottoman Empire by pirates operating from enclaves in the western Mediterranean, such as the Barbary Coast. This form of 'white slavery' could mean a lifetime of servitude if no ransom was raised by family and friends or more usually through public subscription in Scotland – not a prospect readily available to Jacobites, especially those who were diverted to Ethiopia after being captured by 'Turks'. The Ethiopian episode (see the Introduction) was no more than a diversion in the ongoing Jacobite diaspora in the eighteenth century. But it does demonstrate that the diaspora went far beyond Europe and the Americas into Africa, and was indeed to penetrate Asia.

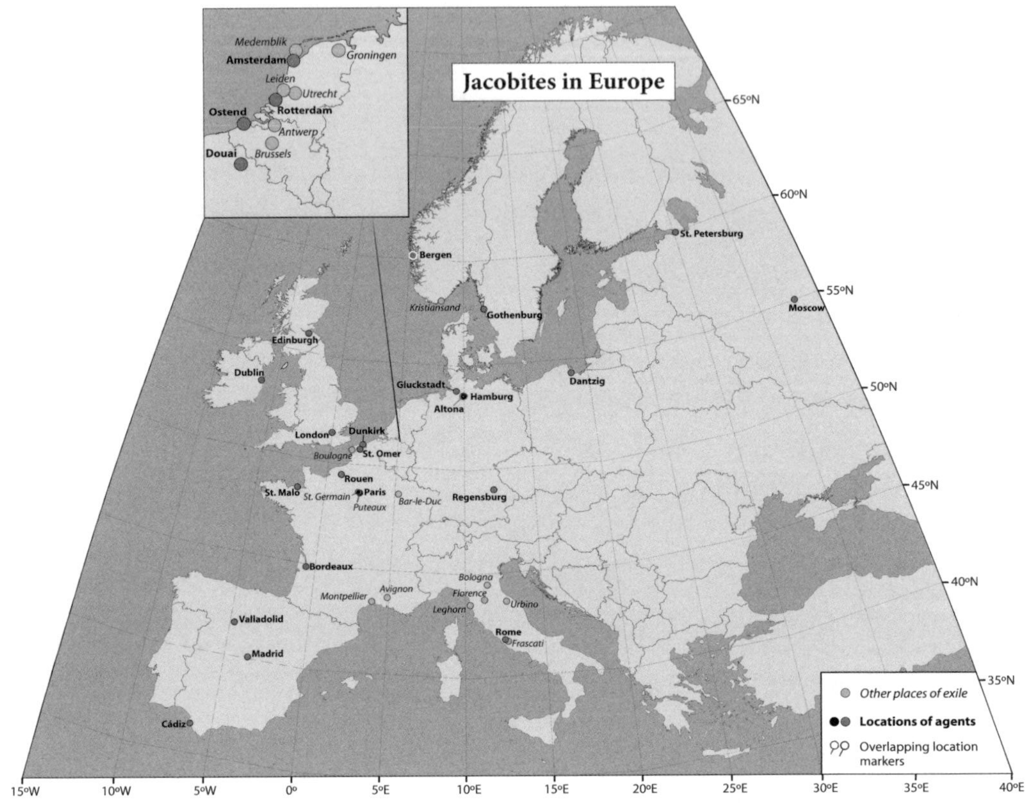

Jacobites in Europe

Medemblik
Amsterdam
Groningen
Leiden
Utrecht
Ostend
Rotterdam
Antwerp
Douai
Brussels

65°N
60°N
55°N
50°N
45°N
40°N
35°N

St. Petersburg
Moscow
Bergen
Kristiansand
Gothenburg
Edinburgh
Dublin
Gluckstadt
Hamburg
Dantzig
Altona
London
Dunkirk
Boulogne
St. Omer
Rouen
St. Malo
St. Germain
Paris
Bar-le-Duc
Regensburg
Puteaux
Bordeaux
Bologna
Montpellier
Avignon
Florence
Urbino
Leghorn
Valladolid
Rome
Frascati
Madrid
Cádiz

15°W
10°W
5°W
0°
5°E
10°E
15°E
20°E
25°E
30°E
35°E
40°E

Other places of exile
Locations of agents
Overlapping location markers

4

# Jacobite Diaspora
# in Continental Europe

Failed risings and a profusion of plots between the 1690s and the
1750s had created a geographic diaspora not just in Europe but in
America, Asia and Africa and a social dispersal that involved artisans, farmers and fishermen as well as nobles, gentry, merchants, clergy
and scholars. Jacobites engaged in commercial, military, colonial, religious and cultural networking. Their interaction, covert as well as overt,
in Europe and beyond was protracted but never pointless for adherents of the exiled Stuarts. The benchmark for analysing the extent and
depth of the Jacobite diaspora is Irish studies. By way of contrast, little
of substance has been done to investigate the nature of English engagement. Current scrutiny of Scottish engagement in the Jacobite diaspora
has gained much from exemplary Irish scholarship. An appreciation of
the spread and diversity of networking is vital given the manifest incap-
acity of the courts in exile to support Jacobites displaced from Ireland,
Scotland and England in the wake of the major risings. Neither James
VII & II nor James VIII & III had the financial resources, the diplomatic
means or the political motivation to find remunerative employment for
all exiles lingering around their courts in France and Italy. A frustrated
James VIII & III reputedly suggested in October 1716 at the court in exile
in Avignon that Jacobites lacking gainful employment should consider
fighting against the Turks. Émigré communities in continental Europe,
including those active in commercial networking, were often no more
than passively Jacobite. Nevertheless, exiled Jacobites from France to
Russia were actively involved in state formation and imperial expansion.

## Scottish Networking

Irish brigades established in France and Spain from the flight of the 'Wild Geese' continued well into the 1690s and extended to military service in Austria, Poland and Russia. This enforced diaspora was complemented by mercantile networking in Italy as well as France and Spain that involved banking and shipping to the Americas, Africa and Asia. The Irish brigades in France and Spain had clauses in their contracts releasing them for Jacobite service, which was only activated during the Forty-Five, when more Irish than Scottish troops provided the professional military backbone to Lord John Drummond's French Regiment. Ongoing recruitment to the brigades, which was facilitated by the Roman Catholic clergy as a grassroots and not just an elite expression of Irish Jacobitism, was a continuing feature of French and Spanish forces in the Americas and Indies as well as Europe until the Napoleonic Wars at the end of the eighteenth century. Scottish Jacobites exiled in France, even in the aftermath of the Forty-Five, had resisted the creation of a Scottish brigade that would diminish the prospects of the court in exile countenancing further risings.

Ciphers in Jacobite code books obtained by the British government give a partial insight into diplomatic and military aspects of Jacobite activity in Europe in the run-up to the minor, Spanish-backed rising in 1719. Selective hints are also given on trading activity in Europe and beyond. In terms of locating Jacobite activities, the courts in exile in Paris and Rome are prioritized. The main European powers that treated with them in anticipation of the rising are mentioned, notably in relation to discreet diplomatic discussions at The Hague in the Dutch Republic involving ambassadors from the emperor in Austria, the Spanish king, the regent of France and the tsar in Muscovy. Passing mention is given to the kings of Prussia and of Poland. The presence of the British ambassador attending on the States-General at The Hague is also noted. Cadiz in Andalucia, together with La Coruna and Vigo in Galicia, were codified as ports of departure for the Spanish invasion fleets. Ostend in the Austrian Netherlands and Dunkirk in northern France, along with Saint-Malo in Brittany, were also deemed significant as naval and privateering bases close to Britain suitable for the embarkation of Irish brigades should France countenance their participation. That Porto in northern Portugal and Bordeaux in southwestern France were also sited had less to do with military logistics than their commercial importance as centres of the wine trade through which documents, money orders and even arms were regularly couriered. There was a significant presence of Irish émigrés in both ports, with some English in the former and Scots dominant in the latter. An Irish presence, as well as its importance as a supplier to Cadiz in the Spanish coastal trade, explains the inclusion of Barcelona in Catalonia. Although secondary to its Mediterranean trading, Barcelona was allied to Cadiz and La Coruna in furthering the Spanish colonial trade to the Americas and Asia. Ostend and the ports cited on the French Atlantic were engaged to a greater or lesser degree in trade as a global undertaking. Jacobite interest in such trade explains the mention of Amsterdam, Rotterdam and Hamburg as the foremost European colonial entrepôts along with London. Two other ports, Gothenburg and St Petersburg, were included partly as prospective participants in the rising, but primarily as the trans-oceanic gateways on the Baltic to Sweden and Russia, respectively. Both ports had a Scottish as well as an Irish and English presence of merchants and soldiers.

The code books suggest that the Scottish diaspora played a vital role for the sustenance of Jacobitism through commercial networking, which involved landowners as well as merchants, in trading ventures around the North Sea, the Baltic, Atlantic Europe and the Americas. Scottish mercantile communities engaged distinctively in tramp trading, a practice which they exported from the Baltic to the Caribbean in the seventeenth century and on to the East Indies in the eighteenth as associates of the Austrians, Swedes and the Prussians as well as the Dutch, Danes, French and English. The expansion of Scottish commercial networks into North America and the Caribbean complemented rather than superseded long-standing networks that operated from Bergen via Gothenburg, Danzig, Stockholm and Koenigsberg on to St Petersburg. The Atlantic connection contributed to the reinvigoration of Scottish networks in Bordeaux and their installation in Lisbon and Cadiz well in advance of 1707. Networks linked not only the Scottish cities of Edinburgh, Glasgow, Aberdeen and Dundee, but lesser ports such as Ayr, Greenock and Dumbarton in the west, Bo'ness, Kirkcaldy and Montrose in the east, and Inverness and even the Shetland Isles in the north to the trans-oceanic hubs of London, Hamburg, Amsterdam and Rotterdam. Mercantile communities of Scots in London, Norwich, Newcastle, Belfast, Dublin and the Isle of Man colluded in privateering, disguised ownership of shipping, smuggling, tax evasion and other illicit commercial practices that facilitated free trade between Scotland and the American colonies as well as helping to sustain Jacobitism as a political movement well beyond the Treaty of Union. The purging of customs and excise officers was an integral aspect of British government reprisals in the wake of the Forty-Five.

Jacobites easily fitted into the distinctively clannish behaviour of Scottish commercial networks based on kinship and family association. These networks had a high degree of literacy and entrepreneurship among merchants and lawyers acting clandestinely, as when counterfeiting shipping documents and judicially packing colonial courts. Commercial networks inclined towards Jacobitism notably deployed women of social standing as couriers to and from the courts in exile. Indeed, three were mentioned in the code books captured before the minor rising of 1719: Mary Fleming (née Keith), Countess of Wigtown; Margaret Maule (née Hamilton), Countess of Panmure; and Margaret Hamilton (née Hamilton), Lady Orbiston. Not all women couriers who claimed titles were actually ennobled: notably, Christian Scott, Lady Largo, courier for the Duke of Hamilton at the making of the Union. The daughter of the financially straightened laird of Ardross, near Elie in Fife, she married into the seafaring Wood family in the neighbouring coastal town from which she took her reputed title. Her title mattered less than her capacity to dress as a noble lady, which allowed her to conceal letters and bills of exchange and wear tradeable jewels.

In comparison to the Irish, the Scots had better and more inventive mercantile banking and credit transfer, partly as a product of interlocking networks and partly as a consequence of greater engagement with colonial trade both before and after 1707. By the 1720s the Scots were not only retrenching their position in France but expanding into Spain, hitherto the dominant preserve of the Irish. The Scots, though a lesser presence in Italy, were actively competing with the Irish in Livorno (Leghorn) and Venice, which also opened up trade to Turkey and the

Levant. However, it was an Irish network that facilitated Prince Henry Benedict's pawning of the exiled Stuart's crown jewels, acquired from his late mother Maria Clementina Sobieska, at Genoa in 1745. It was also an Irish network at Saint-Malo in Brittany that provided the two ships whose arrival in Scotland with Prince Charles Edward instigated the Forty-Five. The much-vaunted naval blockade of Scotland during the last major rising was consistently breached by overseas Jacobite networks. Around thirty ships carrying arms and supplies docked at the northeast ports of Arbroath, Montrose, Stonehaven, Aberdeen and Peterhead, and at Stromness in Orkney.

## Active and Passive Émigrés

The courts in exile had no power to exact levies on trading conducted by commercial networks sympathetic to Jacobitism. However, the mercantile communities engaged in tramp trading preferred to minimize customs on goods by making paper transfers through bills of exchange discounted through private banks. Likewise, they tended to use easily disguised transportable commodities such as pearls rather than specie or bullion, which opened up opportunities for Jacobites to move funds into and out of Scotland without attracting too close surveillance.

British government surveillance did expose a Scottish commercial network operating from Glasgow and Edinburgh to Paris and Rotterdam. Between May and July 1722, the network was charged to transfer the equivalent of £2,000 from Scotland to agents of the Earl of Mar in Paris. British surveillance was designed less to apprehend the Scottish participants than to stop their funding after the transfer process revealed the extent of their continental operations. Funding was raised in Glasgow by Episcopalian merchants associated with Atlantic trading in sugar and tobacco – principally Walter Graham or Houston, who operated mainly in the West Indies; John Buchanan, a lawyer connected to the foremost family engaged in the sugar and tobacco trades; and William Nelson, a banker who absconded when threatened with arrest. Attending on them was a Mr Fisher, a Jacobite agent from Paris, ostensibly in Glasgow to purchase lace. The cash equivalent was then passed to two Edinburgh merchants for transfer to Paris: Thomas Gordon, a senior magistrate in the city, and William Erskine, the only member of the network arrested and sent to England for questioning. The cash transfer by bill of exchange was received in Paris by two bankers, a Mr Gerard and a Mr Watters, acting in association with Robert Arbuthnot, a merchant banker in Rouen. The court in exile at Saint-Germain was represented by its banking company, Messrs Baxter, Finlay and Falconer. This transfer to Mar was conducted covertly without involving General Dillon, the principal Jacobite agent in Paris, where Harry Maule of Kelly was acting as the Scottish alternative to the Irish resident. He was in regular contact with the exiled Scottish community in Rotterdam through John Walkinshaw of Barrowfield and William Dundas, the principal distributor of pensions sent from Paris.

Information from the financial network to support Mar discloses further features of the Jacobite diaspora in France and the Dutch Republic. First, Robert Arbuthnot's activities in Rouen went beyond merchant banking into financial speculation. His clients were by no means exclusively Jacobite. He was linked both to French émigrés and a network of London Scots from a Jacobite hinterland. Second, the payment of pensions in the Dutch Republic raises questions about how and why they were made to Jacobites in a state notably hostile to their cause. Third, the career of Harry Maule, who became the titular 5th Earl of Panmure in 1723, personifies the transition from active to passive Jacobitism as exiles sought and gained pardons to return home to Scotland.

After having fought for the Jacobites at the Revolution, Robert Arbuthnot fled to France where he established himself as a merchant banker at Rouen. He was from a nonjuring family in the Mearns. He became a principal conduit for the transfer of funds from Scotland to Jacobites in exile – a position consolidated from 1732 by his partnership with Alexander Alexander, a banker in Paris. Thirteen years earlier, his brother, Dr John Arbuthnot, a celebrated physician, statistician and satirist in London, had recommended him to John Brydges, Duke of Chandos, who wished to invest in the Mississippi Project promoted from Paris by the émigré Scot John Law with the backing of Regent Orléans. Chandos, who had secured his fortune while serving as paymaster for the Duke of Marlborough's forces in the War of the Spanish

Succession, became a major if not always successful investor in the Royal African, East India and South Sea companies. He went on to become an enthusiastic promoter of the York Buildings Company on its acquisition of forfeited estates in Scotland. A significant patron of the arts and an active slave trader, Chandos in 1724 became chancellor of the University of St Andrews, the first Englishman to hold such a position post-Union. As well as underwriting the problematic, if substantive, investments of Chandos in the Mississippi Project, French government bonds and the French East India Company, Robert Arbuthnot facilitated a correspondence between Chandos and Regent Orléans. He also retained Chandos's diminishing profits in France until exchange rates with Britain improved to the duke's advantage. However, Arbuthnot was not receptive to the duke's proposal that he become the French agent for marketing of coal mined by the York Buildings Company in Scotland, which was inferior to coal from Newcastle for firing kitchens and furnaces. Although Chandos was not directly associated with Jacobitism, he was most willing to work financially with those such as Law, who had helped the cause financially, and others like Andrew Drummond, a goldsmith, who provided him with private banking facilities. Drummond had founded his own bank in 1717 mainly to serve Scottish exiles and the armed forces. His brother William, 4th Viscount Strathallan, fought in the Fifteen and was killed at Culloden in 1746. Drummond's bank was closed for the duration of the Forty-Five.

Robert Arbuthnot gained further from the Chandos connection when John Drummond, a Perthshire kinsman of Andrew the goldsmith, was despatched to France to lead the duke's negotiations with John Law, a stint that was to last seven months until the financially overextended Mississippi Project began to crash in May 1720. Having begun his career as an Edinburgh merchant, John Drummond moved to Amsterdam where he established himself as a prominent financier prior to the Union. He became the leading continental financier for the British forces during the War of the Spanish Succession and commenced a long association with the future Duke of Chandos. Following the conclusion of the war in 1713, Drummond spent the best part of the next decade shuttling between Amsterdam, Edinburgh, Paris and London. He had rather mixed success as an investor in the Royal African and the South

Sea companies and had substantial losses from the Mississippi Project. By 1724 he had settled in London to help shape the direction of the East India Company and acquired the estate of Quarrell in Stirlingshire. Three years later he became MP for the Perth Burghs. A committed unionist, he nonetheless had strong Episcopal and Jacobite connections. With backing from Prime Minister Walpole, Drummond used imperial patronage both to rehabilitate Jacobites and to reward Whigs. He did so in association with two brothers from a mercantile family in Montrose, George and Alexander Ouchterlony, who had become leading mortgage brokers and investors in the Scottish land market for returning exiles. They regularly imported French wines brokered by Robert Arbuthnot and acted as bookkeepers for his transactions through London. They were also prominent financiers for Scots seeking to enter the British armed services or engage in overseas ventures. Without compromising themselves in the eyes of successive British governments, the Drummonds and the Ouchterlonies discreetly networked their patronage and financial expertise to redeem Jacobite fortunes through imperial placements either for the sons of exiles and former activists or even for the reprieved and the repentant. Placements were primarily in India, with more limited patronage exercised in the West Indies, in Virginia and South Carolina, and in Sierra Leone, the Gambia and Angola.

The immediate concern for exiled Jacobites was their financial welfare, for which the payment of pensions was a pressing matter. The merchant banker paying pensions through William Dundas in Rotterdam was William Gordon, a designated Jacobite agent in Paris, who oversaw the payment of pensions to Scottish exiles in three designated areas – in Rotterdam for the Dutch Republic and Flanders, in Saint-Omer for Normandy and in Bordeaux for southwestern France. The Jacobite court had been moved out of Paris to Bar-le-Duc in Lorraine and then on to Avignon when James VIII & III lost the backing of Regent Orléans. However, his French government paid Mary of Modena, the queen mother, still resident at Saint-Germain, a pension amounting to 50,000 livres (£100,000) a month, of which 12,000 livres were passed on as running expenses for her son, who also received a pension of 83,000 livres per year from the papacy. Queen Mary at Saint-Germain and Mar at Avignon scaled monthly payments to exiles to pressing needs, service records, social standing and military rank that ranged from 10–15 livres for the lower ranks in the Jacobite forces on to 30–150 livres for commissioned officers and 200 livres for all exiled nobles. After expenses for the running of the courts in exile in Paris and Avignon were deducted, there was less than 2,250 livres monthly for distribution to exiles in the three designated locations. In June 1718, Dundas notified Gordon that the monthly payment in February and March to 22 exiles came to 1,690 livres, of which five officers accrued from 45 to 100 livres, two lairds received 60 livres each, and the remaining payments of 25–35 livres were paid to professionals and artisans.[1] However, the death of Mary of Modena in May 1718 and the movement of James VIII & III from Avignon on to Urbino in February 1717 and then on to Rome the following year severely curtailed pensions available to Jacobite exiles, especially those not prepared to move to Italy. John Law and his brother William did step in temporarily in 1719–20: John initially to supply 24,050 livres and to underwrite 600,000 livres in arrears due to the late Mary of Modena; William to establish a fund of 9,000 livres for three months for the relief of exiled widows and orphans. In the interim, the Dutch Republic remained attractive to Jacobite exiles of a staunchly Protestant persuasion, with prospects of gainful employment in the merchant cities of Rotterdam and Amsterdam as well as in garrison towns like Utrecht and Groningen, bases for the Scottish-Dutch brigades, which were noted for deserters to Jacobitism in all three major risings. Leiden was also an attractive university town, particularly for the study of law and medicine.

Jacobites in receipt of pensions were essentially underemployed, much given to factional bickering – which occasionally was resolved by duels – and prone to boredom, which could be relieved by travelling. For those inclined to travel rather than retire to French provincial towns, William Gordon's financial support for exiled Scots in France extended to the provision of banking services in various French cities. Alexander Blair of Kinfauns, who had commenced his exile in Rotterdam after the Fifteen, had moved on to Avallon in Burgundy by October 1718. Gordon not only provided him with the equivalent of £180 to meet pressing debts but arranged letters of credit in Lyon and Montpellier as Kinfauns travelled on to explore southern France.

Gordon was also the main conduit for bank transfers from Scotland for Sir John Erskine of Alva, who spent no more than seven months at Saint-Germain before returning home on being pardoned in July 1716. Erskine of Alva had a chequered political career while serving in both the Scottish and British parliaments. He moved from being a supporter of the Revolution and the Union to becoming an electoral agent for his kinsman the Earl of Mar, whom he joined in the Fifteen, more in a logistical capacity to secure supplies than as a military commander. He was twice sent to France in advance of, and then after the arrival of, James VIII & III in Scotland to establish whether Henry, Viscount Bolingbroke, as the co-ordinator at Saint-Germain for the Fifteen, had secured arms and ammunition for the Jacobite forces. On the second occasion, as Bolingbroke continued to fail in his commission, Alva obtained arms and ammunition on his own initiative. However, James VIII & III had returned to France from his six-week sojourn in Scotland before they could be despatched. Alva, who stayed on at Saint-Germain, was subsequently involved in diplomatic negotiations with Sweden and Spain following the dismissal of Bolingbroke. While the former Jacobite secretary of state cut his contacts with the court in exile as a precursor to securing a pardon, this was not accomplished until 1723. Bolingbroke only returned to England when his attainder was rescinded in 1725.

Alva was far more successful in working his passage home. He was well connected to the Scottish judiciary through his brother Charles, the Lord Justice Clerk, and Mar's brother James Erskine, Lord Grange. This judicial connection ensured that Alva was not included in lists of the attainted during his exile. Since 1712, Alva had been secretly working a promising silver mine discovered on his estate in Clackmannanshire. When news of this mine, which potentially offered a return of one-fifth of all profits to the Crown, was leaked during his exile, his brother and his judicial associates were able to secure a pardon for Alva. He accepted on condition he was not required to take an oath of allegiance forswearing the exiled Stuarts. He slipped back into London pending royal ratification by George I, for whom it proved a poor bargain. Alva failed to sustain the silver works productively, ploughing his profits into speculative ventures in agriculture, canals and other mines. Although he no longer publicly espoused Jacobitism, he was not entirely passive, helping to raise funds for Lockhart of Carnwath's Commission of Trustees in Scotland.

While the circumstances of Alva's reprieve from exile were exceptional, pardons were becoming a more attractive option as pension funds contracted and the means, if not the impetus, to travel around France and Italy declined. However, as Alva's case demonstrated, political connections were all important, especially as pardons were by no means guaranteed or unconditional. Their granting made Jacobitism vulnerable to British government interference, especially as pardons were weaponized by John Dalrymple, 2nd Earl of Stair, during his six-year stint as British ambassador in Paris. Prior to the Fifteen, patronage awarded to families with wavering political allegiances had not always produced favourable outcomes. When James Macfarlane, brother to John Macfarlane of Arrochar, was confirmed in December 1714 as a naval surgeon on the *Dartmouth*, a ship of the East India Company, his clan's wavering support for the Hanoverian succession was consolidated. At the same time, James Paterson, with almost ten years naval service, was recognized as suitable for promotion to lieutenant on a man-of-war. However, his brother, Sir Hugh Paterson of Bannockburn, one of the Stirlingshire gentry on manoeuvres during the aborted rising in 1708, remained committed to the Jacobite cause and became an exile in the Dutch Republic after the Fifteen. Stair, prior to his departure from Paris in 1720, was intent on turning underemployed Jacobites in exile into passive Jacobites once home. The contrasting fortunes of the 4th and 5th Earls of Panmure reveal changing Jacobite perspectives on the weaponizing of pardons.

James Maule, 4th Earl of Panmure, who served as a lieutenant colonel at Sheriffmuir, escaped to France in the wake of the Fifteen. He was duly attainted in June 1716. As the court in exile moved from Avignon to Urbino and then to Rome, he felt increasingly marginalized, despite the Earl of Mar being his nephew. Instead of moving directly from Avignon to Urbino in 1717, he embarked on a grand tour at the rather advanced age of 58, guided by his tutor, a Dr Blair, and accompanied by his nephew James, son of Harry Maule. On 8 February, they progressed from Avignon to Pesaro via Marseilles, Nice, Genoa, Bologna, Rome and thence to Urbino by 14 July. The fourth earl stayed there for eight months, then set out on 12 February 1718 for Venice via Fossombrone and Ravenna and on to Milan, Turin, Lyons and Fontainebleau, returning to Avignon on 19 March. Having completed his two-stage tour, he went to Paris, where he contacted John, Earl of Stair, with a view to procuring a pardon. As he refused to give up Jacobitism, his pardon was blocked. Panmure died in Paris in April 1723, being succeeded in the Jacobite peerage by his brother, Harry Maule of Kellie.

Harry Maule had also fought at Sheriffmuir and went into exile in the Dutch Republic, where he enrolled as a mature student at Leiden under the name of James Campbell. In July 1717, a spy for the British government claimed that Harry Maule had been back in Scotland as a Jacobite agent and brought this to the attention of the university authorities. However, Maule, then aged 56, was able to mobilize support from five fellow Scottish students – none of whom were committed Jacobites – that he had never been absent from Leiden for more than three days in Rotterdam or Amsterdam since he commenced his studies in May 1716. His claims were upheld by the university authorities and town magistrates. In correspondence with Mar in 1718, Maule expressed considerable frustration that he could not return to Scotland to redress the mismanagement of the forfeited Panmure estates. Their purchase by the York Buildings Company was being fought tenaciously through the courts by his sister-in-law, Countess Margaret Maule (née Hamilton), with covert backing from Lord Grange. Her endeavours to limit the company's asset stripping was not aided by her inveterate gambling on speculative ventures such as the Mississippi Project, but principally on the South Sea Bubble. Having already become an informer for the British government before Stair left Paris, Mar was able to exert some influence with the Whig ministry on behalf of his uncle, who had never actually been attainted. Within a year of succeeding his brother, Henry Maule was back in Scotland assisting Countess Margaret secure a lease of the Panmure estates from the financially troubled York Buildings Company. In securing his pardon, the titular fifth earl swore allegiance to George I. Yet he never entirely abandoned Jacobitism, serving on Lockhart's Commission of Trustees as a pacific rather than a belligerent presence.

Nevertheless, his two surviving sons became associates of Archibald, Earl of Islay and pillars of the Whig establishment. William Maule became MP for Forfarshire (Angus) in 1735 and sat in the Commons for 47 years without ever making a speech. Having served with distinction in the British Army in the War of the Austrian Succession, he was made Earl of Panmure in the Irish peerage in 1743 and began the full recovery of the Panmure estates from the bankrupt York Buildings Company, which he eventually achieved in February 1764. In the interim, his younger brother, John Maule of Inverkeillor, an advocate by profession whom Islay made his confidential political secretary in 1730, was placed as MP for the Aberdeen Burghs in 1739, a position to which he was re-elected in 1747 despite a challenge to his political sympathies by Cumberland in the aftermath of Culloden. In the following year he became a baron of the Court of Exchequer in Edinburgh and held this sinecure until his death in 1781.

## Conditional Pardons

Political connections notwithstanding, pardons no less than placements usually required patience, as evident from the experience of George, the son of John Mackenzie of Delvine, clerk and later president of the Court of Session in Edinburgh, the highest civil court in Scotland. The family estate in Perthshire was supplemented in Fife in 1711 when George, a year after qualifying as an advocate, married Margaret Malcolm, heiress to Balbedie. Concerned about the impact of English law, language and customs on Scotland in the aftermath of Union, George MacKenzie was drawn to the Jacobites in the Fifteen. He was attainted, but his wife retained Balbedie in her own name while he lost his claim to succeed to Delvine. In France, he initially attempted to set himself up in the wine business at Bordeaux, where he had dealings with the Ouchterlonies. After he moved to Paris in 1718, he extended his financial contacts to include William Law, the main conduit for Scottish investment from Whigs as well as Jacobites in his brother John's Mississippi Project. Mackenzie remained a fringe figure in the Jacobite émigré community in and around Paris. He corresponded with, but seemingly did not visit, the courts in exile. While at Leghorn in an attempt to establish a

Scottish market for Italian wines, he had preferred to travel to Florence rather than Rome. He did develop a warm relationship with the courtier Alexander, Lord Pitsligo, who, having discovered that he had been inadvertently left off the lists of the attainted after the Fifteen, had slipped back to Britain by March 1720, returning over the summer to live peaceably on his Aberdeenshire estate.

Finding it increasingly difficult to live on irregular payments of his monthly Jacobite pension of 60 livres and having made only modest gains from his investments with the Laws, George MacKenzie prepared for a return home after he moved to Boulogne on the Normandy coast at the outset of 1722. Boulogne had become a base for hard-pressed Jacobite exiles such as Sir Hugh Paterson of Bannockburn as well as a convenient location for crossing the Channel. While in Boulogne, Mackenzie received a more regular transfer of funds from his family in Edinburgh, mainly through Robert Arbuthnot in Rouen and William Gordon in Paris. He eventually moved covertly via London back to his wife's estate in Balbedie by April 1722. There he lived quietly until he was apprehended in July and imprisoned in Edinburgh Castle. Concerted lobbying of Sir Robert Walpole and his Whig ministry had already begun by friends and family. Of all the well-connected Scottish politicians professing Mackenzie's interest, the most assiduous and persistent was the Earl of Stair. Momentum behind his petition for a pardon in May 1724 slowly gained traction over the next twelve months. He attained his liberty and a full pardon from George I on 2 July 1725.

Finding productive employment problematic, George MacKenzie had moved to London by June 1732, relying initially on Scottish contacts to improve his social standing. He spent some time in the West Country and in Oxford to cultivate the image of a gentleman scholar. As a political facilitator for Scots in London, he ensured clan chiefs profiting from the black cattle trade paid their debts to bankers like Andrew Drummond. With the assistance of the Ouchterlonies, he secured posts in the armed services or as imperial adventurers for the Mackenzies and other kinsmen. Having married another heiress in 1739, he gained possession of several properties in London. In 1743 he moved to Cambridgeshire. Ready access to its university allowed him to resume the life of a gentleman scholar now dabbling in agricultural improvements. Although he dismissed the Jacobites as 'rebels' at the Forty-Five, he was appalled that prisoners were shipped to England for trial.

While George MacKenzie first encountered Stair's weaponizing of pardons in October 1717, Jacobite exiles had been appraised of this policy by December 1716, when Alexander Robertson of Strowan led a party of exiles through France to join the Earl of Mar at Avignon. Contacted by Stair when passing through Burgundy, Robert Stewart of Appin returned to Paris. Both Stewart of Appin and Robertson of Strowan had fought in the first two major risings and been forfeited in their wake. Appin's sentence was relaxed within five years. Although Strowan was exiled for over twelve years in the Dutch Republic and France, he had returned in 1703 and lived unmolested around Loch Rannoch in the Perthshire Highlands. Neither Appin nor Strowan made any serious endeavour to secure a pardon until the general amnesty that accompanied the restoration of forfeited estates in the Highlands in 1726: an amnesty strongly promoted by General George Wade in his endeavours to pacify the clans. In Appin's case, the pardon certainly neutralized his own Jacobite commitment and that of his son and successor, Duncan Stewart. But it did not prevent their clan mobilizing again for the cause in the Forty-Five under Charles Stewart of Ardshiel, whose estate was forfeited after he escaped to France. Rents from Ardshiel were paid intermittently to him in Paris until his death in 1757. Being pardoned did not stop Strowan becoming the only man to fight for the Jacobites in the three major risings. He effectively ignored his subsequent forfeiture by continuing to live without serious challenge on his Perthshire estate until his death in 1751.

Where pardoning did have a more significant impact on clan commitment was among the MacKenzies, whose chief William, 5th Earl of Seaforth accepted the amnesty of 1726 to reverse his attainder and facilitate the recovery of his estates, which stretched from Easter Ross to the isle of Lewis. His return paved the way for leading gentry of his clan to seek commissions in the Royal Navy and the British Army. The clan was divided in the Forty-Five. The reluctance of Kenneth, 6th Earl of Seaforth, and some of his leading gentry to come out for Jacobitism did not prevent a sizeable clan contingent mobilizing in defiance of them under George MacKenzie, 3rd Earl of Cromartie. Following capture while on manoeuvres in the northern Highlands, Cromartie was brought to London, tried for treason and condemned to be executed. He was spared after extensive political lobbying by Scottish Whigs not unsympathetic to the patriotic dimension to Jacobitism despite their own pragmatic siding with the Hanoverian forces. After three years imprisonment, Cromartie was pardoned in 1749. His estate remained forfeited, and he was kept under house arrest in London until his death in 1766.

After both the Fifteen and the Forty-Five, exiled Jacobites occasionally slipped home clandestinely to attend to pressing family business or in anticipation of a pardon: a process beset by uncertain outcomes, as was notably evident in relation to the differing experiences of the two brothers from the ducal house of Atholl. William, Marquess of Tullibardine and Lord George Murray had both reneged on their military commissions – the former in the Royal Navy, the latter in the British Army – to join the Fifteen, after which they were both attainted. They subsequently interrupted their exile in France to participate in the minor rising of 1719. Tullibardine based himself at Puteaux on the outskirts of Paris. He rarely travelled, though he did accompany James, Earl of Panmure on the first stages of his journey from Avignon into Italy in February 1717. Following his return to exile in 1719, his finances became increasingly reliant on bank drafts authorized by his father, John, 1st Duke of Atholl, whose death in 1724 compounded Tullibardine's financial difficulties. Along with Seaforth and other leading Jacobite exiles in and around Paris, Tullibardine had contemplated seeking an indemnity from the British government if granted permission by James VIII & III. However, as he was attainted, Tullibardine was barred from succession to the dukedom, which passed to his younger brother James, a committed Whig, who did not accord a high priority for bank drafts to France. Tullibardine suffered a further blow when his brother Lord George Murray returned to Scotland just prior to his father's death. Unlike Tullibardine, Lord George had stayed clear of Jacobite intrigue and had preferred to spend his time in exile travelling throughout France and into Tuscany before the minor rising of 1719. Thereafter, he spent time in the Austrian Netherlands and the Dutch Republic. He also dealt directly in Rouen with the merchant banker Robert Arbuthnot for the channelling of funds from Edinburgh to himself and Tullibardine. His father having initiated proceedings that were condoned by James VIII & III, Lord George was eventually pardoned in 1725. His political standpoint in Scotland remained equivocal. He did swear allegiance to George II in 1739, reputedly to participate in that year's general election. But after his marriage in 1728 to Amelia Murray, a Perthshire heiress, he had insisted that his wife's inheritance remain in her name and thereby not be liable to forfeiture should he again commit to Jacobitism.

In the interim, a memorandum of understanding between Tullibardine and his brother James, 2nd Duke of Atholl that they would behave respectfully and fairly towards each other soon broke down. Tullibardine claimed in 1726 that his allowance from James of 50 livres a month, a quarter of that for a Jacobite noble in exile, was insufficient. After lobbying from William Law on Tullibardine's behalf, James agreed to 3,000 livres per month in 1732. But he was in no hurry to ensure that the revised allowance was paid in a timely manner, which stretched Tullibardine's lines of credit with Alexander Alexander, now his banker in Paris. Tullibardine faced eviction from his house in Puteaux for rent arrears and was imprisoned for two months for unpaid debt at the outset of 1733. His finances were set on a more regular footing from 1737 with the assistance of Andrew Drummond, banker in London. However, Aeneas MacDonald, a banker in Paris who came from the Kinlochmoidart branch of the Clanranald, commented on Tullibardine's declining health in June 1742. The next year Tullibardine became embroiled in a protracted dispute with James Innes, rector of the Scots College in Paris, over payment of funds sent over from Scotland on his behalf. In poor shape financially and physically, Tullibardine along with Aeneas MacDonald joined the small party accompanying Prince Charles Edward to Scotland in late July 1745. Twelve months later, Tullibardine, who was captured after Culloden, died while imprisoned in the Tower of London.

His brother Lord George Murray, knowing full well that his participation in three major risings would lead inevitably to his execution if captured, escaped to the Dutch Republic in December 1746. As in his first period of exile, he embarked upon an extensive period of travel, moving across the Rhine and basing himself principally in the duchy of Cleves. Although he again visited France and Italy and journeyed through Switzerland, his main travels were along German waterways and to Silesia, Poland and Prussia. While James VIII & III, whom he visited in Rome in 1747, proposed a pension for him, his main support came from the Perthshire estates of his wife, Amelia, who later joined him on his travels. In 1759, they retired to Medemblik in the Dutch Republic, where Lord George died in 1760. During his journeys, he commented perceptively on economic, military and social affairs. In periods of reflection, he justified his conduct as the leading Jacobite commander, supported principally by other Scottish commanders, in taking battlefield decisions independently of Prince Charles Edward when the occasion required during the Forty-Five.

By the time of the death of Lord George Murray, the Jacobite cause was eclipsed politically. Payments of rents from Scotland were becoming occasional rather than regular. The Scots College in Paris was being transformed from a base for clandestine Jacobite activity into a support agency for Jacobite exiles and, like the Scots College at Rome, a stopping off point for Scottish travellers. With the Hanoverian dynasty secure, British governments were in no haste to grant pardons. At the same time, French governments provided limited opportunities for military employment and were not particularly generous in awarding pensions to escapees from Culloden. Pensions for those not actively involved in the Scottish regiments in French service fell from 50,000 to 34,000 livres per month – a drop of 32 per cent – and entrusting their distribution to Prince Charles Edward until his removal from France in 1748 did not expedite payments.

Lord George's close associate during the Forty-Five, David Wemyss, Lord Elcho, had succeeded to the command of the Royal Scots in French service on the titular 4th Duke of Perth's death in 1747. After his retirement in 1770, he lived out the rest of his life in France and Switzerland before dying in Paris in 1787. His overtures to return home had been rejected repeatedly by British governments. His Jacobite associate David Ogilvy, titular 4th Earl of Airlie, was fleetingly in Scotland in 1752 laying the ground for the Elibank Plot and recruiting for his own regiment in French service. He had attained the rank of lieutenant general by the time he was allowed to return home in 1778, though he had to wait another ten years for a full pardon. Aeneas MacDonald, the banker, was captured at Culloden and tried for treason in London in December 1747. His sentence to be executed was remitted for testifying about his Jacobite activities and associates. He resumed his banking career on returning to exile in Paris, where he died in 1770. Francis Farquharson of Monaltrie, also captured after Culloden, was tried, condemned to death and reprieved in London. Instead of exile, he underwent prolonged house arrest for twenty years in Derbyshire. Neither exile nor imprisonment was to the taste of Lord Pitsligo. After Culloden, he hid out in coastal caves and other safe havens on his estate until his death in 1762.

The Jacobite diaspora threw up two notable exceptions to the general pattern of émigré careers in France. John Holker from Lancashire had been a member of the Manchester Regiment captured at Carlisle on the Jacobite retreat from England. Duly sentenced to death in London, he escaped from Newgate prior to his execution and made for France, where he utilized his extensive experience in textiles to promote industrial-scale developments in and around Rouen. He brought over skilled workers and machinery from Britain to introduce new production methods, becoming inspector-general in charge of foreign manufactures from 1755, a post which he held for three decades. Neil MacEachen MacDonald, who had aided Prince Charles Edward's escape from Scotland after Culloden, also went into exile in France. His son Etienne, who started his military career with the Irish forces in 1784, supported the French Revolution in 1789 and went on to become a prominent general helping Napoleon Bonaparte fulfil his imperial ambitions. In 1809, for his outstanding service in Italy, Napoleon made Etienne MacDonald the first Marshal of France promoted in the field. He was also created Duke of Taranto in the Kingdom of Sicily. Long retired, he journeyed back to South Uist in 1825 to trace his family's roots in the township of Howbeg.

## Imperial Service

In contrast to France, state service and empire building were features of the diaspora through Scandinavia into Russia. Rather than escape directly to France or the Dutch Republic, many Jacobites after the

Fifteen, the minor rising of 1719 and the Forty-Five sailed across the North Sea to Bergen in Norway or to Gothenburg in Sweden. There had been a Scottish mercantile presence in Bergen since the mid-sixteenth century, though in the early eighteenth century the port was a base for French privateers. The Scottish mercantile presence in Gothenburg went back to the town's foundation in 1621 and continued as it became Sweden's premier trans-oceanic seaport. Other than a few exiles who merged into the mercantile community in Bergen, most moved on. Yet, the most enduring community of Scots in the whole Jacobite diaspora was established at Kristiansand in southern Norway, where merchants from Dundee and fishermen from Angus pooled their expertise and contacts to establish the town as a major centre for herring fishing. As exiles were not able initially to return for their families in Scotland, they contracted bigamous marriages and produced second families, which brought them into conflict with the local Lutheran church. Jacobites landing in Bergen were rarely confined for extensive periods as desired by British diplomats, and either made their way to France with the aid of privateers or were conveyed by French and Scottish ships, usually tramp traders in the latter instance, sometimes via Gothenburg and then through the Øresund into the Baltic. They sought military employment in Stockholm or mercantile engagement among Scottish communities, most notably in Danzig (Gdansk) in the Polish-Lithuanian Commonwealth, or both military and mercantile opportunities in St Petersburg as the western gateway to Russia.

After the Forty-Five, David, Lord Ogilvy, who had arrived in Bergen from Angus in a shipload of merchants and fishermen, proceeded via Gothenburg to France. James Moir of Stoneywood was expected to journey to Paris also to seek a military career in French service. Instead, he chose to stay in Gothenburg, from where he had participated in overseas trade in 1740 and developed the mercantile skills that he and his family had long practised in Aberdeen. He was eventually pardoned and allowed to return to Scotland in 1762, considerably more prosperous than when he had left. A more circuitous route brought Kenneth Sutherland, 3rd Lord Duffus, to Russia in the aftermath of the Fifteen. Duffus, a commander in the Royal Navy, had defected to join Mar before escaping from Caithness to Gothenburg where, in 1709, he had married Charlotta Christina, daughter of the governor, Admiral Erik Siöblad. Duffus informed the British government in 1717 that he wished to be reconciled to the Hanoverian monarchy. After setting out, he was seized at Hamburg by the resident British agent. Brought to London and imprisoned pending his trial for treason, he was liberated but effectively banished. After returning to Gothenburg, he decided to accept the position of rear admiral in the Russian Navy in 1722. He was also appointed superintendent of the naval construction yard at Kronstadt on the island of Kotlin in the Gulf of Finland, which guarded the western approaches to St Petersburg. Peter the Great had erected his new capital there in 1703 after securing access to the Baltic at the expense of Sweden. Duffus was promoted to admiral in 1724.

While Russia had long featured in the military diaspora of Scots in the seventeenth century, its role in the Jacobite diaspora was primarily the creation of Patrick Gordon of Auchleuchries. Having served initially in the Swedish (from 1655) and Polish (from 1659) armies, he entered Russian service in 1661. His extraordinary skills as a military engineer secured his promotion to full general, the highest rank in the Russian Army, by 1686, when he briefly returned to Britain as a diplomatic envoy to James VII & II in London, from where he progressed north to visit his family estate in Aberdeenshire. By 1689, as dean of the foreign officers in Moscow, he led them to join Tsar Peter in overthrowing his half-sister, Sophia. Until his death in 1699, he was principal foreign adviser to Peter the Great in his endeavours to modernize Russia by promoting trade and cultural links with Western Europe and building up a strong professional army and navy. As a committed Roman Catholic, Patrick Gordon adamantly opposed the Revolution of 1689–91 in England, Ireland and Scotland. But he was never an active participant in the first major rising or in subsequent plots against William of Orange. However, he maintained a regular correspondence with Jacobite merchants, bankers and booksellers in London, Paris, Rotterdam, Hamburg, Danzig, Riga and Narva. Melfort and Middleton were his principal contacts at the court in exile in Saint-Germain. One of his sons, James, was severely wounded at Killiecrankie in 1689 before returning to military service in Russia, and a son-in-law, Major General Alexander Gordon, was commander of foot at Sheriffmuir in 1716.

Alexander Gordon had enlisted in Russian service in 1695, retiring with the rank of major general to his estate of Auchintoul in Banffshire in 1711. He was persuaded out of retirement at the Fifteen, taking charge of the diminishing Jacobite forces after James VIII & III and Mar departed Scotland in the spring of 1716. Gordon did not pursue an effective guerrilla campaign before his departure from the West Highlands with clan chiefs and other leading Jacobites in the autumn. In France he opted to live not as a courtier in Paris but as a retired émigré in Boulogne, from where he mounted a successful legal campaign in both Scotland and England to have his attainder of 1716 reversed on the technical grounds of serious misinformation. He had been named as Thomas not Alexander Gordon, effectively confusing him with a naval commander who subsequently went into Russian service. In anticipation of a pardon, Alexander Gordon had slipped back into Scotland by 1726. He spent his last three years in quiet obscurity without giving allegiance to George II.

Thomas Gordon from Aberdeen had a varied seafaring career in mercantile, privateering and convoy services for the Scottish state prior to 1707 and thereafter as a naval commander in the British Royal Navy. Like Duffus, he had refused to take the oath of allegiance at the Hanoverian succession. Unlike Duffus, he was not involved in the Fifteen. Instead, Gordon moved around Jacobite circles in London before travelling surreptitiously to France, having a presence at Saint-Germain until he secured a Russian naval command in 1717. He was able to take advantage of a further recruiting drive by Peter the Great to expand his armed forces during the Great Northern War of 1700–1721. At the behest of John, Earl of Mar, Gordon became integral to Jacobite endeavours to seek support from both Russia and Sweden to counter the attempts of George I, as the land-locked elector of Hanover, to secure access to the North Sea. Spain was also brought into play when the new king's British ministry sought to curtail the Spanish recovery of Italian territories lost by the Treaty of Utrecht in 1713. However, neither Russia nor Sweden was prepared to divert resources for the Spanish-initiated rising in 1719. Following renewed attempts to get support from Spain and Russia, Gordon and Duffus did test British sea defences in June 1725 when three ships allegedly bound for Spain called in to Scotland and Ireland. Two of the three ships that moored off Stornoway in Lewis were captained by men who spoke in broad Scots rather than English, though one captain claimed to be French, the other Irish. Gordon's full power to treat and conclude a deal with Russia on behalf of James VIII & III was checked but not eclipsed by the appointment of James Fitzjames, Duke of Liria, son of the Duke of Berwick and grandson of James VII & II, as Spanish ambassador to Russia in 1727. Also commissioned to negotiate for the court in exile at Rome, Liria's Jacobite endeavours were undone when Spain made peace with Britain and France in 1729.

In the interim, Gordon, who was promoted to rear admiral in 1727, went on to become the leading admiral based at Kronstadt after his celebrated victory at the battle of Danzig during the War of the Polish Succession in June 1734. This was a defeat not only for the French Navy but for the French candidate for the elected kingship of the Polish-Lithuanian Commonwealth, which was secured by the Austrian candidate, who became Augustus III, with the backing of the Russian Empire and the electorate of Saxony. Thereafter, Gordon focused on his role as commander-in-chief at Kronstadt. But he maintained his contacts with Jacobite merchant bankers in Paris and the court in exile at Rome and, above all, with the Scottish manager of his finances, John Gordon, merchant in Edinburgh, to provide patronage not only for Jacobite families but for their kinsmen and local associates. Although his patronage was sought for medical appointments, his main placements were military and naval. They included Alexander, the son of John Gordon of Glenbucket, who moved from the British to the Russian Army in 1737 but was killed four years later. Returning to Scotland to attend to family concerns in 1736, Admiral Gordon was publicly honoured by the city of Aberdeen in the same way as Patrick Gordon of Auchleuchries had been fifty years earlier. He died in April 1741. Throughout his time in Russia and latterly at Kronstadt, he was supported by his son-in-law, Sir Henry Stirling of Ardoch, a leading facilitator for Scottish connections, who married Anna Gordon in 1726.

Sir Henry Stirling's route to Russia had been convoluted. In the first general election after the Hanoverian succession, he stood as the parliamentary candidate for Perthshire in February 1715. Although he won the majority of votes, procedures were managed irregularly by the returning officer, John, 1st Duke of Atholl, to secure the election of his own son, Lord James Murray (the future 2nd Duke). Stirling of Ardoch spent considerable time in London contesting the validity of the election, but to no avail. He was not an active participant in the Fifteen. He became a person of significance in the Jacobite movement after he volunteered to deliver the pardon accorded to his uncle Sir John Erskine of Alva in July 1716. When they met up, Alva was planning a journey to Copenhagen to liaise with Peter the Great and his brother, Dr Robert Erskine, the tsar's physician and principal political adviser since 1712. Alva persuaded his nephew to take on this assignation while he returned to Britain. Stirling of Ardoch was well received by both the tsar and his uncle Robert. The court in exile, on moving to Avignon, assigned Ardoch a watching brief over the start of the peace negotiations between the Swedes and Russians at The Hague. At the Earl of Mar's prompting, he was despatched as resident Jacobite agent at St Petersburg in the autumn of 1717. In placing Jacobites and their Scottish associates, his brief extended from military to cultural affairs, particularly after Dr Robert Erskine died in 1718. Although his presence at Danzig had been monitored by British diplomats in 1719, Ardoch confined his Jacobite activities to Russia and corresponding with the court in exile, now in Rome. Nevertheless, after returning briefly to Scotland to sort out family affairs, he became involved in commercial placements to advance the career of his nephew Mungo Graham, son of the laird of Braco in Perthshire, who returned with him to Russia.

At the new year in 1736, Stirling of Ardoch sponsored Mungo Graham's apprenticeship to a Scottish-Dutch merchant house in St Petersburg headed by George Napier, another Lowland Scot. Mungo initially dealt in furs and textiles before engaging with a consortium of Scottish, Dutch, English and German merchants in St Petersburg intent on an exploratory trading venture to Persia. His participation was again sponsored and underwritten by Stirling of Ardoch. As the representative for Napier's firm, Mungo Graham set off in January 1739 via the Caucasus across the Caspian Sea to the centre of Persian silk production at Rasht. Noted more for his enterprise than his experience, Mungo was abandoned and left indebted to an English associate from another firm, a Captain Elton, who had returned to Russia on the excuse of raising more capital to purchase silks. Having faced an outward journey in which hostile Armenians suspected them of being spies rather than traders, his return was delayed by a year after a revolt in the Caucasus by Dagestan Tartars. He eventually made it back via Astrakhan to St Petersburg in September 1741 to find that Stirling of Ardoch and his family had returned permanently to Scotland after the death of Admiral Gordon.

Despite his accumulating debts, Mungo's remunerative trade in silks had stimulated considerable interest in reopening Persian trade by the Russia Company, a reincarnation of the Muscovy Company that had lost its trading monopoly in Russia in 1698 but had resurfaced in Moscow before moving to Archangel in 1717 and then settling in St Petersburg by 1723. Notwithstanding that the overthrow of the Safavid dynasty had left Persia in constant turmoil since 1722, the British Parliament had reinstated the Russia Company's right to trade there in 1741. At the end of that year, Mungo Graham started out on a second venture to Persia with associates from the Russia Company. His activities on behalf of Napier's trading house were again underwritten by Stirling of Ardoch. This venture, which continued until late 1745, was a considerable success, leading to the company establishing a Persia House in London. It made substantial profits from the sales of silks, with handsome dividends for investors and on exchanges of Persian currency. Unfortunately, Mungo Graham was killed in Persia in late 1743. Disputes over his share of the venture's profits and the underwriting of his debts that dragged on until 1764 had ruined the personal relationship between Ardoch and George Napier by 1753. In the interim, the former played no active part in the Forty-Five other than contributing to initial Jacobite fundraising in Perthshire.

Peter the Great's modernizing programme resulted in Russia becoming a major player in European wars for the rest of the eighteenth century. However, the two decades that followed his death in 1725 were marked by political instability with uneasy successions for four rulers, the capital switching between St Petersburg and Moscow, and a growing reaction against western influence at the imperial court. Irish Jacobite General Peter Lacy served Tsar Peter and his successors for fifty years from the outbreak of the Great Northern War. Nevertheless, the military presence of other Jacobites in Russia had been all but eclipsed by the conclusion of the War of the Austrian Succession in 1748 – an eclipse personified by the career of General James Keith.

Along with his brother George, 10th Earl Marischal, James Keith fought in the Fifteen and the minor rising of 1719. Unlike his brother, James Keith was not attainted. While in exile between the risings, Mary of Modena sponsored his attendance at the French military academy in Paris. For their pursuit of Spanish interests, Keith and his brother had been made colonels in 1719. However, James Keith experienced considerable difficulties in having his commission confirmed on his return to exile. Without a regimental command, he served as a volunteer at the abortive Spanish siege of Gibraltar in 1727. Realizing that his Protestantism 'was an invincible obstacle' to his continuance in Spanish service where senior posts were exclusively for Roman Catholics, he looked to further his military career elsewhere.[2] Acquainted with the Duke of Liria, who had accompanied James VIII & III to Scotland at the Fifteen, Keith was able to use the duke's appointment as Spanish ambassador to Russia to his advantage. He was appointed a major general in the Russian Army in 1728.

His Russian career flourished after the accession of Empress Anna in 1730. She appointed him lieutenant colonel of the Izmaylovsky Guards in a reorganization of her regiments of foot. Two years later he became one of three inspectors of the military districts of Russia, being based in Smolensk where he covered the territory along the rivers Don and Volga, which involved extensive travel along the Russian frontier in the Caspian and Black seas. But he was back on active frontline duty by 1733, participating in the War of the Polish Succession, where he distinguished himself in the pacification of southeast Poland. This was soon followed by a campaign in the defence of Ukraine from an invasion across the Black Sea by the Turks assisted by the Crimean Tartars. He was badly wounded in the leg at the battle of Ochakov in 1737. He had to be carried around on a litter to command his troops with the new rank of General of the Infantry. As the wound began to fester, he faced amputation. However, the arrival of the Earl Marischal in St Petersburg in 1738 convinced James Keith to go with his brother to Paris, where his leg was saved by skilled surgeons.

As Sweden was threatening war with Russia, James Keith left Paris for London in February 1740 as the empress's envoy to George II, by whom he was received as a Russian general. But Prime Minister Walpole was still convinced of Keith's Jacobitism. This difference of opinion had blocked a parliamentary motion in 1738 to allow Keith to succeed to the title and Aberdeenshire estates of his kinsman, John Keith, 3rd Earl of Kintore, who had no legitimate offspring. This decision was upheld before Keith's departure in March. Keith had remained in contact with the court in exile as well as with Admiral Cunningham and Stirling of Ardoch as Jacobite agents in Russia. His brief visit gave him the chance to gauge the commitment of leading English Jacobites in the event of another rising.

On his return to Russia, Keith was made governor of the Ukraine. When war broke out with Sweden in 1741, he played a decisive role in the Russian victory at Wilmanstrad near the Baltic port of Viborg. However, he was not involved in the court intrigues that brought Empress Elizabeth to power at the expense of the regency government which had run Russia since the death of Anna in the previous year. By the termination of the war to Russia's advantage, he was sent as Elizabeth's envoy to the royal court of Adolphus Frederick at Stockholm, where he helped to lay the ground for a peace treaty that essentially reaffirmed the Peace of Nystad, which had ended the Great Northern War in 1721. Russia retained the Baltic provinces of Estonia and Livonia and parts of Karelia won by Peter the Great. During the Forty-Five he was on active service assisting Poland fend off an invasion from Prussia. Keith decided to leave Russian service in 1747. In part this can be explained by Elizabeth's refusal to let the Earl Marischal migrate to Russia, but primarily by the empress undermining his operational command of the army he was assembling in Livonia in 1746 to support the Austrians in Germany. He had found it more congenial to work for Anna than Elizabeth, even though both empresses had confirmed him in an extensive estate in Livonia. Leaving Russia, his first port of call was Copenhagen, from where he offered his services to Frederick II (the Great) of Prussia, an opponent of Britain in the War of the Austrian Succession. Prussian agents, much to the chagrin of British officials in Berlin, had been recruiting actively in the north of Scotland from the summer of 1743. Frederick promptly accepted James Keith's offer and promoted him to field marshal.

## Tilting at Windmills

For Jacobites in exile as at home, there was a plethora of covert associations, societies and clubs for the furtherance of a whole range of human activity from intellectual inquiry to sexual gratification. In Scotland, as in England, Jacobite clubs served mainly as safety valves to confound rather than conspire against the British government. Clubs also became a means of channelling Jacobite endeavours towards the Enlightenment or Romanticism rather than rebellion. Clubs abroad acted as ethnic anchors for Scots in general and not just Jacobites in particular. This was particularly true of Freemasonry, which advocated a just, perfect and regular society reinforced by harmonious fellowship regardless of political differences at home and abroad.

Episcopalians were the driving force behind Scottish Freemasonry, which also furthered continental links for Jacobitism through such influential exiles as Chevalier Andrew Michael Ramsay, who became intellectual leader of French Freemasonry from 1734 to 1743. Lodges for the practice of speculative Freemasonry had strong links with the supporters of James VII & II even before the Revolution, notably Lodge Dunblane attended by Drummonds from Perthshire and Camerons from Lochaber. These links were maintained with the court in exile in Rome, which had its own specific Jacobite lodge from the 1720s to well beyond the Forty-Five. Unlike England where the ritual of Freemasonry was purged of its Jacobite associations in the Whig reconstitution of its Grand Lodge in 1723, speculative Freemasonry in Scotland continued to cut across political and denominational barriers. Prominent members of landed and commercial classes involved in the separate reconstitution of the Grand Lodge of Scotland in 1736 had flirted or were flirting with Jacobitism. Masonic traditions of fellowship, vows of secrecy and silence enabled James Hay, the titular Earl of Inverness, to move freely around the sympathetic lodges and report back to Rome at the launch of Scottish Jacobite Association in 1739. Elections for office-bearers to the Scottish Grand Lodge were held without interruption in November 1745. Although shunned by the papacy on the death of James VIII & III in 1766, Prince Charles Edward Stuart maintained his royal position through continental Freemasonry, especially in France, Poland and

Sweden. Marshal James Keith was a noted Freemason, helping establish lodges in Russia, Sweden and Prussia.

The association of Jacobitism with Freemasonry was not particularly fruitful in England, as evident from the chequered political career of Philip Wharton, Duke of Wharton, who was elected Grand Master of English Freemasons in 1722. Wharton was the personification of aristocratic arrogance, entitlement and self-indulgence. Apart from a personal history of prolonged debauched and dissolute behaviour, he was reckless, financially and politically. In short, he was a waster. He had thrown over the Whig principles of his father, Thomas Wentworth, who had played a leading part in the making of the Union of 1707, which contributed to his elevation from a lord to a marquess. Philip Wharton had first approached the court in exile at Avignon in the aftermath of the Fifteen. In November 1716, he had briefed the Earl of Mar on the corrupt and contemptible exercise of power by George I, Walpole and the Whig ascendancy, which had included the shipping of Jacobite prisoners to the West Indies as indentured labourers. The restoration of James VIII & III would be an act of liberation. He was duly rewarded with a Jacobite peerage as Duke of Northumberland. On his return to England, his undoubted abilities as a political orator led to his being raised from 2nd Marquess to Duke of Wharton at the outset of 1718. However, he suffered major losses, including monies borrowed from Jacobite bankers, in the South Sea Bubble of 1720. For the next three years, he irregularly opposed the Whig ascendancy; his position could be purchased to side with Walpole. However, he appeared to firm up his Jacobite credentials with a powerful defence of Bishop Atterbury of Rochester in the House of Lords in May 1723. Although he accompanied Atterbury into exile, he returned to parliamentary opposition until he accepted a diplomatic post from James VIII & III to serve at the imperial court in Vienna. His departure from England in 1725 was expedited to avoid his many creditors. As a diplomat, he was inexperienced and indiscreet. Plans for an Austrian-backed Stuart restoration had foundered by February 1726. Wharton departed for Spain. His revised design for a restoration through a grand alliance of Austria and Russia with Spain was betrayed to the British government. He served without distinction in the failed Spanish endeavour to lay siege to Gibraltar in 1727. Subsequently attainted and forfeited, his endeavours to secure a pardon from George II in return for revealing Jacobite sources of intelligence were rejected. His public denunciation of James VIII & III in 1730 shredded his credibility at the court in exile.

Speculative Freemasonry was not a covert agency for Jacobitism. But in Scotland, it was an integral part of the country's shared culture as allegiance to the *patria* and communal solidarity. There was one overtly masonic fraternity for Jacobite exiles, with lodges in Italy, France, the Austrian Netherlands, the Dutch Republic, Russia and Prussia. That was the Order of Toboso, inspired by the chivalric adventures of *Don Quixote* (1605–15) as chronicled by Miguel de Cervantes. Named after Don Quixote's imaginary amour, Dulcinea del Toboso, the order clearly drew an analogy between the continuing pursuit of a Jacobite restoration and tilting at windmills. However, the order had a more serious purpose. The far-flung Jacobite diaspora had a very real potential for alienation and despondency that tested loyalty to the exiled Stuarts as well as ties of family and friendship.

Nevertheless, the capacity of the order to offer fraternal association was undermined by the vicious factionalism within the Jacobite community in Rome. The order's origins can be traced to Jacobite negotiations at the Spanish court in the 1720s. It was particularly associated with the supporters of the Duke of Ormonde, the Earl Marischal and Bishop Atterbury of Rochester. The Grand Master of the order, the Reverend Ezekiel Hamilton, from an Ulster Scottish family in Donegal, served as the Protestant chaplain to the court in exile, where he was a noted protagonist. He actively loathed the influence exerted at Rome by the titular Earl of Inverness and his successor as secretary, James Murray, the titular Earl of Dunbar. Having lambasted the conversion of Inverness to Roman Catholicism in 1731, Hamilton had Dunbar banned from admission to the order in 1734. Hamilton himself was dismissed from service at Rome on Dunbar's prompting that same year. He attempted to reassert his position by establishing lodges among the retired Jacobite émigrés at Boulogne, the academic community at Leiden, and aristocratic English Jacobite sympathizers regularly taking the waters at Spa in the Austrian Netherlands. These groups were not in the vanguard of campaigns for a Stuart restoration. Increasingly, in Russia and Prussia if not in Rome, the lodges of the order consisted of members of the diaspora, such as Sir Henry Stirling, the Earl Marischal and Field Marshal James Keith, who were no longer active. They were content to reminisce about, rather than die for, a Jacobite Scotland, a sentiment gaining increasing traction beyond the order among overseas adventurers in America, Asia and Africa.

Provinces/states/countries
Locations for adventurers
Settlements
Commercial hubs
Jacobites in the Americas
N
W E
S
90°W
80°W
70°W
60°W
50°W
90°N
80°N
70°N
60°N
50°N
40°N
30°N
20°N
10°N
Quebec
Glengarry County
Montreal
Prince Edward Island
Louisbourg
Pictou
Halifax
Albany
Boston
Newport
Pittsburgh
New York
Perth Amboy
Annapolis
Princeton
Alexandria
Philadelphia
New Castle
Kent County
Sussex County
Tennessee
New Bern
Chattanooga
Cape Fear
Stuart's Town
Wilmington
Charleston
Savannah
New Inverness
St Augustine
Bermuda
Atlantic Ocean
Havana
St Christopher's
Antigua
Campeche
Montserrat
Argyll Colony
Kingston
Nevis
Guadeloupe
Jamaica
Barbados
Cartagena
Grenada
Porto Bello
Tobago
Pacific Ocean
Darién on Panama Isthmus

# 5

# Adventuring in the American Colonies

Outside Europe, the Jacobite diaspora had its most significant presence in the Americas, not so much in Latin America as in the British colonies in North America and the Caribbean. Jacobites had easily merged with existing Scottish, Irish and English communities from the late seventeenth century. Scottish Jacobites were to be found in the commercial hubs of Boston, New York, Philadelphia and Charleston. They also played an important role in the colonial consolidation of New Jersey, North and South Carolina and Georgia in the early eighteenth century. They did so as settlers, prisoners, prospectors, clergy, soldiers, sailors, frontier fighters and traders. Scots were particularly involved in the tobacco, sugar and fur trades. Those arriving as prisoners, soldiers and sailors can be viewed as episodic migrants or sojourners, a classification also appropriate to the upper echelons of the tobacco and sugar trades intent on the accumulation and repatriation of capital. Labourers in plantations, in the mines or iron works, and in the forests rarely returned and can be classified as permanent migrants. Jacobites in particular, like Scots in general, enhanced their colonial experience by socializing in a variety of clubs from the charitable to the intellectual. They promoted Freemasonry without establishing distinctive Jacobite lodges in North America or the Caribbean.

The raising of clan regiments to serve in American theatres of war after the Forty-Five that transformed Jacobites into British imperialists also cleared the glens, the straths and the islands. Parliamentary legislation to abrogate personal authority and associations within the clans was actively supported by chiefs and leading gentry, Jacobites as well as Whigs, who saw political mileage for their own careers in denigrating clanship as a Scottish anachronism hindering the formation of a unified and imperial British state. Scots in general – and Jacobites in particular – were divided in their support for the American Revolution from its outbreak in 1775 to its conclusion with independence for the United States in 1783. They were also divided over the abolition of slave trading in and to British colonies in 1807. While Jacobites – like other Scots and Britons engaged in the tobacco and sugar trades – had exploited slavery for their financial gain, this was not necessarily the case in their clannish and tribal bonding with Native Americans, especially with the Cherokees.

## Jacobite Foundations?

As Duke of York, the future King James VII & II had played a key public role in upholding an imperial perspective for monarchy that included Scottish and Irish as well as English interests. James used his prerogative powers to suspend or dispense with laws restricting Scottish and Irish participation in English ventures overseas. The issuing of letters of marque to Scottish privateers, the pressing of Scots into service in the Royal Navy and the conscription of Scots seamen to serve in the Second (1666–7) and Third (1672–4) Dutch Wars further encouraged a laxity in the application of the Navigation Acts, which restricted trade to the American colonies to English ships sailing to and from English ports. Having been awarded New York as a proprietary colony on its wresting from the Dutch in 1664, James had been an assiduous promoter of a durable Scottish and Dutch commercial network from 1673 that was based in Albany, named after his Scottish ducal title. James also took the initiative in encouraging the extensive settlements of Scots on the lower Delaware, a district hitherto settled mainly by the Dutch, Swedes and Finns. He also upheld two significant exemptions from the Navigation Acts: in Delaware, which was of particular significance for Scottish commercial networks breaking into the tobacco trade of Virginia and Maryland, and in Newfoundland, where there was a lucrative trade in fish to Spain, Portugal and Italy. In the Canadian north, he also opened up participation in the Hudson's Bay Company, with Scots actively recruited from 1682.

James was notably responsive to steady pressure from the colonies for Scots to serve as frontiersmen in Delaware and the Chesapeake, and as servants in households, fields and militias in the Caribbean. Highlanders were viewed as excelling on the frontiers and in militias, but able-bodied men from all districts were welcome to rebuild settlements devastated by hurricanes and increasingly fearing internal upheaval from revolts as slavery expanded exponentially with the profits of sugar and rum. External threats were also forthcoming from the French, the Spanish and the Dutch. Barbados, which was to the fore in providing settlers to consolidate the acquisition of Jamaica from Spain and to extend Stuart dominions in North and South Carolina, was then the main promoter of Scottish immigration and trade through Scottish commercial networks.

Having established his court in Edinburgh when faced with Whig moves to exclude him from succeeding his brother Charles II to the English throne, James targeted the pursuit of Scottish colonies as the commercial alternative to union with England that had hitherto been advocated by his Stuart predecessors. James duly authorized Scottish ventures to South Carolina in 1682 and East Jersey from 1685. Of the two colonies, South Carolina was the more transient. This venture, which was ostensibly promoted by Presbyterian Nonconformists, actually resulted from extensive commercial networking on the Scottish western seaboard. The Scots planters along the Ashley River were based at Stuart's Town, named in honour rather than in defiance of their royal patron. They were intent on breaking into the 'Indian trade' in furs and extending their commercial contacts with Native Americans into Spanish Florida. This policy, which was to be enforced by a trading monopoly within the precincts of the Scottish settlement, ran into jurisdictional disputes with the existing colonial government as well as English trading rivals. It further strained tensions instigated by their insistence on separate administration according to Scots law rather than incorporation with the English colonial government. After fomenting Native American assaults on Spanish settlements in St Augustine, the Scots faced a serious backlash. Spanish raids mounted from Florida and Cuba in the course of 1686 effectively wiped out the Scottish settlement.

Nevertheless, the Scottish presence in South Carolina did not terminate with the razing of Stuart's Town. The surviving Scots regrouped at Charleston. They formed the nucleus of a commercial network that established Charleston after Boston, New York and Philadelphia as a hub for Scottish engagement in the Caribbean.

While the East Jersey colony had drawn off some settlers from South Carolina, this enhanced and deepened the colonial expertise among a commercial network that drew support from the Highlands and the northeast of Scotland. Its principal patrons were well connected at court: namely, the Drummond brothers, James, Earl of Perth and William, Earl of Melfort. In their honour, the principal town where the Scots settled was named Perth Amboy. Another close associate of James VII & II, the English Quaker William Penn, who had established the colony of Pennsylvania in 1683, was very supportive of ensuring the viability of a neighbouring Scottish colony in which religious toleration was a noted feature. Associated with East Jersey was the English colony of West Jersey, which also benefited from Perth Amboy being built as a colonial port of entry independent of New York. As East Jersey was moved by its proprietors in the direction of Scottish legal practice and procedure, its settlers attained a secure livelihood from corn and cattle. By 1688, the colony was not only self-sufficient, but the storehouse and granary for the West Indies in tandem with New York, a situation that entrenched and sustained the Scottish presence.

However, once James became monarch in 1685, his proprietary colony of New York came under the direct rule of colonial officials in London. They were notably critical of proprietary colonies for their laxity in applying the Navigation Acts and pushed for their inclusion within the Dominion of New England (created in 1643). On the eve of the Revolution, James VII & II consented to its expansion to include New York, then East and West Jersey. The merging of proprietary colonies within the Dominion of New England clearly signalled a limited tolerance for Scottish commercial networks continuing to circumvent the Navigation Acts. Also ruled out was any distinctive constitutional accommodation with Scottish colonies in the Americas. These colonial adjustments weakened rather than strengthened the foundations for Jacobitism in North America.

At the Revolution, political agitation on the streets of Boston and New York contributed to the collapse of the Dominion of New England into its constituent colonies. Agitation in Maryland led to the removal of the governor. However, agitation in New York was by no means one-sided, and the change from James VII & II to William and Mary was not universally welcomed in Pennsylvania. Considerably more support was expressed for the Revolution after the failed assassination attempt on William in 1696, when copious subscriptions were made to Whig associations in the West Indies as well as North America, notably in the city and colony of New York, New Hampshire, Virginia, Barbados, Antigua, St Christopher's, Nevis, Montserrat and Bermuda. In doing so, the colonies were following subscriptions in England that could be counted in their thousands. Subscriptions were also considerable in Ireland but less prevalent in Scotland, which was in the midst of a famine that lasted from 1695 to 1700 and was proclaimed by Jacobite polemicists more taken with biblical retribution than numeracy as 'the seven ill years of William'. Justifiable blame by all Scots, not just Jacobites, could be attributed simultaneously to William of Orange for the collapse of the Darien venture.

William's Scottish government was by no means averse to schemes for economic growth, especially those that took the political heat out of the massacre of Glencoe in February 1692. Building upon an Act of 1693 for the encouragement of foreign trade through co-partneries based on joint-stock investments, the Scottish Estates had licensed as a flagship endeavour in 1695 the Company of Scotland trading to Africa and the Indies. When subscription lists were opened in 1696, the Company of Scotland attracted individual and corporate pledges for £400,000 and sums in hard currency amounting to £34,000. William Paterson, a Scottish merchant based in London who was a founder of the Bank of England in 1694, then became a far from benign influence. He persuaded the Company of Scotland to concentrate its endeavours on an American settlement that would serve an entrepôt capable of attracting trade from the East and West Indies through its location at Darien on the Isthmus of Panama. Panama was also the overland route for silver mined in Peru that was shipped to Spain from Portobello and Cartagena in the Caribbean. Despite initial efforts to raise venture capital and shipping in London, Rotterdam, Amsterdam and Hamburg, the Scottish directors were obliged to proceed unilaterally. This requirement, which turned Darien from a visionary enterprise into a fiasco, was attributable primarily to William of Orange.

Notwithstanding his sanctioning of the Company of Scotland in 1695, William could not endorse the Darien venture without the support of the English Parliament, which had preferred to tighten up its Navigation Acts to the detriment of Scottish commerce in 1696. The proposed colony did fit the legislative requirement that commercial activity was to be conducted in any part of the world not then at war with William of Orange. But the Scottish Company was conceived as a rival to the English East India Company, whose members in the English Parliament were more than capable of impeding William's need for financial supply. As the legality of English residents investing in the Scottish Company was ambivalent, the East India Company successfully pushed through the Houses of Lords and Commons a series of hostile measures in December 1695. The threat of impeachment as interlopers for any investor resident in England aborted subscriptions to the Company of Scotland in London. William accorded higher priority to the balance of power in Europe over the balance of trade in Scotland. As he sought to broker a military alliance against Louis XIV, he was determined to appease Spain, which claimed sovereignty over Panama. Scottish interests were deemed expendable. Darien was reduced from a confederation of Scottish, English, Dutch and northern German commercial interests to a separatist endeavour.

The Council for Trade and Plantations, together with the Commissioners of the Customs in London, were determined that the colonial governors implement the Navigation Acts with rigour and offer no assistance to the Company of Scotland. Scots resident in the colonies were to be stripped of public office and treated as aliens. There were concerns within government circles that if the Darien venture succeeded, the Scots would lay claim to a settlement in the counties of Newcastle, Kent or Sussex on the southern shore of the Delaware Bay. English diplomats and colonial officials lined up to sow doubts at home and abroad about the legality of the Scottish enterprise. Their concern for the sovereign rights of Spain over the Isthmus of Panama was somewhat tempered by the lack of current Spanish settlement in the area and by its suitability for an English entrepôt. Indeed, private ventures there by English entrepreneurs had recently come to grief prior to the Scots embarking for Darien. After successive expeditionary fleets that sailed in 1698 and 1699 failed to establish a permanent colony, endeavours to settle Darien were abandoned in 1700. Funded as a national enterprise – as a commercial compact between God and the Scottish people – surveying, provisioning and leadership were deficient, notwithstanding additional assistance provided by Scottish mercantile networks in Boston, New York and Barbados. The defeat of Spanish forces at Tubuganti on 15 February 1700 by a combined force of Scots and Native Americans (Cuna Indians) under the command of Colonel Alexander Campbell of Fonab, a veteran of the Nine Years War, offered no more than a brief respite. English polemicists mercilessly ridiculed the audacity of the Scottish enterprise. Duly glossed over was William's instruction in December 1699 to the governors of Jamaica and the other Caribbean colonies to offer no assistance to the Scots.

Measures to repair Scottish losses became integral to the political discourse on British state formation. The commercial impact of Darien was a critical but not a crippling loss of venture capital: less than £200,000 from the £434,000 pledged or paid in cash. Scottish commercial networks of merchants and planters continued to operate clandestinely in the Americas. Nonetheless, the failure of Darien made the Scots more reliant on access to English domestic and colonial markets. The Darien fiasco contributed to the national sense of defeatism that facilitated the English drive for parliamentary incorporation achieved in 1707 – an accomplishment that immensely boosted Jacobitism even though Scottish Jacobites were only involved marginally on the Isthmus of Panama.


## Pirates, Frontier Fighters and Traders

Developments arising from Darien impacted on Jacobitism in relation to piracy, frontier settlement and colonial trade. In May 1700, charges of piracy were brought by the Spanish government against a handful of Scottish survivors from Darien. They had been captured at Cartagena and taken as prisoners to Cadiz and then on to Seville for trial. As a petition of concerned relatives to the Scottish Estates in October made clear, the only grounds for the charges of piracy, brought after fifteen months' imprisonment, was that William of Orange had disowned the Darien venture. Some Scottish survivors had, however, opted to engage in piracy after ships taking them from Darien were assailed by mainly British pirates based in Madagascar. The Company of Scotland, supported by James Douglas, 11th Earl of Morton, sought to capitalize on this situation by promoting a pardon for the Scottish pirates who, in return for promising to live peacefully within the law, were expected to join a venture to root out pirates, protect shipping to the West and East Indies, and profit by trading ventures to the South Seas. Morton lobbied George MacKenzie, 1st Earl of Cromartie, initially in his capacity as Justice General in Scotland, and then as Secretary of State to Queen Anne, not just for a pardon and indemnity, but for letters of marque that would give the royal seal of approval to any ventures. However, Morton had already made an agreement with English entrepreneurs led by a Captain John Breholt, who would secure shipping and manpower and direct all naval activities, from which Cromartie was promised a quarter share of net profits. Cromartie even claimed that in return for an outlay of £10,000 the pardon to the pirates would yield vast quantities of gold, silver and diamonds to the value of £4 million. However, Breholt and his leading associates had a piratical past and were hoping to use the promise of a pardon and indemnity for Scots at Madagascar to resume their careers as buccaneers. In the event, the pardon and indemnity, though conceded in principle, got bogged down mainly over the issue of reparations that the Scottish pirates would be due to their former victims: an issue not resolved by the Union of 1707. Nevertheless, Breholt, having temporarily relocated from London to Scotland, attempted to revive the project in 1709 primarily as an English venture. Despite further lobbying of Queen Anne by gullible nobles hoping to turn a handsome profit, the venture never put to sea.

The notion of turning pirates into productive servants did not disappear. Captain George Camocke, who was seeking to leave Spanish service, sent a proposal to Queen Mary of Modena in March 1718 claiming that friends in England had signified that pirates in the Bahamas had two ships of fifty guns, two of forty guns and sixteen sloops and brigantines armed with six to twelve guns each. They had built a citadel for their defence with 24 guns. Their numbers were in excess of 5,000 and daily increasing. They had rejected a pardon from the British government and were prepared to declare for James VIII & III. Camocke suggested that he be commissioned by the exiled king to recruit officers and men clandestinely from the Royal Navy to man a fifty-gun ship which he would purchase in Cadiz for the equivalent of £15,000. They would join the pirates in the Bahamas to attack ships trading from Guinea in West Africa to the West Indies. In return for a notional pardon for the pirates, James VIII & III should accrue sufficient royalties to finance a future rising for his restoration. While this venture was too speculative and beyond the resources of a monarch who struggled to pay pensions to his followers in exile, it was not beyond credibility. Five months later, the Jacobite court in exile was informed that the British government had offered to pardon all the buccaneers in Providence Island if they would support endeavours of the Royal Navy to deploy ten or twelve men-of-war to seize all shipping passing through the Gulf of Florida to Spain.

A more feasible maritime project to redeploy exiles in France to the Caribbean had been implemented in the aftermath of the Fifteen. The project was devised by Robert Gordon, merchant and distributor of Jacobite pensions in Bordeaux, and Robert Arbuthnot, merchant banker in Rouen, following the latter's involvement in outfitting the ship *Vandosme* to bring arms and ammunition from Le Havre to Scotland in January 1716. While the arms and ammunition were actually loaded from supply boats once the ship had left harbour, its official cargo – mainly of salt, biscuits, brandy, flints and bread – was almost identical with the goods shipped by the port's merchants to the French fishing community in Cape Breton. A further stimulus to the redeployment of the *Vandosme* to the Atlantic trade was the pressure on paying pensions being conveyed in Bordeaux, especially when Jacobite prisoners to the West Indies on two ships managed to overpower the crews and re-route to France. The first to arrive was commanded by Andrew Ramsay, a son of a pre-Revolution Bishop of Edinburgh, that had returned harmoniously to Bordeaux in December 1716. The second was steered by the more abrasive Laurence

Charteris of Kinfauns in Perthshire, which had struggled into La Rochelle in January 1717. While some of those who had returned were tradesmen who found local employment, less skilled labourers were clandestinely shipped back to Scotland. Faced with finding pensions for nearly seventy additional exiles, Gordon and Arbuthnot had the *Vandosme* fitted out for the French West Indies. Largely crewed by the former prisoners, the ship, commanded by an Englishman, David George, arrived in the Caribbean in June 1717. But on their return journey, George attempted to withhold six months' pay from the crew and became particularly abusive when drunk. In December, Gordon was able to recover the equivalent of £100 from the estate of the now deceased George. In the interim, a second venture to the Caribbean was terminated at considerable loss to Gordon and his associates when the ship was captured by pirates.

Darien also impacted on subsequent Scottish settlement in North America and the Caribbean. Around 1709, a proposal came before the recently formed Scottish Society for the Propagation of Christian Knowledge (SSPCK), which was stridently anti-Jacobite in its commitment to Presbyterianism and the Union. The proposed colony had two major differences from Darien: it was not in the proximity of major Spanish forts and its climate was more equitable and less afflicted by torrid rainfall. Served by rivers feeding into Tampa Bay, its location was to be on the west coast of Florida, considerably distant from the fortified Spanish town of St Augustine in the coastal northeast. But its isolation from other British colonies in the Americas meant the proposal was never executed. However, settlers departing from Darien did boost the Scottish presence in Jamaica, where Campbell of Fonab helped to establish a colony in the western parishes of Hanover, Westmorland and St Elizabeth that was to be consolidated as the Argyll colony by 1729. Fonab, though a member of the Jacobite-leaning Campbells of Glenorchy, soon returned to Scotland as a committed Whig, fighting for the Hanoverian succession at the Fifteen. Migration from Argyllshire, which gathered pace from 1713, was not so much a Jacobite endeavour as an opportunity for clans to break free of the ducal house of Argyll's feudal constraints on their estate management.

New approaches to frontier protection in the aftermath of Darien emanating from South Carolina sought to engage Highlanders, which inevitable meant Jacobites. In June 1712, John Stuart argued that sustaining the British Empire in America and the wealth arising therefrom was dependent on whether Britain or France had the more warlike Indians. If the British were not able to mobilize sufficient Native American support to take Nova Scotia and Quebec, all the northern colonies could be lost. Given that the Indian tribes supporting the French were stronger around the southern colonies, North and South Carolina, Virginia and Maryland could also be lost. Stuart claimed to be the legitimate heir to Patrick Stewart, Earl of Orkney, expropriated and executed in 1615 for his oppressive behaviour in the Northern Isles of Scotland. He also claimed to have travelled extensively in Europe, the Americas and Asia. He contended that among the races of mankind, the Native American tribes were the most savage, fierce and brutal. The only fighting force fit to go against them were those of the Highland clans. Robert Johnson, the governor of South Carolina, put this into practice in the aftermath of the Fifteen, when he had Jacobite prisoners armed and despatched to the colony's frontiers to fight the Yamassee Indians.

By the outset of the Whig ascendancy in the 1720s, Sir Robert Walpole, the first acclaimed prime minister, had decided that British interests could be well served by recruiting Jacobites as expendable frontier fighters in North America. The first American colony where Highlanders were specifically deployed to guard its frontiers was Georgia in the 1730s. This endeavour was promoted by General James Oglethorpe, a British Army officer from a prominent English Jacobite family. His sisters, Fanny and Anne, gleaned political intelligence and gossip for the Jacobite courts in exile. Although critical of the Whig ascendancy, Oglethorpe, whose endeavours were backed by the Patriot party, was more noted for his philanthropic than his political commitments. He recruited mainly from the Clan Chattan and the Munros in the central and northern Highlands, respectively. Prominent among the leaders of this venture, which settled from Savannah down to New Inverness (defiantly named Darien) on the eastern seaboard, were younger sons of the clan elite with limited prospects at home to demonstrate their enterprise, none more so than John Mor Mackintosh, whose father, Brigadier William Mackintosh, had been the prominent Jacobite commander in the Fifteen. Their remit to secure Georgia from hostile Spanish incursions led to the formation of General Oglethorpe's Highland Rangers based on the Independent Companies reinvigorated by General George Wade to police the Highlands. Although significantly outnumbered, the Highland Rangers gained a heroic reputation for their defeat of invading Spanish forces from Florida at the battle of Bloody Marsh on 7 July 1742, which secured St Simon Island for Georgia.

In the meantime, another Argyll colony – instigated by a prominent Jacobite, Sir James Campbell of Auchinbreck, and supported by MacNeills from Knapdale and Kintyre disaffected with the feudal overlordship of the ducal house of Argyll – was established from 1739 along the Cape Fear River that bordered North and South Carolina. Jacobite as well as Whig entrepreneurs were involved as promoters and planters. Around the same time another Argyll settlement, led by Captain Lachlan Campbell from Islay, failed to take root to the north of Albany around Lake George in New York colony. Nevertheless, the three Highland-dominated colonies in Jamaica, Georgia and North Carolina tied Jacobites into the expansion of the British Empire.

An earlier attempt by John Campbell, 1st Earl of Breadalbane, a reluctant Jacobite, to promote Highland resettlement in Nova Scotia was sidetracked by the outbreak of the Fifteen. Nevertheless, Breadalbane and, subsequently, his son and heir (also called John), the second earl, used their heritable jurisdictions to effect the summary removal of disruptive or distrusted tenants to the American colonies, a practice of people trafficking in which they were joined by neighbouring chiefs in the southern Highlands. Alexander Robertson of Strowan, noted as a poet and Jacobite, even threatened in 1709 to deport his sister Margaret for her interference in his estate management. The continuous demand for labour in North America and the Caribbean led to clandestine clearances when young women and children were trafficked out of Skye, Harris and North Uist. This nefarious provision of a one-way passage to America by Sir Alexander MacDonald of Sleat and John MacLeod of Dunvegan, in association with Aberdeen merchants, was stymied when the ship carrying the abducted sank off the west coast of Ireland in 1739. Both these clan chiefs subsequently switched from Jacobite to Whig at the Forty-Five, although many of their clansmen defied them to fight for Prince Charles Edward. Political rivalry as much as clan division were behind the charges John, 2nd Duke of Argyll, laid against Campbell of Auchinbreck in 1740, writing off his endeavours to supplement Highland recruitment to Jamaica as a notably heinous example of people trafficking in offering free travel and six months' provisions after their arrival in return for selling their labour.

Apart from those transported by compulsion, there was a considerable voluntary movement of tradesmen to Jamaica, other Caribbean islands and the Carolinas, Virginia and Maryland, where they integrated into slave-owning commercial networks that occasionally but not always included Jacobites. These networks were primarily engaged in the accumulation and repatriation of capital from the tobacco and sugar trades, not the financing of a Stuart restoration. For these Scottish networks, circumventing the power of the state went hand in glove with commercial innovation. Glasgow merchants used both consignment and store systems first to break into the staple Atlantic trade in tobacco and then to secure dominance in it. Their participation in this trade since the 1630s seemed compromised by the restrictive English Navigation Acts. Under the consignment system the planter bore the risk of marketing, whereas the risk was borne by the merchant under the store system, which tied advances of credit on tobacco sales in Europe to the purchase of merchandise from the colonial store. This latter system, which was particularly suited to the expansion of small plantations along the Chesapeake Bay and into the hinterlands of Maryland, Virginia and the Carolinas, carried higher risks but greater profits. Whitehaven, hitherto third after Bristol and Liverpool in the Atlantic trade, was so eclipsed by Glasgow merchants' use of the store system in tandem with smuggling tobacco through the Isle of Man that the Cumbrian town actually petitioned for repeal of the Treaty of Union in 1710. Scottish entrepreneurs duly extended the store system into the Caribbean in order to enhance profits from sugar and rum.

The foremost tobacco lord in Glasgow during the 1720s was Andrew Buchanan. He and his family operated not only in Virginia and the Chesapeake but in the trade in sugar and rum from Jamaica. Notwithstanding Glasgow's reputation as a Whig city, Buchanan and his family were Episcopalians but not active Jacobites. By 1725, they had established the Buchanan Society, ostensibly to provide education and poor relief for impoverished clansmen who had migrated to the city from Loch Lomond. The society was a front to sustain the meeting house run by Alexander Duncan, the nonjuring Bishop of Glasgow. Having acquired an extensive estate at Drumpellier in Lanarkshire by 1735, Buchanan served as lord provost of Glasgow in 1740–41 when his brother Neil became an influential MP representing the city and other western burghs. The Buchanan network in 1726 was joined by William Simpson, an Aberdeen merchant who dealt principally through Rotterdam, Amsterdam and London with occasional shipments of salmon to Livorno in Italy. During the Fifteen, he supplied gunpowder to Jacobite forces assembled in Aberdeen and served on the Jacobite town council. A committed nonjuror, he escaped censure on the strength of his political connections in the city and shire. He expanded his commercial activities, initially into the Baltic and then the tobacco trade. From being an agent supplying tobacco from Glasgow, he was directly shipping tobacco from Virginia by 1729. By 1734, the Buchanans, whose patronage was not tied to denominational or political affiliations, had moved from nonjuring Episcopalians to jurors in the Anglican communion in Glasgow and had sided openly with the Patriot party rather than covertly with the Jacobites. By 1741, the Buchanans were instrumental in promoting legislation to encourage the formation of commercial co-partneries for manufacturing and colonial trading.

A more overt Jacobite network was less successful in both North America and the Caribbean. The American adventuring of the Camerons of Lochiel stretched back to their participation as colonizers in East Jersey in 1685 and continued as land speculators in association with Bristol merchants. The forfeitures of both Sir Ewen Cameron of Lochiel and his eldest son, John, in 1690, which were confirmed in the wake of the Fifteen, led to protracted legal disputes over their American estates until their enforced sale in 1725 by the Commissioners for Forfeited Estates in England. Nevertheless, two of his grandsons, Donald, who had succeeded as chief in 1719, and John, laird of Fassifern, developed the garrison town of Fort William as a centre for trans-Atlantic trade. By 1734, their entrepreneurial activities ranged from droving cattle to London and other urban markets to providing timber for Cumbrian ironmasters through Whitehaven and smuggling contraband wines from

France, as well as trading legitimately through Fort William, Belfast and Glasgow to Philadelphia, New York and Boston. Despite initial cargoes of French wine not being corked properly, their switch to trading through the Portuguese island of Madeira ensured sales of durable wine in North America. These sales were then used to finance provisions for Jamaica, from where their two ships, the *Neptune* and the *Charming Molly*, returned with sugar and rum. This venture was repeated in 1735, with a younger brother, Evan, again overseeing as supercargo. Evan subsequently moved to Jamaica, taking advantage of a colonial enactment of 1736 to encourage the settlement of white people. Rather than purchase a sugar plantation, he leased a cattle ranch or pen which he worked in the mountains with a contingent of slaves. He was not a shrewd businessman. The venture was struggling before his death in 1741 brought about its collapse. Thereafter, Lochiel and Fassifern concentrated on their core business as commodity traders rather than colonial adventurers. Notwithstanding Donald Cameron's forfeiture after the Forty-Five and continued surveillance of Fassifern as a known Jacobite financier, their sons were re-engaged in colonial ventures in New York as well as New Jersey by 1750. They did so primarily to retrieve family fortunes not to promote Jacobitism, thereby bringing the Camerons into line with others whose colonial engagement in North America tended to distance themselves from Jacobitism. Three instances will suffice.

Networks put economics and kinship over politics. Sir Ewen and John Cameron had granted another planter in New Jersey, Phineas Mackintosh, the brother of Brigadier William Mackintosh of Borlum, power of attorney over their American estates, which endured until their enforced sale in 1725. Another relative of the Jacobite commander, his nephew Ludovic Gordon, a merchant in Inverness, had been involved in the Baltic trade with a base in St Petersburg. Financial disputes in Russia led him to switch focus to the West Indies by 1740. Having weighed up his established connections in Jamaica against more promising opportunities in the Leeward Islands, Ludovick, then aged forty, settled in St Christopher's in 1741. His anticipated opportunities remained largely unfulfilled. Jacobite fortunes in the Forty-Five concerned him less than the prospects for his relatives in its aftermath in Boston and Newport in Rhode Island, and of breaking into the slave trade in Charleston.

Geographic detachment could lead to political detachment. The involvement of Iain Ciar MacDougall of Dunollie in the Fifteen led to his forfeiture and exile in France. Having come back for the minor rising of 1719, he did not return abroad but stayed in hiding on his estate in the Lorn district of Argyllshire and in Ireland before being pardoned in the general amnesty for clan chiefs arranged by General Wade in 1726. However, as he held his estate from John, 2nd Duke of Argyll rather than directly from the Crown, he was unable to secure its freehold prior to his death in 1737. By the following year, a younger son, Duncan, was seeking to establish himself in a shop selling merchandise in Antigua. In his occasional letters to his brother Alexander, the new chief of Clan Dougall, Duncan was notably concerned, like other members of Scottish commercial networks, about the threat posed by the Spanish and the French to British shipping in the Caribbean. Assaults by the Royal Navy on Cartagena and Havana in 1741 were neither victorious nor glorious, with heavy casualties more from disease than military engagement. Duncan was particularly pleased that Alexander had found Archibald, 3rd Duke of Argyll, more amenable to restoring Dunollie, which was accomplished at the outset of August 1745, just before Prince Charles Edward raised his standard at Glenfinnan. Duncan was no less delighted by reports of his clan's participation in the Forty-Five, Alexander having switched away from Jacobitism to side with the Whigs and the house of Argyll.

Geographic detachment diminished awareness of political involvement. On 14 April 1752, Alexander MacDonald from Westmorland parish in Jamaica wrote to his cousin Alexander MacDonald of Glenaladale, having come to the resolution that 'after a long silence' he wished 'to acquaint you that I'm in the land of the living'. He had been out of contact with his relatives in Moidart for ten years and was unaware whether his father and mother were still alive. In the interim, he had regularly shipped goods to and from Glasgow merchants. The Jamaican adventurer had been persuaded to move to the Caribbean by Aeneas MacDonald, the merchant banker from Paris, of whose misfortunes in the Forty-Five he was aware. He was particularly concerned to learn from Glenaladale 'how all you are reinstated since the year forty-five'.[1] He made no mention that Glenaladale was one of the first to join Prince Charles Edward, that the prince had raised his standard on Glenaladale's estate at Glenfinnan on Loch Shiel in August 1745, and that Glenaladale had played a leading role in the prince's escape from Scotland in September 1746. Glenaladale, who had served as a major in the Clanranald Regiment, had not gone into exile, nor was he attainted. He had maintained a low profile in the West Highlands until he was included in a general indemnity of 1747. The Jamaican adventurer hinted that he would return in two to three years. He was looking for opportunities to purchase land. Having amassed a fortune through sugar and slaves, he returned eventually to Scotland in 1770. Three years later he bought Glenaladale.

## Smoke and Mirrors

Political distancing between adventurers in America and Jacobites in Scotland was part of a pattern of political engagement that lacks clear definition. No convincing evidence has yet been revealed that commercial networks in North America or the Caribbean had levies imposed on them to finance Jacobite risings or made regular contributions to funding a Stuart restoration. Unlike Russia, there appears to be no record of Jacobite agents resident in America reporting back to the courts in exile. Indeed, Jacobites were rarely evident when Dr Alexander Hamilton, a medical practitioner in Annapolis, made an extensive four-month tour from Maryland to Maine in 1744. Hamilton left Annapolis on 30 May, reached as far as York in New Hampshire on 11 August, then returned by a different route back to Annapolis on 27 September. On his travels, he took particular interest in fellow members of the Scottish diaspora and especially in their clubs. The only overt reference to Jacobitism came on 30 June, when he was in Albany, the colonial capital of New York. He conversed with an old man known as 'Scots Willie', a veteran soldier who had fought with the Jacobites at Killiecrankie in July 1689 and claimed to have witnessed the death of Viscount Dundee.

Nonjurors, who formed the liturgical bedrock of Jacobitism in Scotland, did receive funds repatriated from the Americas. Financial legacies, especially from the slave plantations producing tobacco, sugar and rum, sustained spiritual and material support for Episcopalians from Perthshire to Shetland. John Anderson, an Episcopalian priest and plantation owner in St Christopher's, had invested £6,000 for hospitals, schools and clerical support. His bequest of 1735 allowed considerable latitude to his trustees, drawn mainly from nobles and gentry in Aberdeenshire. Instructions that clergy in the university towns of Scotland be supported in their use of the Anglican liturgy were set aside by 1744 in favour of nonjuring schools and clergy in the northeast. Scottish Episcopalians recruited in the aftermath of the Revolution into the service of the Church of England in the Caribbean were noted for their incorruptible rectitude and their reliance on support networks of fellow countrymen regardless of denominational or liturgical difference. These support networks in New York, New Jersey, Pennsylvania and Massachusetts were also utilized to promote charity for colonial clergy, predominantly nonjurors, in straightened circumstances.

However, political complications arose from the failure of colonial governments to distinguish between English and Scottish nonjurors: the latter being predominantly if not exclusively Jacobite while the former were more aligned with 'High Church' Anglicans and Tories. This discrepancy led to unsubstantiated charges and counter-charges of Jacobitism being presented against governors and they, in turn, against their opponents in and out of colonial councils from South Carolina to Maine between the Fifteen and the Forty-Five. Among the first of these cases was the accusation by Sir Nathaniel Johnson against Captain Thomas Nairn, an assemblyman in South Carolina and agent for Indian affairs there. Johnson claimed in June 1708, in the wake of the abortive minor rising in Scotland, that Nairn, who was Scottish by origin, should be charged with treason for calling for the removal of Queen Anne and her replacement by James VIII & III. Several of Nairn's colleagues rebutted the charges, affirmed that his principles were directly opposed to Jacobitism, and raised grounds for his release on wrongful imprisonment in September. Nairn himself fronted his case for wrongful imprisonment in October to the Lords Proprietors for the colony and to Queen Anne and her British ministry. Of the two Indian traders whom Johnson had used as principal witnesses against him, Nairn affirmed one was a lunatic and the other was convicted of buggery! Nairn won his case and Johnson's term as governor was ended in the following year.

The most protracted case of alleged Jacobitism concerned Governor Robert Hunter and a group of English nonjurors contesting his direction of New York and New Jersey. It ran for almost two years from August 1716 to July 1718. Hunter's opponents formed a nonjuring network that stretched from New York to Boston and were in receipt of funds from nonjurors in London. They aimed to advance the High Church interest among Anglicans. Their subversive branding as Jacobites was more emotive than being designated Tories. While this controversy certainly contributed to the Jacobite and anti-Jacobite polemical discourse in the British Atlantic Empire, it does not constitute clear evidence for Jacobite organization, networking or agenda setting in the colonies.

In New England, as in England, the drinking of toasts and swearing of oaths suggest no more than a presumed cohesion among Jacobites, not incontrovertible evidence for any political agenda to fundamentally alter or overthrow colonial government. Governors impugned for their Jacobite sympathies were primarily Scots during and after the Fifteen, which cast a shadow over the loyalty of the Scottish nation in America as in Britain. Political smearing applied not only to Robert Hunter, but to Lord Archibald Hamilton in Jamaica, Robert Lowther in Barbados and Alexander Spotswood in Virginia. Around the Forty-Five, James Glen in South Carolina and Gabriel Johnston in North Carolina faced charges based on the false equivalence that all Scots were Jacobite sympathizers. Charges raised against Gabriel Johnston in December 1748 were not resolved for seven months. He was held to have appointed suspect persons to offices of trust. Yet the only instance cited was a William MacGregor, who had fought in the Fifteen, being appointed a justice of the peace and colonel of the colony's militia during the Forty-Five. MacGregor had twice refused to take oaths of loyalty to George II before relenting on the third occasion he was asked. Governor Johnston had allegedly received news of Culloden 'very coldly' and expressed concerns for the many 'Rebel chiefs killed and taken prisoners'. Only two political opponents in the colonial assembly pressed charges against him. Johnston was exonerated from their accusations of Jacobitism in July 1749.

Political smearing notwithstanding, a case can be outlined for a Jacobite presence of significance in the American colonies beyond that of polemical discourse. In April 1716, a New England ship with a Scottish master licensed to carry powder from London to the colonies readily diverted to Scotland to supply declining Jacobite forces. In August 1740, Ranald MacDonald of Clanranald negotiated with a Scottish network in Philadelphia, with links to Aberdeen nonjurors, for a Captain Keith to bring a cargo of firelocks, pistols and flints to Holland, from where they were carried to Norway. The arms aboard the *William and John* were then concealed in a cargo of timber shipped to the River Clyde in August 1740. During the Forty-Five, among the ships attempting to breach the naval blockade of Scotland was one commanded by a Captain Sinclair that had carried arms and supplies from Boston. It was apprehended at Stromness in Orkney in early April 1746.

## British Imperial Service

In the aftermath of Culloden, clanship was to be emasculated as the enemy within Great Britain. This entailed the decanting of Highlanders to North America to secure and populate territories that the British were to take from the French, who posed a threat from Canada to the Gulf of Mexico. But the French had a more systematic location of forts and settlements linked by waterways and they had better relations with the Native Americans. British troops recruited in America were reluctant to serve for prolonged periods on offensives beyond their own colonies, as was notably evident in Cape Breton during their successful siege of Louisbourg in 1745 and its retention until 1748, when it was returned to the French at the conclusion of the War of the Austrian Succession. As well as being of immediate benefit to New England, the wresting of not just Nova Scotia but Canada from French control was key to the protection of the western flank of all the British colonies in North America.

Whig as well as Jacobite clans were affected by the post-Culloden legislation to disarm and to proscribe such cultural identifiers as the wearing of tartan. Enforced pacification of the Highlands in the interests of civility was marked by the commercial promotion of agriculture, fisheries and manufactures, integral to which were enhanced construction of roads, bridges and harbours; the planting of villages and towns;

and the greater provision of schools. State-sponsored terrorism gave way to state-sponsored improvement. Thirteen forfeited estates of Jacobite chiefs and gentry were annexed inalienable to the Crown in 1752. The Annexed Estates were to be corridors of improvement from the southern through the western Highlands with intersections in western and northern districts. Another eight years elapsed before the commission to manage the Annexed Estates became operational. In addition to promoting loyalty to the Hanoverian dynasty, the commission was charged to diversify the Highland economy and promote Presbyterianism. The task of linking vocational education, basic English literacy and rigorous moral instruction to uphold the British establishment was carried out in conjunction with the SSPCK.

This internal programme was to be complemented by imperial service. Notwithstanding the discriminatory exclusion of Scotland from the Militia Act that applied elsewhere in Britain and Ireland, six Highland regiments were raised from 1757, primarily for their usefulness as a highly mobile and hardy light infantry during the Seven Years War, in which Britain and France were the principal antagonists in North America. This deployment of Highland troops regardless of previous Jacobite affiliations has been accredited to William Pitt the Elder in his capacity as prime minister. But this initiative, which gave substance to John Stuart's suggestion as to the suitability of Highlanders as Indian fighters in 1712, was actually advocated by John, 2nd Earl of Stair at the close of the Forty-Five. It was also raised and rejected on grounds of trustworthiness by William Shirley, governor of Massachusetts and commander of the British forces at Louisbourg. These proposals were further stalled by the reluctance of loyalist clans, who had been treated with contempt by Cumberland during and after the Forty-Five, to mobilize for the European theatre of war when the Whig ministry was still condoning repression throughout the Highlands.

But the switch to an imperial theatre of war, initially under the command of John, 4th Earl of Loudon in North America, offered not just continuity of employment for the Black Watch (raised from the merger of the Independent Companies in 1739) and the other Highland regiments which Loudoun had raised from loyal clans at the Forty-Five. The additional six Highland regiments secured a military channel for the resumption of the cultural trappings of clanship: wearing tartan, carrying arms and playing bagpipes. Although not specifically proscribed, bagpipes had come to be associated with the legislation banning the clans' use of warlike instruments. Probably the most ferocious battle of the Seven Years War involving Highland regiments was that fought at Ticonderoga on 7 July 1758: a bloody endeavour to seize a fort on the main route from the New York colony to Upper Canada by way of the Hudson River and Lakes George and Champlain. The Black Watch sustained particularly devastating casualties as they charged into a sustained storm of gunshot. Highland regiments also served in the Caribbean from 1759, where troops were required to dislodge the French and establish naval bases in Guadeloupe and Havana. Given their relatively successful, if expendable, deployment as light infantry in Canada, particularly at the taking of Quebec in 1759, as well as their involvement in reclaiming Nova Scotia and acquiring Prince Edward Island, Highland regiments offered an imperial avenue for the public rehabilitation of the chiefs and leading gentry of the clans. Setting a precedent, Simon Fraser, Master of Lovat, was restored to his forfeited estate in 1774.

Jacobite exiles in France were also to fight against their former compatriots in the Forty-Five during the Seven Years War – most notably James Johnstone, from a mercantile family in Edinburgh, who had joined the Jacobites in Perth in September 1745. He worked as a facilitator within the Jacobite military command, being considerably closer to Lord George Murray than to Prince Charles Edward. He eventually escaped after Culloden to the Dutch Republic before moving to Paris. Finding his pension insufficient, he enlisted as an ensign in the Compagnies Franches de la Marine, being promoted to lieutenant when he arrived at Louisbourg in 1754. When Louisbourg was recaptured by the British in June 1758, Johnstone moved to Quebec; he was involved in the French defeat in the battle of the Plains of Abraham on 13 September, when he was directly confronted by clansmen serving in the Highland regiments, who treated him leniently. Two years after returning to France in 1762, he was created a chevalier and embarked upon *A Memoir of the 'Forty-Five*. While his military service in Britain and Canada was not undistinguished, his memoir, which was translated from French and published in 1822, was considerably livelier and more memorable.

With the end of the Seven Years War in 1763, the Annexed Estates had primarily become an agency to relocate demobilized soldiers and sailors, a task not infrequently achieved by the removal of clansmen and their families. The commission's fourteen years of effective planning ended in 1774 with the abandonment of all industrial ventures. Offers of long leases giving greater security of tenure for farmers implementing agricultural improvements were curtailed to facilitate the movement of labour into the industrializing Lowlands and to conserve landed interests in anticipation of a full restoration of the disinherited Jacobites. The British government had also sanctioned the settlement of half-pay officers, non-commissioned officers and private men after the conclusion of war in 1763. Through the allocation of land grants, which varied from 50 acres for private soldiers to 5,000 acres for commissioned officers, episodic migration became permanent. Among the initial grants were lands to the north of Albany in the colony of New York. Their allocation instigated the first substantial wave of Highland migration and settlement. But these grants of land needed further cultivation if their value was to appreciate, which, in turn, encouraged further emigration from Scotland in general and the Highlands in particular to Nova Scotia and Prince Edward Island (PEI) in the Canadian Maritimes and to North Carolina.

The pioneering exodus, primarily from the bounds of the MacDonalds of Clanranald in Moidart, Arisaig and South Uist to PEI, was orchestrated in 1772 by the Gaelic entrepreneur Captain John MacDonald of Glenaladale, who had carefully planned and generously budgeted with respect to the voyage and settlers' immediate needs. To further finance his colonial undertaking, he sold his family estate in the West Highlands in 1773 to a close relative, Alexander MacDonald, the Jamaican entrepreneur. Captain John's colonial undertaking was subject to continuous carping from migrants, particularly those from South Uist who had been evicted for refusing to turn Protestant and had limited resources to bargain for settlements in PEI. Nevertheless, Glenaladale, though often an absentee from PEI, remained convinced that he had improved the lot of all his Roman Catholic and former Jacobite migrants both materially and spiritually.

Migration to North Carolina, which involved families formerly associated with Whig as well as Jacobite clans drawn from diverse parts of the Highlands and Islands, was in full flight by 1771. Among the migrants was Allan MacDonald of Kingsburgh in Skye, who had held a commission in an Independent Company mobilized for the British Army during the Forty-Five. With him was his far more celebrated wife, Flora MacDonald, who had aided the flight of Prince Charles Edward from South Uist over the sea to Skye in June 1746 – an episode which led to her arrest and imprisonment in the Tower of London, where her celebrity ensured lenient treatment and frequent visits from Jacobite sympathizers until her release under the amnesty of July 1747. She married Allan MacDonald in November 1750, but their farming endeavours in Skye had mixed fortunes prior to their departure for North Carolina in 1774. For the MacDonalds as for all other recent migrants to North America, the ordinary setbacks of pioneering were compounded by the extraordinary circumstances of war. All colonial migrants faced uphill struggles at the American Revolution, which provided a further avenue for Scots to demonstrate their military credentials as British Loyalists. Chiefs and clan gentry were again to the fore in raising ten Highland regiments for service in the American War of Independence from 1775 to 1783.

Other former clansmen were recruited into the 84th Highland Emigrant Regiment, mainly from the Carolinas. These recruits were soldiers discharged from Highland regiments at the end of the Seven Years War. The prospect of a full-scale restoration of the disinherited Jacobites was a significant incentive to recruitment in 1775. But showing loyalty to the British government often proved an expensive business for hard-pressed chiefs and clan gentry. Conversely, many of the rank and file recruited for the defence of the American colonies used military service as a free ticket to cross the Atlantic for their personal advancement. As in 1763, the prospect of land at the end of the war was a powerful inducement. The more frugal recruits were able to repatriate small sums, usually no more than £6 yearly, to aid their families meet escalating costs of rent and stave off evictions.

For Highland migrants, one of the most important engagements of the American War of Independence was the battle of Moore's Creek near Wilmington, North Carolina, on 27 February 1776, in which some 1,400 Loyalists faced 2,000 American Patriots. However, the Loyalists, drawn mainly from Highland settlers, were poorly armed and easily routed.

A delayed assault on Charleston a few months later was repulsed and all the southern colonies were effectively lost to the British Crown. Allan MacDonald of Kingsburgh fought and was captured at Moore's Creek. He was finally jailed in Philadelphia, 700 miles away, until released under a prisoner exchange. Disciplinary proceedings brought by the Patriots against Flora were suspended. She was eventually allowed to go to New York to join up with her husband in April 1778. After Allan rejoined his regiment in Nova Scotia, Flora returned to Britain in poor health by the end of 1779. Located back in Skye, she was joined by her husband in 1785. His intention had been to settle in Nova Scotia, but as for many Loyalists the compensation he received fell well below his actual losses.

Notwithstanding the defeat of the British forces in the American War of Independence, the sterling service of the Highland regiments in North America and the Caribbean provided the ostensible excuse to restore the remaining disinherited chiefs and clan gentry. By disannexation in 1784, there was a general recognition that the former Jacobite estates were distinguished because of their comparatively bad condition, especially for their neglect of agricultural improvements. The burden of inherited debts, which had been continued rather than cleared by the commissioners, varied from the equivalent of 13 to 35 years. The latter figure was tantamount to bankruptcy. The commission was not a major force in transforming, far less in civilizing, the Highlands. But the Annexed Estates had an exemplary role in accelerating the break-up of traditional townships through the creation of single-tenant farms, planned villages and crofting communities.

After the American Revolution, several Scottish regiments were rewarded with land in Canada. Though settlements were established with some difficulty in the inhospitable land allocated at Pictou on Cape Breton, Loyalist Highlanders flocked north to join their countrymen not only in the Maritimes. Glengarry County in eastern Ontario attracted a continuous stream of migrants originally from the estates of the MacDonalds of Glengarry and other Jacobite clans in Lochaber. Highlanders were among the skilled Scottish artisans who went out to Quebec and other parts of British North America to serve as ships' carpenters and wrights with the intention of remitting money back to their wives and families pending their eventual emigration. Those who lost their lives in British service left destitute widows and children who were thrown back on parish provision of poor relief.

Jacobites, or their offspring, who had arrived between the Fifteen and the Forty-Five were more likely to be Patriots than Loyalists. Thus, William Mackintosh, the eldest son of John Mor, a leader among the Highlanders settled in Georgia during the 1730s, went on to become a colonel of the 1st Regiment of Georgian Cavalry. His two sons, John and Lachlan, also served as commissioned officers for the Patriots. In like manner, not all Jacobite combatants who made their way to North America on escaping from or being exiled after Culloden were chastened by their intimate knowledge of the dire consequences of rebellion against the British Crown. They were able to take advantage of the decision by the Scottish Grand Lodge to charter lodges in North America and the West Indies at the outbreak of the Seven Years War, notably in Boston in Massachusetts, Charleston in South Carolina and Fredericksburg in Virginia. A member of the last lodge was George Washington, the tobacco planter who went on to become the first President of the United States established after the American Revolution. In addition to Washington, the lodge provided another seven generals for the Patriots. One of these generals and a close friend to Washington was Hugh Mercer from Pitsligo in Aberdeenshire, who had served as a surgeon on the Jacobite side at Culloden and escaped eventually by ship from Leith to Philadelphia later in 1746. Serving as a medical practitioner in Pennsylvania, he joined the colonial troops fighting with the British against the French in the run-up to the Seven Years War. He and Washington participated in the expedition that replaced the French Fort Duquesne with the British Fort Pittsburgh in 1758. With the support of Washington, Mercer moved to Fredericksburg to resume his medical practice after the war; he joined Washington in Lodge Fredericksburg in 1767. During 1775, he became an active Patriot in Virginia. Initially a colonel in the 3rd Virginia Regiment, in June 1776 he was appointed brigadier general in the Continental Army raised by the Patriots in the thirteen colonies united in their opposition to British rule. He went on to serve with distinction in New Jersey and New York, but at the battle of Princeton on 3 January 1777 he was mortally wounded and died nine days later.

## Race Relations

Another group of Jacobites who came to North America in the aftermath of Culloden were actually to fight against the French, the American Patriots and then the United States of America. They were mainly but not exclusively Highlanders – Stuarts, Rosses, MacDonalds, Camerons, Buchanans, MacNairs, MacGillivrays, Macintoshes, Chisholms, Duncans and Watts – who intermarried with Native American tribes, most notably the Cherokee and the Creek, whose matrilineal lines of succession enabled their offspring to become chiefs and leading warriors, as well as Indian agents and traders like their Jacobite fathers. Lachlan, the son of Alexander MacGillivray of Drumnaglass, who was killed at Culloden, married a Creek princess in Georgia. Their son John became an acquisitive but celebrated Creek chief and an adviser to President George Washington on Indian affairs. John Ross and John MacDonald, who assimilated into the Cherokees in Georgia, were the grandfathers of John Ross, who became the principal chief of the Cherokee nation from 1828 to 1866. He led his people through the Native American removals west beyond the Appalachian Mountains, as well as planning and establishing a textile village at Chattanooga in Tennessee, which introduced his people to industrialization on their own terms.

Scottish interaction with Native Americans predated the Union of 1707 and was sustained by Scottish traders and their firms in the extraction of deerskins, beaver and other animal pelts from the Carolinas to New York. Scottish traders were tolerant of Native American customs and did not seek to impose their versions of Christianity. Traders were supported by wider Scottish commercial networks that extended credit to importers of goods that were exchanged for furs and to Native Americans who wished to purchase these goods. But the Highlanders had a particular affinity not only as traders but as frontiersmen, which was notably evident in Georgia from the foundation of the colony in 1735. Relations with Native Americans were cordial from the outset and were consolidated in expeditionary forces against the Spaniards in Florida and Cuba. They were continued in succeeding generations through the American Revolution. The Highlanders in Georgia kept their feather caps, plaids, targes and claymores. At New Inverness (later

Darien), the chiefs and warriors of the Cherokees and Creeks and the clannish contingents of Highlanders emulated each other in hunting and sports, particularly those involving stick and ball, such as lacrosse and shinty.

There were certainly tensions between the soldiers in the Highland regiments and the Native Americans. Like soldiers in other British regiments, the Highlanders treated Native American warriors with contempt, dismissed them as savages and sexually exploited their women. Highland regiments were used to suppress a Cherokee uprising from 1759 to 1761 against the intrusion of settlers on to their lands in the southern colonies. Like the demobbed Highlanders given land after the peace of 1763, the rights of Native Americans were recognized by a proclamation of George III. In return for permitting colonial settlements east of the Appalachian Mountains in recently acquired lands in Florida and Quebec, lands to the west of the Appalachians were reserved for Native American tribes. The unwarranted intrusion of colonial settlers along the Ohio River and into territories that became the states of Tennessee and Kentucky encouraged the Cherokees and the Creeks to side with the British Loyalists over the American Patriots in the War of Independence. When the British lost and the Americans won in 1783, the Cherokees and the Creeks were among the Native Americans who continued to wage war against the fledgling United States until 1794, when a peace was brokered by President Washington assisted by chiefs with a Jacobite hinterland.

The generally tolerant relationship between Scots and Native Americans from Darien in Panama in the 1690s to Darien in Georgia from the 1730s was not extended to Africans sold into chattel slavery in the British American colonies. One notable exception to this occurred in Georgia. General Oglethorpe and his trustees at the outset of the colony in 1735 had prohibited importing, employing and trading slaves in Georgia. However, a vocal group of Lowland Scots in and around Savannah were soon pressing for the importation of slaves and rum to encourage trade with the West Indies. John Mor Mackintosh and seventeen other heads of Highland families firmly opposed any relaxation of the 1735 prohibition on pragmatic and principled grounds. Slavery, they argued, was not cost-effective in a frontier colony, especially when

Spaniards in Florida were offering sanctuary to slaves who ran away from their masters. The returns from slave labour would soon be overtaken by the costs of guarding them. Accordingly, they argued for further migration from the Highlands, which would enhance productive labour as well as uphold rather than undermine frontier defences. At the same time, they affirmed their opposition to chattel slavery: 'It's shocking to human Nature, that any Race of Mankind, and their Posterity, should be sentenced to perpetual slavery.'[3] While the prohibition held for another decade, it was gradually undermined by the illicit importation of slaves by Lowland Scots and other British colonists coming from the Carolinas and the West Indies. It was rescinded in May 1749 with no further protests from the Highlanders.

Relations with black communities, particularly in colonies producing tobacco, sugar and rice, rarely rose above the exploitative for Highlander or Lowlander, Jacobite or Whig, Loyalist or Patriot. In North Carolina, slaves to Highland settlers and merchants were taught Gaelic as a means of controlling the market and curtailing runaways in the Cape Fear district. At the outbreak of the American Revolution, Loyalists and Patriots between the port of Wilmington and the colonial capital of New Bern were prepared temporarily to set aside their differences when the colonists' dispute with Britain appeared to open a door to a slave insurrection.

Jamaica accounted for most Scots in the West Indies – about one-third of the white inhabitants of the island in the mid-eighteenth century were thought to be Scots by birth or descent. Slave-holding was part and parcel of life in the fields, households and shops. There was no difference between Jacobite and Whig families in this respect. However, bringing slaves back to Scotland proved problematic for a Jacobite family. In 1778, the Court of Session, the highest civil court in Scotland, ruled that slavery was not recognized by Scots law. This landmark case was brought by Joseph Knight, a former slave baptized and legally married in Scotland, against his former master John Wedderburn of Ballindean, who had fought at Culloden and escaped to Jamaica. The judges determined that dominion over a Negro in Jamaica was unjust and could not be supported in Scotland. It was agreeable neither to humanity nor to Christianity.

John Wedderburn was joined in Jamaica by his brother James, who had also fled after Culloden. Their father, Sir John Wedderburn of Blackness near Dundee, was captured, executed and forfeited. John and James Wedderburn became successful sugar planters in Jamaica. On returning to Scotland, John Wedderburn acquired the estate of Ballindean in Perthshire in 1768 and James bought Inveresk in Midlothian in 1773. Despite their success as imperial adventurers, the Wedderburns retained a profound sense of injustice from their family's losses for Jacobitism. John Wedderburn's determination not to suffer a further loss of property led him to pursue his case against Joseph Knight. This intensified sense of injustice was carried into the anti-abolition movement by their descendants at Ballindean and Inveresk and by another Jacobite family related by marriage: the Johnstones of Westerhall near Dumfries, who owned a plantation in Grenada. They were among a significant group of Scottish dissenters to abolition of the slave trade within the British Empire in 1807 and then of slavery itself in 1833. The anti-abolitionist cause was organized through networks of West Indian planters, merchants and financiers. Acting in concert with English counterparts, they resolutely resisted philanthropic calls for the abolition of slavery. The Wedderburns and the Johnstones numbered among those families with a Jacobite history who were the most assiduous pursuers of reparations for the loss of their property rights in slaves. They had bitter memories of forfeiture without compensation after the Fifteen and the Forty-Five.

In the midst of the abolitionist controversy, an iconic monument to commemorate Prince Charles Edward Stuart raising his standard for the Forty-Five was constructed at Glenfinnan. Built in 1815, seventy years after the actual event, its erection and design was funded by Alexander MacDonald of Glenaladale, whose father was the Jamaican adventurer who had purchased Glenaladale in 1773.

The monument at Glenfinnan was a product of sugar and slavery as well as Jacobitism. The monument, over 18 metres in height, had a larger-than-life statue of an unknown Highlander added in 1835. Its sculptor, John Greenshields, whose artistic patron was Sir Walter Scott, claimed that his inspiration was Prince Charles Edward Stuart. The monument has become a global symbol for Jacobite Romanticism.[4]

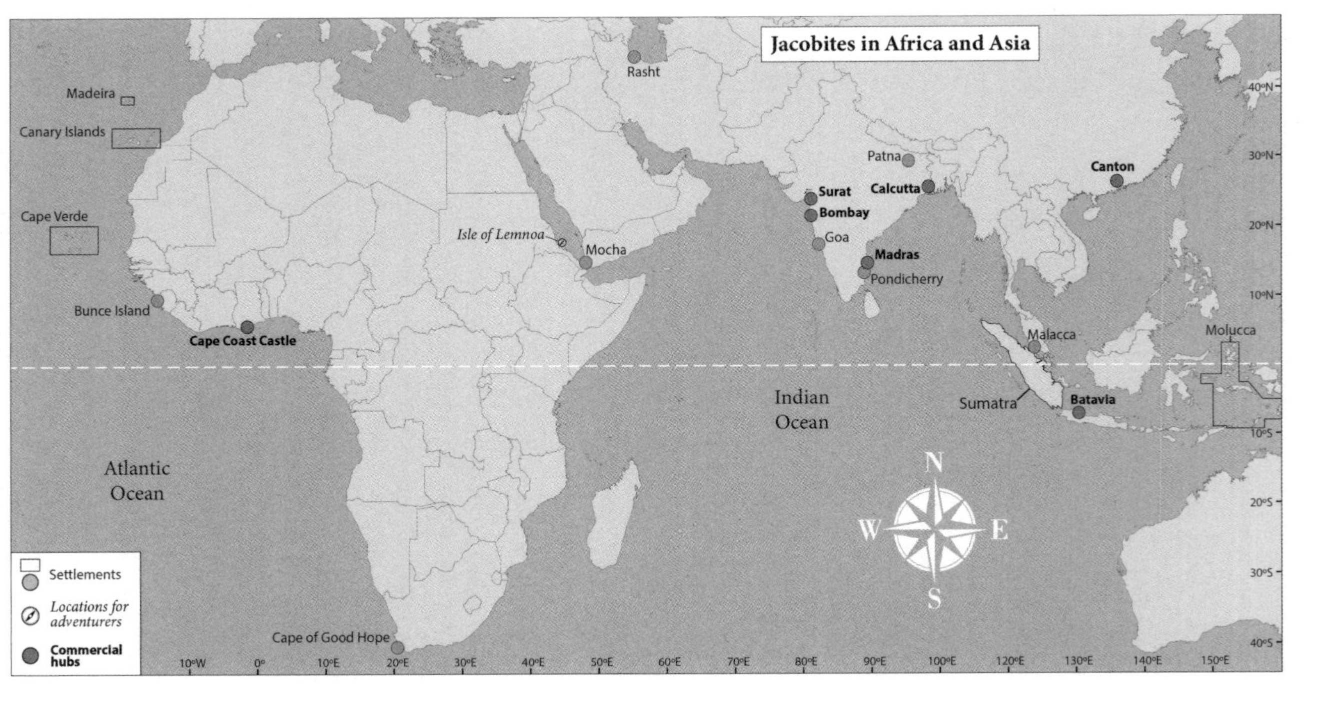

Jacobites in Africa and Asia
Settlements
Locations for adventurers
Commercial hubs
Canton
Batavia
Malacca
Sumatra
Molucca
Patna
Calcutta
Surat
Bombay
Goa
Madras
Pondicherry
Rasht
Mocha
Isle of Lemnoa
Indian Ocean
Atlantic Ocean
Cape of Good Hope
Cape Coast Castle
Bunce Island
Madeira
Canary Islands
Cape Verde
N
E
S
W

# 6

# Africa, Asia and Global Adventuring

Jacobite adventuring overseas was by no means restricted to North America and the Caribbean. Whereas adventurers in the British American colonies were usually integrated into settled communities in town and country, this was not the case for adventurers in Africa, whose slave trading, mineral prospecting, foraging for game and searching for medicinal roots were secured by forts. In Asia they could expect protection from forts, although commercial networking in the East Indies, especially in India and China, was based in longestablished merchant communities trading in such commodities as textiles, drugs and tea. Adventuring in Africa and Asia was mainly but not exclusively channelled through chartered companies – most notably the Royal African, South Seas and English East India companies operating from London. Jacobites had no managerial role nor did they direct policy, but some were recruited as expendable manpower into the military forces that protected and expanded commercial ventures emanating from West Africa via Jamaica into Latin America in the case of the Royal African and South Seas companies and from Mocha in Arabia to Canton in China for the English East India Company. These ventures were also open to Jacobites as commodity traders on behalf of the respective companies or as freelance tramp traders. Jacobites were less likely to be engaged as overseas adventurers in the chartered companies of the Dutch and Danish states, which were consistent allies of the post-Revolution British monarchy. But they had a distinctive presence in French, Spanish, Austrian and Swedish chartered companies from states periodically, if not always consistently, opposed to the Hanoverian succession. Indeed, Jacobites had founding roles in the East India Company of the Austrian Netherlands operating from Ostend and later in the Swedish East India Company operating out of Gothenburg.

Jacobite adventurers from Scotland, as from England and Ireland, did not restrict their commercial activities to one continent, developing global trading from Latin America via the West Indies to the East Indies and profiting notably from the Spanish and Swedish as well as British empires. Monies accrued from the French, Dutch and Danish empires in America, Africa and Asia were rarely repatriated by Jacobite exiles. But monies repatriated from the British, Spanish, Austrian and Swedish empires were used for the political and social rehabilitation of Jacobite families and for the recovery and improvement of their estates at home. Adventurers also reinvested profits of East Indian ventures to expand their interests in Caribbean plantations. Active adventuring on a global scale carried high risks not just from missed or failed opportunities, but from incidental deaths caused by epidemic diseases, natural disasters and battlefield casualties. Jacobites were also passively engaged in global adventuring through investments in stocks and shares of chartered companies. Jacobite families in the aftermath of Culloden, from whom Highland regiments were raised for service in India, were not averse to becoming serious critics of the management and direction of the English East India Company when returns from dividends did not match their expectations.

## Africa and Latin America

Between the first and second expeditions to Darien on the Isthmus of Panama, the Company of Scotland to Africa and the Indies had actually fitted out a ship, the *African Merchant*, which sailed via Madeira and Cape Verde for the Grain, Ivory and Gold coasts in West Africa. Although the captain (William Bell) was charged to look for a convenient site for a fort when on the Ivory Coast, this was not necessarily as a future base for slave trading, which was more associated with Guinea along the Gold Coast. This was the only trading venture of the Company of Scotland that actually returned a profit: the *African*

*Merchant* brought back to Edinburgh extensive quantities of rice, ivory and gold dust in July 1700. As the Darien scheme was collapsing, two proposals were considered, but never executed, to bolster the company's finances. The first, in April, which was to be undertaken in association with the Dutch on Cape Bonne Esperance at the Cape of Good Hope in South Africa, was projected as a colony for the supply of slaves. The second, in August, was for the company to license a private venture for no more than five undertakers to invest £5,000 in a ship to be built and outfitted in London and thereafter another £2,000 to trade with coastal Guinea. The ship was designed to operate out of London in the slave trade. Two years later, Glasgow merchant adventurers were beginning to dabble in the slave trade using ships operating out of London, Bristol, Liverpool and Whitehaven to stay within the scope of the English Navigation Acts. A consortium of lairds and merchants from in and around Inverness and Aberdeen, acting in association with the Royal African Company (RAC), made an initial venture in May 1713 to Cape Coast Castle in Guinea.

None of these ventures can be deemed Jacobite endeavours. However, opportunities in Africa and Latin America did open up for the supporters of the exiled Stuarts. By the Treaty of Utrecht, which concluded the War of the Spanish Succession in 1713, Scots also gained a significant foothold in the African slave trade through the concession of the Spanish *assiento* to British suppliers, notably the South Sea Company (SSC) working in tandem with the RAC. In the 1720s their contract for carrying slaves to Campeche in Mexico was devolved to a Scottish company, Blackwood and Cathcart, whose main shipping agent was the Glasgow firm Dalrymple and Graham. No less significantly, in the wake of John, Duke of Chandos's investment in both charter companies, his Scottish associate Alexander Ouchterlony became a director of the RAC by 1734. Placement in the factories or trading houses of the SSC extended throughout Latin America from Cuba and Hispaniola through Campeche, Cartagena and Portobello on to the coastal districts of Brazil and to Buenos Aires on the River Plate. Placements tended to be limited to officers who had served in the British forces during the War of the Spanish Succession. Limited opportunities for Jacobite families did open up as the RAC expanded its presence in western Africa from Sierra Leone to Angola. Families of Jacobite sympathizers were not entirely excluded from naval commissions, as the Royal Navy protected the shipping of both companies in bringing slaves from Guinea to Jamaica.

The most prominent, if not notorious, Jacobite in the service of the RAC was Robert Balfour, 5th Lord Balfour of Burleigh. A convicted murderer who had escaped from prison in 1709 by exchanging clothes with his sister, he kept a low profile while lingering around his family estates in Fife. He did make a covert trip to Lochmaben in Dumfriesshire in May 1714 to join a Jacobite protest against the impending Hanoverian succession. He came out of hiding to join the Fifteen, for which he was attainted and forfeited. Neither imprisoned nor exiled on the Continent, he seems to have engaged clandestinely in the slave trade from Liverpool before resurfacing in June 1721 as a factor at Cape Coast Castle in Guinea, where he endeavoured, without any conspicuous success, to retrieve his family fortunes. He was reported dead in September 1722.

Although the RAC had been divested of its trading monopoly following the Revolution, it had certainly become more receptive to employing Scots in the aftermath of Union. It was on Alexander Ouchterlony's watch that Scots, including some with nonjuring credentials, became notably influential on the Gold Coast in West Africa as chief agents, treasurers and warehouse keepers at Cape Coast Castle near Accra. They enjoyed fairly amicable and mutually supportive trading relations with the Royal Danish West India and Guinea Company, whose main fort near Accra was Christianborg Castle. Certainly, there were disputes within the territories claimed by the respective companies arising from intertribal slavery and the pawning of free men, women and children. However, the Scots were opposed to the ruthless policy of territorial acquisition which the Danes attempted in 1744. They argued for 'proper evidence' by drawing on personal experience, on working conventions of the European powers engaged on the Gold Coast, and above all on respect for the customs and traditions of the indigenous peoples. Intertribal disputes between the Danish and RAC outstations to the east of Accra were to be resolved through arbitration: a customary process known as a *palaver*, in which the principal protagonists made a *fetish*, whereby they gave oaths to facilitate resolution by paying reparations. This process had much in common with arbitration and assythment to repair friendship still practised among the predominantly Jacobite clans and the landed elite on the boundaries between the Highlands and Lowlands.[1]

Territorial differences notwithstanding, the Danish company set considerable store by good commercial relations not only with the RAC but with Scottish as well as English free traders who supplied provisions, such as foodstuffs, clothing and gunpowder, in return for gold, ivory and even shares in slaving ventures to the West Indies. Ships arriving from Glasgow and the Firth of Clyde tended to be on temporary release from shipping sugar and rum from the West Indies or tobacco from Virginia and the other southern British colonies in North America. Two years after it had been engaged by the Camerons of Lochiel to trade with Jamaica, the *Neptune* arrived in Guinea in 1736, primarily to acquire gold and then to transport slaves at the behest of two Glasgow merchants, James Colquhoun and George Bogle. Unlike the Camerons, they were neither Jacobites nor nonjurors. However, the nonjuring Buchanan and Company from Glasgow did despatch the *Argyle*, under Captain George Hamilton, to the RAC and Danish fortifications at Accra in 1737 and 1738 and again in 1742 and 1743. On all four occasions, the exchange of stores for gold and ivory took priority over opportunities to engage in slave trading. Glasgow merchants remained reluctant to commit to wholesale diversification into slave trading. In the aftermath of Culloden, the stridently anti-Jacobite Alexander Harvie in Barbados attempted to persuade the Glasgow merchant Claud Alexander to outmanoeuvre and supersede Liverpool and Whitehaven in trading slaves directly from West Africa to the Caribbean. But Alexander made no effort to form a consortium in Glasgow for that purpose, preferring to look for remunerative ventures in the East Indies.

There was one subsequent slaving venture with marginal Jacobite as well as Glasgow connections. Bunce Island in Senegal on the Rice Coast, which housed a fort abandoned by the RAC, was acquired in 1748 as a slaving entrepôt by Oswald, Grant and Company operating out of London. One of the two principal partners, Richard Oswald, who had a Caithness connection, had become a tobacco lord, sugar baron and committed Whig in Glasgow before moving to London in the aftermath of the Forty-Five. By 1759, he had purchased the estates of Cavens in the stewartry of Kirkcudbright and Auchincruive in Ayrshire, and later acquired plantations in Florida as well as Virginia and Georgia. Alexander Grant came from a family in Invernesshire sympathetic to Jacobitism at the Fifteen. He went on to retrieve the fortunes of the Grants of Dalvey: first as a doctor and then as a planter in Jamaica before moving to London as a merchant adventurer. He succeeded to Dalvey in his own right in 1755. During their control of Bunce Island, which lasted until 1785, they became major suppliers of slaves to rice plantations in South Carolina and Georgia and to the British, French and Danish West Indies. To emphasize their Scottish credentials, they built a two-hole golf course on the island and had their domestic servants at the restored fort dress in tartan.

## Arabia to China

In the aftermath of the successful venture by the *African Merchant*, the Company of Scotland sent three ships east via Africa to India and China in 1701. Two, the *Speedy Return* and the *Content*, were lost in the Indian Ocean. They were seized initially by pirates from Madagascar and lost subsequently on the Malabar Coast of southwest India. The third ship, the *Speedwell*, foundered on rocks off Malacca in 1702, its lucrative cargo dissipated and its crew dispersed without any capital repatriated to Scotland. In the following year, the *Worcester*, notionally in the service of the East India Company (EIC), arrived at Calcutta from Surat under the command of Thomas Green. Captain Alexander Hamilton, of Scottish extraction, had retired from India with a fortune after 35 years of seafaring in the Far East. His account as a freelance skipper occasionally contracted to the EIC was published posthumously, twelve years after his death in 1732. Hamilton learned from Captain Green and other senior members of his crew that they had sold arms and ammunition to pirates in Madagascar and gone on to plunder a Moorish ship which had carried seventeen Europeans on board. Revelations about their piratical activities on the Malabar Coast give some credence to the capital charges brought against Green and his crew when the *Worcester* sought refuge in Scottish waters on returning from India in 1704. Another ship chartered by the Company of Scotland, the *Annandale*, had already been impounded on the River Thames at the behest of the EIC. With the *Worcester* secured in the Firth of Forth, the Company of Scotland initiated an action for redress in the Admiralty Court that led to Captain Green and several of his crew being executed for piracy in March 1705.

The trial and execution of Green heightened tensions between the Scottish Estates and the English Parliament but did not prevent the accomplishment of Union in 1707. Although the Scots could now trade legally in the West Indies, the East Indies remained a monopoly of the Whig and Tory East India companies that merged in 1708. The new EIC based in London was the only English trading concern able to exclude rival companies or restrict the active participation of anyone wishing to engage in commerce overseas. There was no question of the English becoming the British EIC. Nevertheless, its English predecessors had not excluded Scots before the Union and certainly made no attempt to impose a blanket ban thereafter.

But there was no significant Jacobite presence in the East Indies until the 1720s. That presence can be attributed primarily to John Drummond of Quarrel, with backing from Prime Minister Sir Robert Walpole, for whom engagement with empire became a noted means of rehabilitating Jacobites and integrating them into the British state. Having had rather mixed success as an investor in the RAC and SSC, and substantial losses from the Mississippi Project in France, Drummond of Quarrel settled in London, from where he helped to shape the direction of the EIC from 1724. A committed unionist, he nonetheless had strong Episcopal and Jacobite connections. Until his death in 1742, Drummond placed Scots regardless of their political or religious affiliations in the service of the EIC. Although his death coincided with the downfall of Walpole, Drummond established a framework for Scottish patronage in the East Indies that endured until the 1780s.

From his base in London, Drummond was regularly aided and abetted by George and Alexander Ouchterlony, and occasionally by his kinsman Andrew Drummond, banker and goldsmith. They reputedly secured Scots around a quarter of the patronage dispensed through the EIC. In turn, this may have led to the annual repatriation of capital worth £500,000 by 1750. Scots became particularly prominent in both the military and mercantile branches of the company in Bengal. Drummond also aided Scottish and Ulster Scottish commercial networks in Bombay and Surat on the western seaboard of India and in Calcutta and Madras on the eastern seaboard. As tramp traders, they sourced coffee from Arabia through the Indian Ocean to the South China Seas where they purchased tea in Canton. In between, they traded in textiles including silks, ivory, sugar and candies, peppers and diverse spices, alums and other dyes, porcelain (chinaware), fine woods for furnishings, and drugs (not all of which were as addictive as opium). The separation of military and trading interests in the EIC was not always strictly adhered to, especially for seafarers. There was considerable scope for governors, sea captains, supercargoes and pursers in charge of commodities that were to be marketed in ports to trade on their own account, although their commercial priorities were nominally in the interests of the EIC.

Two of Drummond's most successful protégés became governors respectively at Bombay and at Fort St George at Madras: namely, Robert Cowan from Londonderry and James MacRae from Ayr. Both were part of a stridently anti-Jacobite, Ulster Scottish network. MacRae was integrated into the network by marriage, but his links to the Jacobite clan from Wester Ross were historic, not current. Both Cowan and MacRae had made their initial mark with the EIC as seafarers fighting pirates before being promoted with the assistance of Drummond to the role of governor. Cowan held his position at Bombay from 1729 to 1734, MacRae at Fort St George from 1725 to 1731. They were also reliant on Drummond to stay in office and were relieved of their posts when they lost his confidence. Like other adventurers in India, regardless of their political affiliations as Whig or Jacobite, Cowan and MacRae accrued sufficient capital to live conspicuously in the style of elite native nabobs and returned home with reputed fortunes in excess of £100,000. There were effectively three ways for such British nabobs to repatriate capital between the Fifteen and the Forty-Five. Money accrued from official business could be remitted back to London through bills of exchange at rates determined by the EIC. Rupees could be sent back as silver specie in treasure chests supplemented more discreetly by purses of diamonds. The riskiest but most remunerative option favoured by both Cowan and MacRae was to send rupees as silver specie to Canton, where it was converted into gold and sent back in European ships.

In return for his patronage, Cowan and MacRae delivered regular intelligence on commercial and military affairs to Drummond that appraised the EIC's impact on the political economy of Asia: intelligence that allowed Drummond to sustain his position as an influential governor in the EIC. Drummond had also other motives, more closely tied to maintaining his position as a Member of Parliament for the Perth Burghs from 1727 until his death in 1742. He was particularly supportive of families in Perthshire and Tayside not just to rehabilitate those caught up in the Fifteen, but to win over those families flirting with Jacobitism to British imperial service. But in this context, his record was decidedly mixed. Drummond could secure a placement but not guarantee all adventurers would profit, far less live like nabobs. Attaining placement in India was certainly no guarantee of prosperity. The chances of any adventurer returning with a fortune were one in five hundred, as laid out by Robert Cowan to John Drummond on 18 August 1733: 'fortunes acquired here in these Sickly Climates are deadly earned, not 1 in 50 returning to their Native Country & of these that do, not 1 in 10 with a sufficient Competency.'[2]

Those less fortunate in their placements faced high mortality rates from fevers and other epidemical diseases, while some also struggled to maintain adequate funding for their commercial or military ventures. This could also lead to downward social mobility for those who suffered serious losses, whereby linen drapers and other tradespeople were obliged to become mere sorters of goods or labourers in the service of the EIC. Some deemed from the outset as ill-advised to come out to India or subsequently found unsuitable for commercial trading were encouraged to redeploy with the military. This was the fate of Hugh MacKenzie of Fraserdale, who had arrived at Fort William in Bengal in 1731. His father, Alexander MacKenzie of Prestonhall in Fife, who had a claim to the lordship of Lovat through marriage, had led out his adopted clan for the Jacobites in the Fifteen. But he was undermined by the notorious Simon Fraser of Beaufort, who swung the clan over to the Whigs and duly succeeded to the title of Lord Lovat as the male heir.

A member of another Jacobite family placed in India by Drummond was less fortunate. Sir David Threipland of Fingask had engaged in the Fifteen, for which he was attainted, forfeited and exiled before returning surreptitiously to Perthshire by 1732. Drummond not only assisted his pursuit of a pardon but had already aided the placement of Fingask's son George as a surgeon at Fort William in Bengal in 1724, after other sons who had also featured in the rising had failed to retrieve the family's fortunes in West Africa. However, despite a promising start to his career in India, moving on to Fort St David on the Malabar Coast by 1727, George succumbed to a fever four years later. Despite's Drummond patronage, the Threiplands of Fingask were active in the Forty-Five. While David, the heir to Fingask, was killed at the battle of Prestonpans, his younger brother Stuart served throughout the rising as physician-in-chief to Prince Charles Edward. After a brief spell of exile in France, he was included in the indemnity of 1747 and returned to his medical practice in Edinburgh. It proved so distinguished that he became president of the Royal College of Physicians in 1766 and so profitable that he was able to buy back Fingask in 1783.

The fever to which George Threipland succumbed also affected Alexander Wedderburn from a family near Dundee that flirted with Jacobitism. However, Wedderburn, who was a cousin of Drummond, recovered and resumed his career in the EIC which had started as a purser on a ship from Fort St David to Surat in 1726 and then on a ship from Bengal to China in the following year. Having served profitably as supercargo on a ship from Calcutta to Persia in 1729, Wedderburn had gone on to become a factor at Bengal by 1731, though he chafed at the restriction imposed by Governor MacRae at Fort St George on freelance trading by assistant supercargoes. The fever of that year prevented his opportunity to return to China and diminished his tradeable stocks, which Drummond had replenished from the company's treasury. By the outset of 1733, Wedderburn had established a commercial partnership at Madras that was reported to be thriving in Calcutta by 1735. He continued to prosper there until his return to Scotland in 1743.

Another member of a family that had flirted with Jacobitism was John Fotheringham. He had been operating with his father, George, as a free merchant for five years out of Bombay before soliciting Drummond's help to repatriate money in 1732. Although Drummond helped John Fotheringham secure a mercantile post with the EIC, it had not been to his liking. In March 1739 he told Drummond that his inhumane treatment had persuaded him to seek his fortune elsewhere, notably as a supercargo on a ship of the Swedish East India Company bound for Bengal. He was currently in Cadiz where gold and silver were purchased as specie to be exchanged for tea at Canton. The Swedish company, more so than any other chartered East Indian company, was supportive of Jacobites. However, the initial challenge to the main chartered companies came from the Ostend East India Company founded in the Spanish Netherlands in 1722.

The Ostend company had first been mooted by the Jacobite double agent John Ker of Kersland around 1720 and was supported by freelance traders in the East Indies among Irish Jacobite exiles, such as Thomas Sarsfield. Also drawn in was Hugh Campbell from Edinburgh, a member of the Campbells of Cawdor, a clan of Jacobite sympathizers. As a freelance trader based around Madras, Campbell had engaged in the tea trade from Canton and was to help smuggle diamonds back to London, through a Jewish network, for John Drummond in 1726. Hugh's brother, Colin Campbell, became a significant player in the Ostend company, which he joined in 1723 after fleeing London to avoid being jailed for debts he had accumulated as a stockbroker during the South Sea Bubble. But the two most influential Scots in the company were the brothers Alexander and Abraham Hume from Berwickshire, noted as Quakers rather than Jacobites. The Ostend company had attracted considerable investment from traders in stocks and shares in Antwerp, Amsterdam and London. Nevertheless, after pressure on the Austrian emperor from the other countries more established in the East Indian trade, the Ostend company's overseas ventures were suspended in 1728. The Humes, who ran the main station for the Ostend company on the Coromandel Coast in southeast India, re-engaged with the EIC, mainly as suppliers of ships in London. Until the Ostend company was formally wound up in 1738, adventurers and investors used two other East Indian companies as flags of convenience, initially the Danish and thereafter the Swedish East India Company. Founded in Gothenburg in 1731 by a West Indian trader, sugar refiner and ballistics manufacturer, Niklas Sahlgren, in association with Colin Campbell, who was to continue as a director in the company until his death in 1757, the Swedish East India Company recruited his brother Hugh as well as prominent Jacobites from the northeast of Scotland.

Colin Campbell made his initial and highly profitable journey to China as supercargo on the Swedish East India Company's first ship to Canton in 1732. He was joined three years later by Charles Irvine from the family of Drum in Aberdeenshire. In the aftermath of the Fifteen, Irvine had fled to France, settling in Rouen, the base of the French East India Company (Compagnie des Indes). With the assistance of the Jacobite merchant banker Robert Arbuthnot, who traded with the Compagnie, Irvine had travelled to India and Canton with free-lance traders operating out of Saint-Malo. Irvine, who had returned to Aberdeenshire before his death in 1771, was a key player with Campbell in ensuring that the Swedish East India Company played down friction with other European companies by uniquely not having any stations or factories in India. At the same time, they diversified the Swedish company's markets by promoting the smuggling of tea into Britain. A key player in their recruitment, funding and marketing was George Ouchterlony, based in London, whose son Thomas also ventured to China with the Swedish East India Company. After the Forty-Five, they were joined by a former captain of the Life-Guard for Prince Charles Edward at Culloden, George Carnegie from the family of Pitarrow in Kincardineshire, who served as a merchant adventurer in Gothenburg for nineteen years until his return to Scotland in 1765. Another adventurer from the northeast, George Chalmer, arrived in Gothenburg around the same time. He and his family remained in Gothenburg mainly directing the Swedish East India Company. A bequest from his son William founded the Chalmers University of Technology there in 1829. But no similar bequests were made by Scottish adventurers in the Swedish East India Company, as in the other chartered companies, to finance or sustain Jacobitism.

## Global Adventuring

Families of adventurers associated with Jacobitism did not restrict their activities to single continents. Adventuring in America, Africa or Asia could be pursued profitably as a global endeavour, for which the benchmark was set by the Grants of Monymusk in the Highland foothills of Aberdeenshire. A cadet line of the Grants in Speyside, they were overtly

Whig but had covert financial and insurance deals with Jacobites. The scale of their commercial operations, whether legal or illicit, was undoubtedly trans-oceanic. In 1713, the year after they acquired Monymusk, the Grants were involved in a slave venture to the Guinea Coast in association with Inverness merchants. They had already acquired a landed interest in Pennsylvania in 1701 that was consolidated as the manor of Montjoy by 1730. Trading from the Baltic to the Caribbean, they built up their commercial activities over the next two decades in Boston, Maryland and South Carolina and became substantial plantation owners, first in Barbados from 1716 and in Jamaica from 1723. At the same time, they moved into Latin America, both as adventurers and shareholders in the SSC from 1721, with a particular interest in Campeche, Mexico, from 1729 as a base not only for the *assiento* but for the logwood trade. During the 1720s they also became involved in the East India trade, initially through London, where they occasionally operated on the margins of financial probity with Jacobite speculators. Their Whig credentials were enhanced after they based their trading ventures in India on Bombay from 1735. The family also engaged in the naval and military ventures of the EIC, occasionally from 1728 and regularly from 1744.

At the other end of the scale, families engaged in global adventuring as an occasional pursuit even when they changed their political allegiance from Jacobite to Whig. The Campbells of Barcaldine in Lorn engaged with the Camerons of Lochiel, whom they had fought alongside in the Fifteen, in ventures to New York and Jamaica in 1734. However, Daniel, a younger son of Patrick Campbell of Barcaldine, having just qualified as a surgeon in Edinburgh, was dissuaded by an uncle already settled in Jamaica from venturing there in a professional capacity as the island was reputedly overstocked with surgeons. Instead, he was advised to move to London and get a placement on a mercantile or naval ship bound for Jamaica. He opted for the latter but died ten weeks after his arrival on the *Antelope* in October 1734. Having prospected for gold on their own account in Brazil from 1728, the Campbells of Barcaldine were keen to throw over their past Jacobitism and demonstrate their loyalty to the Hanoverian succession through overseas service in the British Army and the Royal Navy, which took them to the East Indies as well as the West Indies. After the fall of Madras to the French in 1746, Captain Alexander Campbell, along with other members of the Argyll militia who had fought at Culloden, enlisted in an Independent Company sent to win back Madras and lay siege to the French fort at Pondicherry in 1748. It met with limited success in the field before the Treaty of Aix-la-Chapelle, which brought the War of Austrian Succession to its conclusion, restored Madras to Britain and confirmed French control over Pondicherry. That October, Alexander had informed his father, John, now laird of Barcaldine, that he had considered staying on in the service of the EIC, but limited prospects of promotion meant it was better that he come home on half-pay rather than rely on prize money to augment his salary in India.

The Campbells of Barcaldine were cadets of the Campbells of Glenorchy headed by the Earls of Breadalbane, whom they followed closely in matters of political economy. They were particularly influenced by John Campbell, Lord Glenorchy (the future 3rd Earl of Breadalbane), who had notably rehabilitated the former Jacobite clan by becoming a British diplomat. In July 1728 Lord Glenorchy, as envoy to the Danish royal court in Copenhagen, had protested that the Danish East India Company, based at Altona on the River Elbe, was prejudicing British interests and privileges by allowing traders from the Ostend company to participate in their ventures to India and China. Personal adventuring by the Breadalbane earls after the Anglo-Scottish Union had been restricted to finessing land deals in New Jersey, where they also were dabbling in copper mining by 1738. However, their principal financial adviser, John Campbell, cashier to the Royal Bank of Scotland from its inception in 1727, facilitated and enhanced imperial ventures by other cadet families in the shires of Argyll and Perth. Their extensive travels commenced with the indigo and sugar trades from the West Indies after 1707 and continued through to the English tea trade from China by 1753.

The global scale of adventuring by Scottish families and its impact on their commitment to Jacobitism can be measured in more detail through two case studies. Capital accumulation overseas and its repatriation from the East Indies to the West Indies led to the eventual distancing from the cause of the exiled Stuarts by the Stirlings of Keir. They preferred building up their acquisition of plantations in Jamaica to carrying out extensive agricultural improvements in central Scotland. The Duffs from the northeast repatriated funds from the Spanish and Swedish as well as the British empires. In the process they augmented their political and landed position, subordinating but not subduing the family's links to Jacobitism. Although they belatedly acquired plantations in Jamaica, their primary concern with global adventuring was the funding of local enterprises. Agricultural improvements on their burgeoning estates in northern shires were complemented by commercial diversification through extractive industries, manufacturing and fisheries. Reinvesting surplus capital in stocks and shares sustained their gradual switch from direct to indirect engagement in empire.

The Stirlings of Keir were landowners near Glasgow and in the shires of Stirling and Perth. James Stirling, a committed Jacobite, was out for the cause in 1708, 1715 and 1745. Having gone on manoeuvres with other gentry from Stirlingshire in 1708, they were acquitted of treason by a Scottish jury: a verdict which contributed to the imposition of the more severe but less scrupulous English treason law on Scotland. Stirling of Keir felt the force of that law when he was attainted, forfeited and exiled for his involvement in the Fifteen. Around 1719 he slipped back from France and lived privately on his estates until he was apprehended in Glasgow in August 1727. Nevertheless, he was pardoned the following June. Apart from Jacobitism and nonjuring episcopacy, his main claim to fame was fathering 22 children (to one wife) between 1704 and 1729. Despite his attainder, the family were able to reclaim the estate from forfeiture through sequestration, a process supported by their tenantry as well as their friends and kinsmen. John, the eldest son of James, was installed as estate manager on reaching his majority in 1725, though he did not take over the full running of the family estates for another three years. By his own reckoning they were worth over £30,000 but carried a not inconsiderable debt of around £8,600. Nevertheless, John went on to become a manager of a multinational, global concern.

The Stirlings had links to the American colonies prior to the Union, but these were now augmented immensely. Two brothers, James and Robert, moved to Jamaica where they worked their way up from bookkeepers to overseers to plantation owners. Their elder brother Archibald, who had also moved to Jamaica, got his first commercial break through a brief but lucrative engagement with the Glasgow firm Dalrymple and Graham servicing the Spanish *assiento* to Campeche. In 1734, he worked his passage as a purser to Bengal in India through the family connections with John Drummond of Quarrel, whom John Stirling actively supported in his re-elections as MP for the Perth Burghs. Archibald also derived financial assistance from Scottish merchant houses in London, with the Ouchterlonies again to the fore. Having started out with a working capital of around £350, Archibald, by good luck as well as by hard work, prospered through tramp trading in silks and other textiles, minerals, sugar candy, spirits, porcelain and opium. Not only did he associate with other Scottish traders in Calcutta, Patna and Madras, but his principal partnership was with Daniel Lascelles, whose father, Henry, was a notable global trader with trans-oceanic interests that reached out from Yorkshire to the Americas, Africa and Asia.

The Forty-Five interrupted but did not impair the Stirlings' entrepreneurial endeavours. With monies repatriated from empire, James Stirling's purchase of an elaborate uniform at Edinburgh for himself and two of his sons, Hugh and William, prior to the outset of the rising led to them being placed under surveillance. Nevertheless, Hugh and William were active in the service of Prince Charles Edward after the Jacobite Army returned from Derby. They were arrested and confined with their father in Dumbarton Castle after attempting to escape to Rotterdam in the aftermath of Culloden. They were all liberated by the general indemnity granted in July 1747. Hugh was given the chance to rehabilitate himself as a merchant in Calcutta but died at Fort St David in April 1749, ten months after his arrival in India. He left no estate of note. His brother Henry, who commenced his career with the EIC at Fort Marlborough in Sumatra in 1739, transferred from a military to a civil position in Bengal, becoming resident agent at Sillibar, an outstation for Patna, in 1742 until his death in November 1748. He left little more than £1,415 worth of personal effects.

Archibald had left India before the deaths of his two brothers. In his last twelve months as a trader in Bengal, from February 1747 to January 1748, he had a cash turnover of £337,863 – of which £40,570 (12 per cent) was profit. Prior to his return to Britain, he engaged a London Jewish network to repatriate diamonds worth around £18,000. Most of his remaining funds, including £5,000 tied up in high-risk ventures, were despatched from India by 1751. These funds were used by John, assisted by George Ouchterlony, to clear off the debts which had encumbered the family estates, to acquire more lands in central Scotland, and to invest in lead mining in the West Highlands. Rents of around £900 at his father's attainder in 1716 had been pushed up by John Stirling to almost £1,600 by 1742. But arrears owed by tenant farmers had also accumulated to almost £2,400, a situation remedied in part in 1750 when Archibald purchased the estate of Cadder outside Glasgow from his brother.

Capital generated through John's pioneering of agricultural improvements and engagement in extractive industries remained secondary to funds mobilized through global enterprise. Despite their kinship, the Stirling brothers lent money to each other at commercial rates, usually 0.5 per cent below the current market rate. Nevertheless, Archibald and John acted in concert to invest monies accrued in Bengal in the family interests in Jamaica. Their brother Robert, who had acquired a plantation by 1748, also had his debts ameliorated and his cash resources sufficiently enhanced to purchase another plantation, mainly for cattle. His annual returns from the production of sugar and rum were reputedly worth £3,200, of which £2,000 was reckoned clear profit. By 1753, their brother James was also set up with a modest plantation worth £1,200 and the annual prospect of producing £200 worth of sugar and rum. As Scotland's Jacobite past was laid to rest by the abortive Elibank Plot, Robert Stirling recalled from Kingston in Jamaica the family's long, expensive involvement with the exiled Stuarts. He wrote to his brother Archibald on 30 September that as 'the chief use of money is to support our friends & Relations', they were the better quit of Jacobitism: 'We in Jamaica live happy in that respect for we don't trouble ourselves about Kings or any thing else but how to make as much Sugar & Rum as we can & to live friendly with one another.'[3] Archibald, for his part, was long estranged from Jacobitism when he took control over the Stirling estates in Scotland and Jamaica from 1757. He was succeeded in 1783 by his brother William, who had put his participation in the battles of Falkirk and Culloden for the Jacobites well behind him.

In contrast to the Stirlings of Keir, who operated exclusively within the British Empire, the global ventures of the Duffs from the northeast accorded precedence to the Spanish and Swedish empires. Their commercial networking, which was based in the shires of Aberdeen and Banff with further mercantile interests in the towns of Elgin and Inverness, primarily consisted of three families – of Braco and Dipple, of Craigston and of Drummuir. Opposed to the Union of 1707, all three families were more than tainted with Jacobitism. They continued to intermarry with Jacobite landed and mercantile elites. While leading members of the network became pragmatic Presbyterians, they continued to sponsor Episcopalian meeting houses. Their network also included Roman Catholics. Duff fortunes were founded first on private banking and landed enterprise, then on overseas trade. As well as lending on mortgages and annuities, the network traded in debentures and indulged occasionally in lottery tickets. Their members tended to avoid such high-risk, speculative ventures as the South Sea Bubble or the Mississippi Project. They did, however, acquire estates from families who had overstretched themselves by such speculation. They used their extensive Jacobite connections to lay claim to sequestered and forfeited estates, including those of the Earl of Mar on Deeside and of Gordon of Glenbucket in Strathdon. In the process, salmon fisheries, droving, textile manufacturing, the timber trade and slate quarrying featured in their commercial portfolio.

By the 1730s the two most prominent members of the network were William Duff of Dipple and Patrick Duff of Premnay. The litigious Duff of Dipple was MP for Banffshire from 1727 until he negotiated with Sir Robert Walpole for his elevation to Lord Braco in the Irish peerage in 1734. Although no longer attending Westminster, he remained a regional politician of substance. He diligently interacted with the MPs for the towns and shires of the northeast, firmly maintained contacts with Scottish political managers and commissioners for government agencies in Edinburgh, and generally supported the ministry in London, even in their pursuit of punitive policies against Jacobites and Episcopalians. However, his family contracted marriages to prominent Jacobites. His eldest sister, Helen, married William Sutherland of Roscommon in Moray, the brother of Kenneth, Lord Duffus, whom he joined in the Fifteen and in exile. Roscommon clandestinely returned to Scotland in 1729 in an unsuccessful attempt to acquire money from his wife, who had a liferent on his forfeited estate. Braco's sister Mary married William Baird of Auchmedden in Aberdeenshire, and his sister Janet married James Kinloch of Kinloch with estates in Fife and Angus. His daughter Janet married Sir William Gordon of Park in Banffshire. All their husbands were active Jacobites in the Forty-Five. While Baird of Auchmedden came within the scope of the general indemnity granted in 1747, the other two were forced into exile in France, Gordon of Park dying in Douai in 1751 while Kinloch of Kinloch was eventually granted a pardon in 1764. Braco forcibly prevented his estranged elder son, William, from joining the Forty-Five and made no attempt to attend his funeral when he died in London in 1751. Nevertheless, Braco did contribute in 1752 to the re-establishment of St Andrew's Episcopal Church in Banff, which had been destroyed by Cumberland.

A lawyer by profession as well as factor to Lord Braco, Duff of Premnay was the network's business manager. His collecting money for the relief of Jacobite prisoners at Carlisle in 1716 was soon put behind him. He acquired such a reputation as a political fixer in Aberdeen, Edinburgh and London that he came to be recognized as the man in the northeast who acted for Archibald, Earl of Islay (later Duke of Argyll), the principal political manager in Scotland. Nonetheless, his role as a justice of the peace from 1727 was challenged by accusations of Jacobitism that were eventually laid to rest when Premnay was instrumental in securing the return of Aberdeen to civil government and in securing reparations for riotous behaviour by government forces occupying the city in the aftermath of the Forty-Five. In the interim, Premnay assiduously cultivated contacts from the northeast in London merchant houses and Inns of Court, in the Navy Board and in the RAC. These contacts facilitated his repatriation of funds from three empires for the Duff network through London.

Premnay's brother-in-law, Captain John Urquhart, operating as a Spanish naval commander in the Americas and the Mediterranean, made considerable profits that were repatriated in tranches of £5,000–8,000 from Cadiz in the 1730s. As Urquhart was a Roman Catholic, his money was worked through mortgages and annuities with the assistance of Andrew Drummond, the goldsmith and banker, rather than being put directly into the acquisition of landed estates. Using a kinsman, William Urquhart of Meldrum, as a front, Captain Urquhart eventually secured the estate of Cromarty in Easter Ross for just under £9,000 in 1741. Premnay's brother Archibald, with the aid of Jacobite contacts in the Swedish East India Company and initial seed funding from Captain Urquhart and George Ouchterlony, became a successful China tea trader. So confident was he in his capacity to make a profit of 40 per cent on his trading transactions from Gothenburg that he sold his patrimony of Craigston in Aberdeenshire to enhance his venture capital. In 1743, Archibald Duff invited leading members of the network to invest £3,000 in his dealings trading tea from China, a portion of which was then smuggled into Britain. Within five years he sent back £1,030 from Canton in English ships and another 3,000 rix-dollars when he put in to Batavia. Dividends for the network were regularly repatriated from Gothenburg well into the 1750s. Notwithstanding backing from Alexander Ouchterlony, the network's only wasted asset in empire was Premnay's hapless brother Francis, who died while serving as a surgeon and spendthrift trader at Whydah on the Gold Coast in 1738.

Another Duff brother, Robert, progressed productively through the ranks of the Royal Navy, serving mainly in the West Indies until the rising in 1745 enabled him to demonstrate the requisite conspicuous brutality in suppressing Jacobites, which was rewarded with command of his own ship of the line. Further promotions followed from mention in dispatches for manoeuvres against the French fleet in the Bay of Biscay in 1759 and from serving as governor and naval commander at Newfoundland in 1775 and thereafter at Gibraltar until his retirement as a rear admiral in 1781. Successive promotions enhanced his capacity to repatriate sufficient funds from prizes and naval tickets to acquire the estate of Logie in Aberdeenshire by 1764 and then, for £19,000 in 1782, the estate of Fetteresso in Kincardineshire, which had once belonged to George Keith, Earl Marischal. In the interim, Lord Braco had been elevated further in the peerage as Earl of Fife from 1759 and his son George had expanded the Duff interest in Jamaica from naval to mercantile.

George Duff, through his marriage to Frances Dalzell in 1756, acquired within two years several plantations along with a lucrative portfolio of shares and annuities from insurance in, and coal supplies to, London as well as mines in Scotland. Frances was the daughter of Gibson

Dalzell, the surviving child of his relationship in Jamaica with a mixed-race woman. Gibson Dalzell from Nithsdale had progressed from junior army officer to agent for the SSC in Cuba from 1722 to 1733. He was a rather casual bookkeeper who moved to Jamaica to trade on his own account with Cuba and Campeche, Panama and Cartagena in the Gulf of Mexico. He became embroiled in a protracted court case in London with the SSC in 1734 for his failure as an agent to account for £8,680. This case was only settled by George Duff in 1759, when all but £796 of the reputed debt was written off. Legal suits were no impediment to Gibson Dalzell diversifying from trade into plantation ownership in Jamaica, acquiring estates producing sugar and rum prior to his permanent relocation to London with his daughter in 1746. Despite inclement weather, slave revolts and market fluctuations in commodity prices, the estates were reasonably productive, with continuous investment in machinery, mills and slaves. Gibson Dalzell relied on attorneys, usually with a Scottish connection, to run his estates after his move to London: a practice of absentee ownership that was continued by George Duff as his wife, Frances, steadfastly refused to leave the imperial metropolis.

While members of the Duff network continued to serve overseas in the army and navy, their direct engagement with empire, whether as sojourners or absentees, became secondary to their indirect involvement through the acquisition of stock and shares in overseas venture companies. The considerable fortunes the network accumulated under the Earl of Fife's leadership were grounded in indigenous enterprises which imperial capital enhanced, particularly with respect to banking, white fisheries and distilling. Its investment in planned villages to develop local economies and promote regional interdependency in the later eighteenth century marked out the Duff network as progressive and enlightened entrepreneurs shorn of any subversive traces of Jacobitism.

## Imperial Dividends

In the later eighteenth century the situation of the EIC changed dramatically. In India it moved from being a chartered mercantile venture to a company state through territorial expansion mainly, but not exclusively, in Bengal. It developed a substantial civil service as well as expanding its military and mercantile divisions. This transition was made possible by the piecemeal collapse of the Muslim Mughal Empire, which had hitherto dominated most of the Indian subcontinent from its northern capital in Delhi. By 1750, the Mughal Empire had endured external raids from Afghanistan and Persia. It was also fighting off a more sustained challenge from the Hindu Marathas from Deccan and the coastal area around Bombay, which had driven a territorial wedge between the northern and southern districts of the Mughal Empire. Civil wars within the empire had led to the northern districts of Sind, Gujarat, Oudh and Bengal breaking away to form regional states under nawabs. The French and the English East India companies sought to exploit this unstable situation by promoting rival factions in the Carnatic region, which provided the hinterland to their forts and factories, as well as those of the Danes and the Dutch, on the Coromandel Coast. Their skirmishing lasted from 1746 to 1756: that is, prior to the conclusion of the War of Austrian Succession until the outbreak of the Seven Years War, when British forces vanquished the French.

As the Indian theatre of the Seven Years War developed, skirmishes in the Carnatic were overtaken by events in Bengal, where the nawab, Siraj-ud-Duala, captured the EIC fort at Calcutta. Captured Britons were imprisoned in the punishment cell that became notorious as the 'Black Hole' in which 43 of the 64 prisoners died from suffocation or heat stroke in 1756. In June the following year, the nawab, assisted by the French, was defeated by a vastly inferior number of British troops and Indian sepoys under the mercurial command of Robert Clive from Shropshire at Plassey. Clive proceeded to set up a puppet nawab, extracting a considerable personal reward for himself in the region of £234,000. This puppet was subsequently deposed for another of the EIC's choosing in 1760, with a second gratuity in excess of £200,000 extracted for the benefit of the company's Bengal council. A subsequent British victory in August 1764 at Buxar against the combined forces of the Bengal puppet nawab, the Mughal emperor and the nawab of Oudh was followed in 1765 by the Treaty of Allahabad, under which the emperor ceded civil, judicial and administrative tax gathering, the *diwani* of Bengal, to the EIC, which now had effective control of the richest and most populous province in India. The EIC also had a puppet nawab ruling the Carnatic region on its behalf by 1765 and massively built up its armies in Madras and Bombay as well as Bengal.

EIC rule was not benign but mercenary and grasping, which intensified and aggravated the famine of 1770 in which a third of the Bengali population of around 20 million died. A monopoly over the marketing of opium grown in Bengal – and subsequently marketed in Canton by freelance traders paying lucrative commissions in silver to the EIC – was imposed in 1773. That same year, the EIC came close to bankruptcy. Vast sums were extracted from the territories under its control to pursue warfare against the Marathas in the west and Mysore in the east rather than augment the return of commodities to London. EIC governance was marked by corrupt and contending factions keen to exploit India for their personal advantage. This attracted criticism and motions of censure in the British Parliament. But the end of the Whig ascendancy in 1784 led a Tory ministry under William Pitt the Younger to institute a Board of Commissioners for India that was to oversee the political operations of the EIC. Its trading and exercise of patronage were left untouched. Nevertheless, Pitt's close political associate, the Edinburgh advocate and serial holder of cabinet offices Henry Dundas (later Viscount Melville), used the board to build up placements for Scots in India. Unlike his predecessor John Drummond, this was not to rehabilitate Jacobites.

Irish Jacobites were particularly well represented on the French side. Thomas Lally, Count Tollendall, whose family came originally from County Galway, was appointed governor-general of French India at the outbreak of the Seven Years War in 1756. Lally had been prominent as a leader of the Irish brigades in the resounding French defeat of the Duke of Cumberland at Fontenoy in the Austrian Netherlands in May 1745. He subsequently joined Prince Charles Edward in the Forty-Five. The Irish brigades under his command failed to seize Madras in 1758, and on being besieged in Pondicherry, he was forced to capitulate in 1761. He was made the scapegoat for the French military failure in India, being brought to trial, convicted and executed in 1766. His beheading was particularly messy, although he was publicly exonerated by Louis XVI two years later. Scottish Jacobites were notably less prominent, the most conspicuous of Scottish extraction being James Law of Lauriston, the nephew of the celebrated financier and deviser of the Mississippi Project,

John Law. The heir to Lauriston arrived in the midst of the skirmishes in the Carnatic in 1752 and subsequently went on to serve in Pondicherry until its capture by the EIC.

However, Scottish veterans of the Forty-Five did resurface in India. Alexander Grant, from Glen Urquhart on Loch Ness, was part of the contingent who defied their chief in Speyside to fight with Prince Charles Edward. Gaining a military contract with the EIC, he was among the commanders at Plassey who persuaded Clive to engage with the vastly superior number of troops at the disposal of Suraj-ud-Duala. Also at Plassey was Alexander MacLeod from Bernera, whose chief had switched his clan away from Jacobitism towards the Hanoverians prior to the last major rising. Alexander MacLeod, who had joined the naval service of the EIC, captained the *Marlborough* in the fleet supporting the recapture of Calcutta in 1756. Jacobites as well as Whigs were in the Highland regiments sent to India despite being prone to mutiny when faced with such a trans-oceanic posting. Two regiments were sent out belatedly in the Seven Years War in 1761, another two at the tail end of the American War of Independence in 1783 and four more in 1785.

The first contingent sent out continued in India beyond the Seven Years War. The regiment raised under the auspices of the ducal house of Gordon was commanded by Major Hector Monro of Nevar in Ross-shire. He had participated in the Earl of Loudoun's less malign northern campaign against the Jacobites, though he did join in the state-sponsored terrorism in the aftermath of Culloden. Having brutally suppressed a mutiny of Indian sepoys, he went on to lead the British forces to victory at Buxar in 1764, which secured EIC control of Bengal. Unlike the Highland regiments serving in North America, there were no promises of land at the end of campaigns. Discharged troops on several occasions had to make their own way home. Commissioned officers, however, returned with riches accrued from plunder and prize money. Having returned to Britain in 1771 with a considerable fortune, Alexander MacLeod was to purchase outright his family patrimony of Bernera along with the adjacent far larger island of Harris and the far-flung island grouping of St Kilda in 1778. The price paid to his clan chief, Norman MacLeod of Dunvegan, was £15,000. Among the Jacobite families who made fortunes from military service in India were the Murrays of

Glen Girnaig in Blair Atholl, who had fought as MacGregors in the Forty-Five, and the Johnstones of Westerhall. Peter Murray acquired £200,000. John Johnstone made even more, bringing back £300,000 in 1765 to buy three estates in the Scottish Borders and a sugar plantation in Grenada.

Scottish soldiers, merchants and civil servants in India could fraternize through Freemasonry but only at lodges in and around Calcutta (from 1728), Madras (from 1752) and Bombay (1758) that were licensed from England. The Grand Lodge of Scotland did not become active in India until the early nineteenth century. Scots who managed to get into the elite of the EIC's civil service supplemented their salaries with bribes and private trading. However, as nabobs were returning with fortunes at least twice or three times greater than were achieved before 1750, the direction of the EIC in London as well as India became an issue of continuous controversy.

Returning nabobs exerted their influence in London as shareholders in the EIC and built up their parliamentary interests locally and at Westminster. This controversy was personified in the career of Sir John Macpherson from a staunch Jacobite family in Badenoch that had relocated to Skye. He first arrived in India as a ship's purser for his uncle, Alexander MacLeod from Bernera. He progressed his EIC career as a civil servant in Madras. Ingratiating himself with the nawab of the Carnatic, he worked covertly for the Whig ascendancy against the EIC, acquiring a fortune along the way. Although he was dismissed by the EIC when his underhand dealings were discovered, he mobilized polemical support from his kinsman James Macpherson, whose creative writing had provoked a major literary controversy about the heroic Fingalian tradition in Gaelic poetry. Such was their combined impact in the London press that the directors of the EIC were persuaded to appoint Sir John Macpherson as their supreme governor in Calcutta, from where in 1784 he progressed to acting governor-general of the British Raj. The immediate impact of Macpherson's governorship was the accelerated repatriation of capital to around £1.3 million annually. This led to significantly increased investment in landed estates in Scotland by his associates and cronies, notwithstanding the polemical admonition from James Macpherson that such investments could not be recouped quickly. Estates were purchased in the Highlands and Lowlands by returning nabobs. This, on the one hand, advanced the pace of agricultural improvements and, on the other, accelerated the clearance of people from the countryside to towns and cities throughout the United Kingdom or to British territories overseas and the United States.

Notwithstanding past political affiliations of families repatriating capital, no monies from the East Indies were evidently channelled towards reviving Jacobitism, which was politically a lost cause for over three decades prior to the death of Prince Charles Edward in Rome in 1788. This was also the case for capital repatriated through the Swedish East India Company or accrued through its smuggling of tea into Great Britain and Ireland. Certainly, a Swedish fleet had assembled in Gothenburg over the winter of 1745–6 with the intention of providing assistance to the Jacobites in Scotland until becoming trapped in ice. After Culloden, Gothenburg became a significant refuge for Jacobites and a transit port to France. However, Scots from Jacobite families in the service of the Swedish East India Company were not involved in directing or financing the Jacobite cause thereafter. Instead they focused on purchasing estates and furthering charitable enterprises, particularly in the northeast of Scotland. George Carnegie, after his return in 1765, purchased his family's estate of Pitarrow in Kincardineshire, to which he added Charleton in Angus. He also aided his nephew, Sir David Carnegie, purchase Kinnaird in Angus, forfeited by James Carnegie, 5th Earl of Southesk, after the Fifteen. David Lyall, who retired as a Swedish merchant in 1787, came back to Angus to buy the estate of Gallery near Montrose. Following extensive crop failure in Scotland in 1782, Lyall had sent over £20 from Gothenburg for the relief of the poor in his native parish of Farnell. Charitable giving had already been evident in the will of the founding director of the Swedish East India Company, Colin Campbell, who left £100 to the Royal Infirmary in Edinburgh that was paid in November 1758. Six years earlier, James Moir of Stoneywood had collected money in Sweden to help build the Episcopal Church in Banff destroyed by Cumberland.

When the cardinal prince, Henry Benedict, the last male heir in the direct line of the royal Stuarts, died in Frascati in 1807, he was in receipt of an annuity worth £4,000 from George III. His sources of income had either dried up or never materialized. The French Revolution of

1789 had guillotined funding from Louis XVI. Napoleon's invasion of Italy in 1799 had deprived him of his ecclesiastical revenues. Having gained no dividend from Jacobite global adventuring, he was reliant on Hanoverian financial support from 1800. Nevertheless, Jacobitism was not impoverished. The cause had been revitalized culturally through the Enlightenment and Romanticism.

7

# Enlightenment and Romanticism

Jacobitism was an integral aspect of the Enlightenment and Romanticism in the eighteenth century. Jacobitism had opened up new geographic horizons in America, Africa and Asia beyond its traditional stamping grounds in Scotland, Ireland and England and on the European continent. However, its enduring legacy derived from new intellectual horizons that were more cultural than political. This can be attributed initially to the contribution of Jacobite activists to the Enlightenment and subsequently of Jacobite sympathizers to Romanticism. The courts in exile offered limited sponsorship for such endeavours, but James VIII & III did attempt to reset an intellectual agenda which professed that patriotism was at least the equal of his dynastic claims to restoration in the three kingdoms the Stuarts had lost to the Hanoverians. Patriotism and its varied and at times contradictory redefinition became a continuous theme of the Enlightenment and Romanticism. The Jacobite contribution to the Enlightenment has been underplayed by the Whig focus on Edinburgh in particular – and on Scotland in general – as the epicentre of the Enlightenment in a British context. But outstanding contributions in such fields of enquiry as spirituality, state formation and political economy were made by Jacobites, most of whom were required by political necessity or expediency to live beyond Scotland. Romanticism, however, has been widely recognized as the product of Jacobite sympathizers who were for the most part domiciled in Scotland, although their own political hinterland had rarely stretched to active commitment by sword or by pen. The cause they commemorated and even glorified was long lost before the death of Prince Henry Benedict in 1807.

## Beginnings of the Enlightenment

The Enlightenment in Scotland is associated with the common-sense balancing of reason and emotion, with philosophical scepticism, with a holistic view of humanity in society, with the community interest in science and medicine no less than in the liberal arts, and with an experimental methodology for problem solving across the whole range of human experience. Leading luminaries of this Enlightenment were based predominantly but not exclusively in Edinburgh. They have been associated with a progressive Whig influence in Scotland. Not only did they uphold the Hanoverian succession effected in 1714, but they also celebrated the Treaty of Union that created the United Kingdom in 1707 as an enlightened aspect of state formation. Leading proponents of this Whig perspective were William Robertson, the historian; Adam Ferguson, the sociologist; and Adam Smith, who applied moral philosophy to economics. Robertson had been on the losing side at Prestonpans in the Forty-Five, in which, as chaplain to the Black Watch, he had preached against Jacobitism. For such Whigs, British national identity was promoted assiduously as patriotism and prosperity imbued by a common commitment to liberty and Protestantism. However, this perspective on the Enlightenment only began to gather momentum and make an international impact from the 1750s. It is still open to a sustained challenge.

Intellectually, the Whig contribution to learning was distinctive but not detached from the Republic of Letters, the leading intellectual movement driven from the European continent rather than Britain from the late seventeenth century. The Scottish intellectual contribution was made by both Whigs and Jacobites in diverse areas from astronomy to biology and from cartography to jurisprudence. Contributions by Jacobite intellecturals can be differentiated between measurable and inquisitive fields of study. The measurable concerned architecture, agricultural improvement, medicine, mathematics and political economy; the inquisitive involved philosophy, printing and bookselling, Latin, history and liturgy. The measurable and the inquisitive were intellectual tendencies rather than definitive categories. Deism, which laid the philosophical foundations for Freemasonry, could also be located within liturgy for its use of rituals and symbols, but it aspired to measure just, perfect and regular societies, with God being designated the great architect of the universe. Printers and booksellers are included among the inquisitive not for their measurable output or sales, but for the intellectual quality of their publications. Jacobite intellectuals were by no means unique in having more than one field of study. Although most were obliged to periodically leave Scotland for their political activism, few received patronage from the courts in exile.

In measurable fields of study, Jacobites were to the fore in architecture. Sir William Bruce of Kinross as a designer and James Smith of Whitehill in Midlothian, Scotland's first professional architect, were primarily responsible for redefining aristocratic palaces and country houses along classical European lines. Heavily embellished, baroque features in favour in Italy and England were largely confined to landscaped gardens. Sir William Bruce, a courtier under Charles II but not James VII, was suspected of involvement in the assassination plot against William of Orange in 1696 and placed under house arrest during the minor rising of 1708. Trained as a mason in Forres, James Smith had gone to Rome to retrain as a Jesuit priest in the early 1670s but became more interested in architecture and actually turned Protestant. When he returned to Scotland, he enjoyed the patronage of the Duke of York, the future James VII & II, in redesigning the frontage to the palace of Holyroodhouse and completing the chapel for the revived chivalric order of the Knights of the Thistle. Closely associated with George Lockhart of Carnwath in the aftermath of the Union of 1707, he was latterly reduced to constructing barracks in the Highlands to restrain the clans at Inversnaid, Cille Chuimin (later Fort Augustus), Ruthven and Glenelg between 1718 and 1723. By this juncture, the Earl of Mar, retired as a Jacobite schemer, was theorizing about stately palaces and elaborate country houses. The latter were to be supported by landscaped gardens and suitable for the pursuit of extractive industries in association with agricultural improvements. Mar's colleague from the Fifteen, William Mackintosh of Borlum, who had escaped from Newgate Prison in London, had broken his exile in France to return to Scotland to participate in the minor rising of 1719. In less than five years he had slipped back into the Highlands, where he maintained a low profile until he was captured and imprisoned in Edinburgh Castle in November 1727. Having promoted the afforestation of part of his estate on Loch Ness, he began promoting agricultural improvements from prison, arguing the merits of a programme that should take no more than sixteen years in *An Essay on Ways and Means of Enclosing, Fallowing, and Planting Lands in Scotland* (1729).

The most diversely talented Jacobite was Dr Archibald Pitcairne, physician, mathematician, deist, satirist and patron for aspiring intellectuals. Pitcairne wrote extensively on mathematics as well as medicine in attempting to explain the mechanisms governing the working of human organs. As professor of the practice of medicine, he lectured briefly but influentially at the University of Leiden in the Dutch Republic during 1692 and 1693. Pitcairne built up an extensive medical practice in Edinburgh and became such an assiduous collector of books that, after his death in 1713, his library was purchased by Peter the Great of Russia. Never averse to public controversy through his scientific publications, Pitcairne was also noted as a satirist of Presbyterianism and as a prominent Freemason. Another mathematician of international significance was James 'the Venetian' Stirling. Unlike his close kinsmen, the Stirlings of Keir, James Stirling was not active in the Fifteen. Nevertheless, he was expelled from Balliol College in Oxford University at the outbreak of the rising. He subsequently travelled extensively on the Continent to further his reputation as a mathematician, engaging in debates from London to St Petersburg on pure and applied mathematics. He earned a precarious livelihood first in Venice as a professor of mathematics, then in London as a teacher in a city academy and as a recruiting agent for colonial ventures. In 1737, he returned to Scotland to become manager of the mines at Leadhills in Dumfriesshire. Having declined a professorship at Edinburgh University in 1738 and accepted election to the Royal Academy of Berlin in 1746, Stirling's application of mathematics to mechanical engineering culminated in 1752 with his series of surveys of the River Clyde to improve its navigation and its commercial importance for Glasgow.

The most notorious intellectual exile was the international financier and political economist John Law from Lauriston in Midlothian.

His penchant for gambling rather than Jacobitism had taken him from Edinburgh to France, where he devised the speculative Mississippi Project to sustain and grow the French presence in Louisiana. He had not gone directly to France, having moved initially to London to reap greater rewards from his application of mathematical probabilities to gambling. However, he took flight to the Continent after he was convicted and sentenced to death for killing a man in a duel, a crime for which he was eventually pardoned in 1719 as his Mississippi Project was becoming the inspiration for the South Sea Bubble in London. In 1705, in the course of the debates on the making of the Union, Law had presented a proposal for a land bank that was rejected by the Scottish Estates as too adventurous in seeking to issue banknotes as paper credits. Law argued that a bank based on land rather than supplies of silver was far less vulnerable to increased imports of bullion or any debasement of the coinage. Law sought to generate a surplus in exports over imports on the grounds that an expanded money supply would lead to greater employment and enhanced output from manufacturing. This was a highly contentious yet potentially constructive proposition; but only if the consequences of an expanded money supply had been expressed as *should be*, rather than *would be*, economically beneficial. In France, Law realized that financial innovation, in the shape of stocks and shares, had led to new ways to increase the money supply beyond that of security in land. He argued that banking should be fully integrated with the domestic and colonial economies. However, he underestimated the costs of entrenched officeholding in France and the desire of investors to accumulate capital rather than rely on income from dividends. Instead of eliminating the French national debt, the mania he instigated for share dealing led to a financial crash in July 1720.

Prior to this crash, Law was visited in Paris by Alexander, Lord Forbes of Pitsligo, the most prominent of the inquisitive intellectuals, to discuss speculative Jacobite schemes. Pitsligo, who was active in both the Fifteen and the Forty-Five, had used the time he spent in exile on the Continent to travel extensively and develop his philosophical and religious interests. On first visiting France as a youth, he was much influenced by his personal acquaintance with French Quietists, who promoted passive piety over active politics. Despite being drawn to mysticism, Pitsligo neither abandoned his Episcopalianism nor his active Jacobitism. Having retired from the courts in exile and returned to Scotland later in 1720, he reaffirmed his tolerant commitment to ecumenical approaches to religion on grounds of pragmatism rather than deism. His pragmatism was further evident in his writings on political philosophy when he acknowledged that the Hanoverians could be regarded by fact rather than by right as the legitimate British monarchs.

Another spiritual and intellectual adventurer was Andrew Michael Ramsay, a Scottish émigré in France whose commitment to Jacobitism was surpassed only by that to European Freemasonry. Ramsay came from a family in Ayrshire divided by religion: his father was a Covenanter, his mother an Episcopalian. His sympathies were influenced by the latter, but were more substantially shaped by nonjuring intellectuals, like Pitsligo in Aberdeenshire, who tempered their Jacobitism with Quietism. They were in close contact with Flemish and French mystics, which led Ramsay to arrive in Cambrai in 1710 at the household of Archbishop François Fénelon. Over the next two years, not only did the archbishop persuade Ramsay to convert to Roman Catholicism, but he imbued him with his political philosophy to broaden but not dilute the basis of monarchical government in the interest of public liberty. Ramsay spent six years between 1717 and 1723 editing and interpreting the archbishop's works, which brought him to the attention of the Jacobite court at Rome, where he was briefly employed as a tutor to the infant Charles Edward. But he was unceremoniously dismissed after a duel and returned to France to broaden his intellectual interests. He moved on from a universal plan of government that synthesized natural law and divine right theory to uphold absolute monarchy and reject the Revolution of 1688–90. In key publications from 1727 to 1732, deism became the inspiration for his blending of science, education and political economy with mysticism and history to uphold political virtue, unity and order. As a French chevalier, Ramsay had shrewd networking skills but was very much a compromised intellectual. *L'Histoire de la vie de Fénelon* (1723) was adapted by Ramsay to suit Jacobitism rather than remain true to Fénelon's concepts of political virtue. Ramsay was instrumental in tying Scottish Freemasonry into French Freemasonry, which provided not only important political connections for Jacobites in exile, but Prince Charles Edward with a gateway to European courts and intellectual circles well after the Jacobite cause was extinguished in the wake of the Forty-Five.

Ramsay supported the restoration of the house of Stuart; he was drawn into the controversy on the primacy of the dynastic state over the territorial nation, depicted variously as the commonwealth or the community of the realm in Scottish history, on the side of James VIII & III. This controversy was initiated by Patrick Abercromby in his two-volume *The Martial Achievement of the Scottish Nation* (1711–15) and George MacKenzie in his three-volume *The Lives and Characters of the Most Eminent Writers of the Scottish Nation* (1708–22). Both authors were qualified doctors of medicine, and both were committed Jacobites from the shires of Aberdeen and Ross, respectively. Abercromby had initially trained to become a Jesuit priest at the Scots College in Douai, but switched his studies to medicine and practised in France until he returned to Scotland by 1706. Mackenzie was a staunch Episcopalian who practised as a doctor in Edinburgh, where he became an associate of Pitcairne. Their patriotism was rooted in their documentary analysis of Scottish history from the eleventh to the sixteenth century. They were both associated in Edinburgh with the printers and booksellers Robert Freebairn from Perthshire and Thomas Ruddiman from Banffshire, who together and separately since 1706 had printed, published and sold a range of intellectual, spiritual, legal and polemical books. Freebairn was then the royal printer in Scotland. Ruddiman had resigned as a schoolteacher at Laurencekirk in Aberdeenshire to become a librarian in Edinburgh at the prompting of Archibald Pitcairne. They collaborated only in the production of Abercromby's two volumes. But Ruddiman, on his own initiative prior to the Fifteen, had published the poems and other Latin writings of George Buchanan, a leading sixteenth-century scholar of international standing in learning during the Renaissance and in religion during the Reformation. Ruddiman, as the leading Latin scholar in Scotland, was primarily concerned to celebrate Buchanan's poems, not his political philosophy, which justified the killing of tyrannical rulers and the deposition of monarchs deemed ungodly. Buchanan even went on to suggest that such actions taken in the name of the commonwealth expressed the sovereignty of the people.

This publication added fuel to the controversy generated by the patriotic publications of Abercromby and Mackenzie, which had inspired some Jacobites to promote limitations on monarchy in the aftermath of the Union of 1707. That the exiled Stuarts should accept constitutional limitations as the price of their restoration was not endorsed by James VIII & III. In 1716, he commissioned Thomas Innes, a priest teaching at the Scots College in Paris, where his brother Lewis was rector, to re-assert the primacy of the dynastic state as the source of patriotism. This was duly accomplished in *A Critical Essay on the Ancient Inhabitants of the Northern Parts of Britain, or Scotland* (1727). By this juncture, Abercromby was dead; Freebairn had returned from exile for his participation as Mar's printer in the Fifteen and was preparing Mackintosh of Borlum's work on agricultural improvements for the press; and Ruddiman had become publisher and owner of the *Caledonian Mercury* newspaper and was about to become the keeper of the Advocate's Library. This institution had been established in 1682 as part of the cultural enhancements undertaken by James, Duke of York (later James VII). Its holdings, which were not restricted to law books, were to be greatly expanded by Ruddiman, turning it into a copyright library.

Much more than Abercromby in his use of sources and Mackenzie in terms of factual accuracy, Thomas Innes had absorbed the teachings on the writing of history by French and Dutch scholars during the Republic of Letters. It was not sufficient to collate and edit sources prior to publication. They had to be categorized, deciphered, dated and authenticated before analysis could commence. Innes was the outstanding historian in Scotland at the commencement of the Enlightenment. Nevertheless, patriotism, whether territorial or dynastic, was a shared Scottish heritage that cannot be viewed as the exclusive property of Jacobites. Loyalty to the territorial nation became a more pressing concern than allegiance to the exiled house of Stuart or the incumbent house of Hanover. David Scott, an Edinburgh lawyer who came from Haddington in East Lothian, was a Presbyterian who had flirted with Jacobitism and accepted the Union of 1707 more out of pragmatism than principle. In *The History of Scotland* (1728), which pushed historical transactions into the eighteenth century, Scott rebranded territorial patriotism with a British identity. This identity was particularly acceptable to those Scots engaging in empire who supported the replacement of Episcopalianism by Presbyterianism in the Kirk at the Revolution.

But the Revolution, notwithstanding its outing of Episcopalian clergy and their subsequent exposure to penal laws, was to prove a source of liturgical liberation for nonjuring Episcopalians who refused toleration in return for abjuring the exiled Stuarts. Prior to the Revolution there had been some interest among Episcopal clergy and academics in sacramental innovations, based firmly on Greek patristic readings, which emphasized the importance of set prayer and personal piety in preparing to receive the sacraments. (While great store was placed on the authority of the early fathers, the early mothers of the Church were ignored.) Clerics and academics arguing for frequent communion laid the groundwork for the spread of practical mysticism into the northeast of Scotland. Greater liturgical observance in the wake of the Revolution enabled nonjurors to differentiate themselves from Presbyterianism as well as from jurors who had been reduced to adjuncts of Anglicanism. Some nonjurors given more to piety than politics were inclined to move in the direction of Flemish mysticism. Others, with stronger links to English nonjurors, flirted instead with Greek and Russian Orthodoxy or Coptic Christianity, although in the latter case they were open from 1692 to the polemical taunt that the true Jacobites were the supporters not of the exiled king at Saint-Germain but of Coptic Christians in Egypt, Libya and Nubia.

Foremost among the Scots in the cross-border grouping based in London who described themselves as the 'Orthodox and Catholic Remnants of the British Church' were Alexander Campbell and Thomas Gadderar, successively nonjuring Bishop of Aberdeen.[1] Cross-border collaboration was particularly evident on sacramental matters in the rejection of a single Confession of Faith and in the production of the Nonjuring Rite as an alternative liturgy in 1718. There were concerns expressed to the court in exile from Jacobite agents in London as from George MacKenzie in Edinburgh that liturgical innovations were placing nonjuring collaboration under strain despite the determination of Campbell and Gadderar to avoid schism. However, a split was provoked when the Scots, in keeping with the more numerous presence of nonjurors in their homeland, endeavoured to return their English colleagues to the usages they ascribed to the primitive Christian Church. Division was most evident in relation to the mixing of water with wine at communion, which also led to tensions within the nonjuring community in Scotland that were aggravated rather than resolved by the creation of the College of Bishops in 1720. The college not only favoured consecrating bishops to territories which lacked the historical authenticity of established dioceses, but from 1731 it was prepared to annul elections of bishops who favoured the usages. Thomas Rattray of Brechin, who had dissented from his fellow members of the College of Bishops on the appointment of usagers and validity of diocesan elections, was instrumental in a partial regrouping of nonjurors in Scotland and England. This was accomplished in 1744 by those who subscribed to the new spiritual paths he prescribed in *The Ancient Liturgy of the Church of Jerusalem*. This liturgy, based on rigorous patristic scholarship and forensic historical enquiry, united subscribers sacramentally as the true apostolic heirs to the primitive purity of the Universal Catholic Church. Such liturgical innovation was complemented by theological debates on prayers for the dead and the intermediate or middle state between heaven and hell, which was promoted not so much as a revamped purgatory for sinners as a place of reflection and light for departed souls. With Bishop Rattray taking up the mantle of Bishops Campbell and Gadderar, the nonjurors were advocating a distinctive, but not exclusive, Scottish approach to salvation that furthered spiritual Enlightenment.

Despite the repression in the wake of the Forty-Five, the nonjuring tradition was far from eradicated as liturgical practices of Episcopalians were carried from Scotland to the United States of America. A new liturgy of 1764 built on past practice, notably the Prayer Book of 1718 and, above all, *The Ancient Liturgy* of 1744. By permitting the reserving of sacramental elements, this liturgy enabled nonjurors to circumvent reimposed penal laws that restricted the Eucharist to a handful of communicants in one room or meeting place. This liturgy was also testament to the growing rapprochement between the jurors who adhered to Anglicanism and the nonjurors who remained committed to a universal, Catholic and Orthodox Church. This tradition, which had provided the spiritual bedrock for the Jacobite heartlands in the Highlands and the northeast, was exported to America after the surviving nonjuring hierarchy consecrated Samuel Seabury at Aberdeen in 1784 as the first Episcopalian bishop of the fledgling United States. His *Communion Office*, published in New London, Connecticut, in 1786, was based on the Scottish liturgy of 1764.

## Political Virtue and Political Economy

Spiritual Enlightenment was not an issue to appeal to the philosopher and historian David Hume, whose scepticism about religious revelation denied him professorships of philosophy at Edinburgh University in 1744 and at Glasgow University in 1751. As a philosopher, Hume was particularly open to French influences except mysticism. He was a close associate of Chevalier Michael Ramsay in the 1730s and subsequently of the political philosopher Montesquieu, with whom he corresponded covertly in the exchange of letters and manuscripts through the Jacobite wine networks operating between Bordeaux and Edinburgh. This covert connection does much to explain Hume's defence of Archibald Stewart, wine merchant and lord provost of Edinburgh, who was accused and acquitted of surrendering the Scottish capital to the Jacobites in the Forty-Five. However, Hume was not committed politically to the Jacobites or the Whigs. From the 1740s to the 1770s, he was a gargantuan influence on the Scottish Enlightenment as a sceptical philosopher writing on politics, political economy and history. Hume maintained that the science of man that afforded knowledge of human nature should be the basis for all other intellectual disciplines.

For Hume, history was primarily explaining philosophy by examples. His initial major work, the two-volume *The History of Great Britain* (1754–6), covered the conflict between the Stuart monarchy and the English Parliament in the seventeenth century. But it did not extend beyond the Revolution, stopping in 1688. Instead, he went back to the sixteenth century with another two-volume *History of England* (1759) under the Tudors. This was not an uninterrupted history of liberty, though he did commend the remarkable coherence of English history in both centuries. However, he commented adversely on English insularity and exceptionalism. Instead of framing national identities to accord with Whig views of English liberties, he argued instead for the greater progressive task of establishing a civil society in Great Britain. This task was in part undertaken by prominent Scottish Whig intellectuals, notably William Robertson, in relation to state formation. Adam Ferguson, although he was less convinced about the perfect nature of the English constitution, was supportive, as was Adam Smith for political economy. They were well aware that the Revolution in Scotland, unlike that in England, was uncompromised by any accommodation with Tories and was more purposefully anti-Jacobite. James VII was deposed in Scotland, whereas he was deemed, as James II, to have abdicated in England. Scottish Whigs thereby acclaimed the flame of political purity without regretting the demise of the Scottish Estates in 1707. They saw themselves as the moral guardians of the British constitution based on the sovereignty of the monarch in Parliament – not on the sovereignty of the community of the realm, far less on that of the people. They came to equate political virtue with British patriotism that was not so much monarchic as oligarchic, and was territorial as an imperial rather than a purely domestic construct.

Jacobite intellectuals were no less concerned with political virtue and global aspirations. The Jacobite agenda for empire was primarily set by the acclaimed military commander Field Marshal James Keith and refined by the diplomat and spy Sir James Steuart of Goodtrees. By political necessity, both spent much of their productive lives exiled from Scotland. In offering a prescient critique not just of British state formation but of the imperial aspirations of the European powers, Field Marshal Keith stressed the primacy of political virtue over capital repatriation. The material recognition in the shift in wealth creation from land and labour to technology was the achievement of Steuart of Goodtrees. In the process, they linked the Enlightenment to empire and to enterprise.

The global vision of James Keith produced a prescient critique of the imperial aspirations of Britain and other leading European powers. After entering the services of Frederick II of Prussia in 1747, Keith had become governor of Berlin and a member of its Academy of Sciences, but remained inactive in the field until the outbreak of the Seven Years War. His critical writings between 1748 and 1756 emanated mainly from Sans Souci in Potsdam, where Keith was installed as a confidant and counsellor of Frederick II along with his brother, George, Earl Marischal. Also present for three years only was Voltaire, the French philosopher, historian and satirist whose famed wit was not enhanced by his fiery temperament. Having participated in the failed Jacobite risings of 1715 and 1719, Keith had become a military commander of international repute in Russia and Prussia after an initial foray in Spanish service. The field marshal was determined to pass on his accumulated political wisdom to his nephew and adopted son, Chevalier John Drummond, who had taken part in the last major Jacobite rising in 1745. Trained in France as a military engineer, Drummond, a grandson of the Jacobite courtier William, Duke of Melfort, had served in Spanish America, where he was involved in early plans for a canal across Panama to link the Atlantic and Pacific oceans.

Keith was anxious that Drummond continue his mission to destroy the Ottoman Empire for the benefit of Russia and for the freedom of Greece and the Balkans, objectives which he promoted as both rational and liberal. The destruction of the Ottoman Empire in Europe, whether accomplished 'by war, or by negotiation or by cultivating the arts of civilisation', must be consistent with political virtue in order to ensure that Drummond retained the confidence of 'any government whose end is the happiness and prosperity of an empire'. In like manner, the destruction of the Spanish Empire in the Americas was not only advantageous to the leading European powers, but carried the further prospect of moral reformation, without which France, Britain and the Dutch Republic were bound to lose their own empires in the Americas. Keith advised Drummond 'that to study the interests of Commerce' was a rational pursuit 'not unworthy of your genius'. Commerce opened up prospects for both the accumulation and the repatriation of capital. He particularly commended his adopted son for the knowledge he had already acquired of trade during his travels in Spanish America. But he warned Drummond against using this commercial acumen to secure a position of profit from Britain. Keith, who had declined to participate in the Jacobite rising of 1745, was, above all, unconvinced that the British state had practised or encouraged virtuous patriotism since the Revolution: 'its ministry is but a fortuitous mass of corruption.' Patriotism, which was both virtuous and real, was beyond the capacity of the corrupt oligarchy that passed for parliamentary government. Accordingly, Keith had become increasingly sceptical whether the replacement of the Hanoverians by the exiled Stuarts would accomplish the moral reformation achieved by enlightened monarchy in Prussia. Like Hume in relation to France, Keith believed that civilized European monarchies, however authoritarian, were not despotic. He hoped that Drummond should facilitate such civilized monarchy in Russia to conclude the heroic work begun by Peter the Great.[2]

Chevalier John Drummond never went to Russia, however. Having found that he could not attain the rank of colonel, which he had enjoyed after switching back from Spanish to French service, he retired to the West Indies in 1756. Two years later, his uncle was killed when the Austrians defeated the Prussians at Hochkirk. Drummond relocated to London in 1770, where he retained a perceptive interest in Eurasian affairs on the side of the Russians rather than the Turks. He remained particularly wary of interventions lacking in political virtue by British governments.

For the leading intellectuals of the Scottish Enlightenment, progressive moves towards a civil society were based on stadial development. Humanity was held to have passed through several stages of development from barbarism to civility that culminated in the development of commerce and manufactures. But the foundations of their stadial arguments were theoretical, based on readings of classical texts from Greek and Latin, and backed up by historical examples. Field Marshal Keith, on the other hand, based his insights on state formation by allying his global vision to his extensive military experience over five decades. In like manner, Steuart of Goodtrees drew on his personal observation of industrial manufacturing and its technologies from his extended exile on the Continent as a Jacobite diplomat and spy. Goodtrees, commissioned by Prince Charles Edward as Jacobite ambassador to the French court, had slipped out of Stonehaven in Kincardineshire in October 1745 before the Jacobite Army marched into England. But his stint as ambassador throughout 1746 was noted mainly for his irritation about the lack of adequate French backing for the Jacobite cause. Not being attainted, he retained his estates of Goodtrees in East Lothian and Coltness in Lanarkshire. But his exclusion from the Act of Indemnity in 1747 led him to travel extensively in France, Italy, the Austrian Netherlands, the Dutch Republic and Germany, where he commenced his writings on political economy in 1759. He returned to London, then to Coltness, at the end of the Seven Years War, but he was accorded no formal pardon until 1772. In the interim, he published in London his *Inquiry into the Principles of Political Oeconomy* (1767).

This work of intellectual significance has never achieved the same international resonance as Adam Smith's *Wealth of Nations* published nine years later. Smith stressed the importance of labour to wealth creation. Improved divisions of labour were the key to productivity that underpinned the emerging factory system. Smith also broke with the prevailing mercantilist economic orthodoxy that government should promote exports and discourage imports, which he regarded as restricting enterprise. In so doing, Smith ensured the triumph of labour stimulated by overseas trade over landed enterprise in the long-standing debates on wealth creation that stretched back to the mid-seventeenth century. However, he did not anticipate the further transformative role of technology. This was the achievement of Steuart of Goodtrees. He agreed with Smith, and also David Hume, that capital investment was the motor of economic growth. But where Smith and Hume contended that money followed industry, Steuart was more proactive. Like his fellow Jacobite sympathizer John Law, the international financier, Steuart was adamant that a relaxation of the money supply through quantitative easing could stimulate industry. Whereas Smith was an ethical apologist for free trade, Steuart advocated the light touch of government on economic levers. Steuart went far beyond Smith when he associated industrial growth not just with the rational technology that raised living standards as well as productivity but with the responsible patriotism engendered by commerce. This constituted a real safeguard against absolutism or even the enlightened authoritarian monarchy that Field Marshal Keith had extolled.

India was already coming to prominence in imperial discourse before the loss of thirteen American colonies, a loss forewarned by Keith although he did not anticipate that Britain would be more than compensated from territorial and commercial acquisitions in the subcontinent. The imminent loss of the American colonies had stimulated fresh Scottish thinking on engagement with empire. In seeking to provide legislators with a working set of principles for political economy at home and abroad, Smith in his magisterial work of 1776 argued that the payment of high wages for labour was the mark of a progressive state. Protective trade tariffs, corporate monopolies and the accumulation of bullion were rejected. Open commercial transactions, interdependent trading and the pursuit of a favourable balance of trade were commended. Smith was less concerned to concentrate capital investment on export markets and trans-oceanic trade than on agricultural improvements and an internal common market for the mutual benefit of Scotland, England and Ireland. He wholly underplayed the financial significance of the colonial connection in repatriating capital from plantations based on slave labour, which he condemned as archaic and inefficient. In so doing he relied on testimony from entrepreneurs engaged in the tobacco trade, which became defunct as the outbreak of the American War of Independence coincided with the publication of his *Wealth of Nations*. Yet the ongoing integration of the West Indian sugar and cotton trade with textiles and chemicals consolidated the repatriation of capital for use in industrial manufacturing as the lost American colonies became the United States in the 1780s.

While Steuart was primarily concerned with the domestic policy of free nations, he accepted an invitation from the East India Company to comment on currency problems. He duly produced *The Principles of Money Applied to the State of Commerce in Bengal* (1772), which reported on currency deficiencies, on the causes of the scarcity of coin and on methods for expanding paper credit. A secure but flexible currency that stimulated investment in merchandising was important for the internal conduct of trade as well as sustaining the value of repatriated capital. Steuart was also conscious of the advantages that British subjects residing in Bengal could derive from the tea trade to China. A flourishing market economy would afford them the opportunity to deliver competitive rates of exchange to French, Danish and Swedish borrowers, who had to purchase silver as specie, at great expense, in the Spanish port of Cadiz to pay for the tea acquired in Canton. For his politics as well as his economics, Steuart – not Smith – was the inspiration for the first chair of political economy created in Revolutionary France for

Alexandre Vandermonde at the École Normale in 1795. This professorship sought to integrate enterprise and applied Enlightenment in the service of the progressive state committed to wealth redistribution as well as wealth creation.

While Field Marshal Keith and Steuart of Goodtrees were the leading lights of the Enlightenment from a Jacobite perspective, the illuminating contribution of a handful of others should not be discounted. Andrew Gordon, a Roman Catholic from Angus, who was a Benedictine monk at Regensburg in Bavaria before going on to become Professor of Philosophy at Erfurt, made the first electric motor by 1745 and became a renowned physicist specializing in electromagnetics. His Jacobite sympathies were evident in a brief he presented and promoted to the *parlement* at Strasbourg that was published originally in German and translated as *The Origin of the Present War in Great Britain prosecuted by Charles Edward Stuart* (1746). Robert Strange from Orkney, who trained as an engraver in Edinburgh, served throughout the Forty-Five in the Life Guards while designing fans and reproducing portraiture to enhance the public appeal of Prince Charles Edward. At the outset of April 1746, he was asked to produce banknotes for the Jacobites on a copper printing plate of his own creation. Although the banknotes were completed to the design Strange etched on the copper plate two days before Culloden, that defeat terminated their issue. Strange escaped into exile but was included in the Act of Indemnity of 1747. Three years later he settled in London. He won international recognition as a leading engraver. His long association with the court in exile, where his brother-in-law, Andrew Lumisden, became secretary of state in 1764, was cemented by Strange's election to the Accademia di San Luca in Rome. For his successful contribution to the visual arts under the Hanoverians, he was knighted by George III in 1787.

Its classical legacy had made Rome the major cultural centre for artists and architects from all over Europe, who came to study in the city's prestigious fine art academies or in the studios of fashionable painters in the eighteenth century. The Jacobite court in exile, located at Villa Muti on the Piazza dei Santi Apostoli, was not an insignificant source of patronage, especially for Scots, until the death of James VIII & III in 1766. However, the deaths of his sons, Prince Charles Edward in

1788 and Prince Henry Benedict in 1807, opened up an era of cultural adventurism that went underground during the convulsive upheavals of the French Revolution and the Napoleonic Wars throughout Europe. Within Scotland, England and Ireland there had been traditional means of using textiles and other artefacts to signify political allegiance, from buttons, garters and ribbons on personal dress to wine glasses, whisky quaiches and punchbowls for convivial drinking, and on to snuff boxes and customized weaponry. But cultural adventurers were now primarily concerned to acquire and recycle documents, pictures, jewellery and other commemorative artefacts salvaged from the defunct Villa Muti and from the Scots College in Paris, which housed the papers and mementoes of James VII & II until ransacked in 1792. Cultural adventurers in Rome and Paris, whose commitment to Jacobitism was primarily mercenary and far from enlightened, established a lucrative market in memorabilia relating to the exiled Stuarts. Robert Watson from Elgin in Moray, who had a long and chequered career as a political radical in Britain, North America and France, grasped the opportunity to act as the middleman in Rome for the sale of the Stuart Papers to the Hanoverian monarchy in 1817. At the prompting of the Prince Regent (later George IV), some sample papers from Rome had been acquired in 1807. The prince's prompting, backed up by advances of cash, encouraged Watson to use his underground connections to secure a comprehensive collection relating to the courts in exile under James VIII & III, for which the British government paid him a commission of £2,500. Lodged at Windsor Castle near London, the Stuart Papers were archived for occasional and selective use by historians. Ongoing adventuring in memorabilia was driven not just by curiosity or sentimentality for a lost cause. Jacobitism had become a staple of Romanticism.


## Romanticism

The ideological purity of the Enlightened Whig perspective on the Revolution and the Union was treated with sporadic scepticism as successive British governments oscillated between reform and repression in their reaction to the American and French revolutions. The two principal sceptics, famed principally for their creative literary talents, were James Macpherson and Sir Walter Scott. Eschewing the rhetoric of radicalism, their critical doubts were grounded in archival history. Both were to profit materially from their engagement with Romanticism. Macpherson built a mansion called Belleville at Alvie in Badenoch before his death in 1796, while Scott established his in the revived Scottish 'baronial style' at Abbotsford near Melrose in Roxburghshire in 1824.

Macpherson's rich embellishment of Gaelic oral tradition relating to the classical heroes of Celtic mythology, which had instigated the 'Ossianic controversy' from 1761, provided a Scottish template for Romanticism that resonated well beyond Great Britain. Its fascination with the primitive and the irrational fundamentally questioned the Enlightenment as the tempering of reason with emotion. A member of a Highland clan tainted with Jacobitism, Macpherson can be viewed as lamenting the passing of a warrior society in a coded elegy for the Jacobite Highlands. However, this warrior society – having been pressed into the service of the British state in the Seven Years War (1756–63) – became the most reliable light infantry in the service of the British Empire on a global scale through the American Revolutionary War (1776–83) to the Napoleonic Wars (1793–1815). At a time of major agricultural and industrial transformation, Macpherson's Romantic appeal to the past carried echoes not just of epic heroism but of a moral economy, as a counterpoint to extensive social removals and relocations from the 1760s well into the nineteenth century.

Having served briefly as a colonial official in Florida for two years after its acquisition in the Seven Years War, Macpherson's imperial remit as a polemicist was first evident in a staunch defence of British rights against the claims of American colonists for independence. He went on to become a noted polemicist opposed to the Whig ascendancy's regressive and lax oversight of the East India Company, which he attributed to its commercial monopoly and political autonomy. Macpherson was a more thorough historian than William Robertson and far from Romantic in his approach to the British constitution. His *History of Great Britain* (1775) drew on original papers from the archives of both royal houses of Stuart and Hanover. Like Robertson, he welcomed the Union for bringing an end to the fractious Scottish Parliament, but he was highly critical of the clandestine manoeuvres that marked its accomplishment in 1707. More so than Hume, Ferguson and Smith, Macpherson recognized that in an unequal partnership Scotland was not necessarily the beneficiary of subsequent developments in political economy. For Macpherson, the pressing issue for virtuous politics was the more equitable working of the Union to serve Scotland within empire. Political independence may have gone but the Jacobite version of Scottish patriotism, defined by the achievements of soldiers, scholars and adventurers, underwent a moral as well as a Romantic revival.

No less a commitment to the development of Romanticism in Europe and beyond was made by Sir Walter Scott, a leading Edinburgh lawyer with an enduring attachment to his Border background. As a commentator, antiquarian and novelist, Scott strove to restore an appreciation of the enduring validity of Scotland's essentially rural community values. In the process, he wished to rehabilitate the Highland clans that had been the military bedrock of Jacobitism and were now at the beck and call of the British Empire. In the course of the Napoleonic Wars, six new Highland regiments had been raised between 1793 and 1800. A Jacobite by inclination if not by intellect, his confessional commitment moved from Presbyterianism to Episcopalianism. Throughout his poetry, his historical novels and his Scottish history, Scott was concerned to give equal prominence to Highlanders as to Lowlanders. Although he had published an edited collection of Border ballads in 1802, his first literary contribution of international significance came as a Romantic poet, notably from *The Lay of the Last Minstrel* (1805) to *The Lady of the Lake* (1810). Both dealt with historical themes from the fourteenth century in the Borders and the Perthshire Highlands, respectively. Their Romantic elements were especially evident in his superb scene setting, which laid the basis for a thriving tourist industry, particularly to Loch Lomond and Loch Katrine in the Trossachs.

Scott's literary contribution to Romanticism was further enhanced by the publication of 27 historically themed novels. However, only two were directly related to Jacobitism: his first, *Waverley* (1814), whose English hero (Edward Waverley) gets caught up in the Forty-Five, and *Rob Roy* (1817), where Scott exercised considerable dramatic licence on the activities of his Highland hero before and after the Fifteen. Scott's sympathetic portrayal of Rob Roy MacGregor took little account of the bandit proclivities of his immediate family and clan. Another two novels were of incidental relevance to Jacobitism: the *Heart of Midlothian* (1818) covering the Porteous Riot of 1736 and the *Bride of Lammermoor* (1819) concerning the making of the Union of 1707. As a novelist whose work ranged over diverse centuries and territories, Scott applied the concept of stadial development favoured by the Scottish Enlightenment to explore the different stages of social progress that existed side by side within one country. His historical novels explored political ambivalence and moral ambiguity. In the process, his Romanticism can be held to have invented the historical novel. But Scott has been caricatured as a leading fabricator of spurious 'Highlandism' or kitsch 'Caledonianism' through his association with the Prince Regent, George IV, who can be taken to have personified the association of Jacobitism with Romanticism.

With the permission and prompting of the Prince Regent, Scott had led a small expedition to establish that the Honours of Scotland, stored in Edinburgh Castle but locked away since the Union of 1707, had not been lost, looted or stolen. As expected, they were discovered unmolested in a locked box in the castle's Crown Room. Scott was duly knighted after the Prince Regent became George IV in 1820. Two years later, Scott was the principal stage manager for the visit of George IV to Edinburgh. This visit to the Scottish capital in 1822 was a tartan extravaganza. Its association of tartan with military prowess and imperial service constituted a peculiar weave that came in the course of the nineteenth century to represent Scotland's distinctive presence within the British Empire. When George IV's niece, Queen Victoria, and her husband, Prince Albert, acquired and developed Balmoral on Deeside during the 1850s, this led to renewed charges of 'Highlandism' by royal warrant. However, Victoria, especially as a widow, found solace and inspiration in the Highlands. She immersed herself in its history, natural history and culture. Indeed, for her espousal of Romanticism, she can be depicted as the only Jacobite monarch to reside by choice in the Highlands.

Four years after the visit of George IV to Edinburgh, Scott was effectively bankrupted by the financial crash which terminated the trading of his principal publishers and long-standing associates, James and John

Ballantyne, originally from Kelso. From 1826 until his death six years later, Scott wrote his way out of debt by a prodigious output of novels, short stories, plays and works of non-fiction, the most significant of which was his *Tales of a Grandfather*. In this work, originally released in four annual instalments from 1828 to 1831, Scott offered a version of Scottish history from the Wars of Independence to the last Jacobite rising that was rooted in civic humanism and adventurous patriotism. He celebrated rather than anaesthetized heroic traditions. He was no prototype for a film or television director with a distorted view of Scottish history. Scott welcomed the accomplishment of the Union not for its statesmanship but for its validation of Scotland as a partner in empire. On no account did the Union justify the provincial relegation of Scotland or the subordination of Scottish political, commercial and ecclesiastical interests to those of England.

The contributions of Macpherson and Scott to Romanticism with a Jacobite twist were supplemented in the poetry and songs of Robert Burns, James Hogg and Carolina Oliphant, Lady Nairne. Burns from Ayrshire did have a Jacobite pedigree as his family, originally of the name Burness, came from Kincardineshire and were active in the Fifteen. Hogg's connection to Jacobitism derived from literary tradition not political antecedents. Lady Nairne was connected by descent and marriage to three Jacobite families in Perthshire – the Oliphants of Gask and the Robertsons of Strowan, as well as the Nairnes – who had all faced forfeiture and prolonged exile for their participation in all three major risings. Carolina Oliphant (named after Prince Charles Edward) became Lady Nairne by marriage to her husband, William, whose grandmother Margaret was a particularly active Jacobite. This original Lady Nairne, through whom the lordship descended, was a talented and tenacious woman obliged to assume managerial responsibilities during the protracted exile of her husband and son in France. Notwithstanding her flair and competence as an estate manager, she was most celebrated as a Jacobite recruiter and news gatherer at the Fifteen. During the Forty-Five, she entertained Prince Charles Edward and issued commands for men and munitions from her bed just two years before her own death aged 78.

Of much greater and enduring fame was Robert Burns as Scotland's national bard. The poetry and songs of Burns are imbued with the ideas of reform and radicalism inspired by first the American and then the French Revolution. An intended voyage to Jamaica in 1786 was pre-empted by the publication of the first volume of his poetry, the Kilmarnock edition. This most influential volume of poems ever published in Scotland is permeated with visionary voyages which marked the transition in Scottish patriotism from Jacobite to Jacobin. Patriotism was here moved beyond the provenance of the political elite to a shared cultural, literary and territorial heritage of the Scottish people at home and abroad. In the process, Scottish patriotism transcended both cultural Romanticism and contemporaneous discussion of how Scots should contribute to the British Empire. It wholly rejected Scottish absorption into a British identity created from England.

The dominant literary format in eighteenth-century Scotland was the popular art song rooted in oral culture in both the Highlands and Lowlands. Much of this traditional folk repertoire for the popular art song was compromised for polite society by its explicit sexual content. Burns, Hogg and Lady Nairne effectively created a national song from the popular art song and folk tradition by editing material regarded as unsuitable for mixed audiences, and by fashioning new words to tunes old and new. Jacobite songs featured prominently, partly by offering a symbolic code for continuing popular Scottish opposition to the Union of 1707, partly for their Romanticism in lamenting not just a lost cause but a lost world. Their songs fashioned a powerful critique in support of each and every member of humanity in Scotland and beyond: a critique of wealth, social standing and privileged political position. Their songs were a moral corrective to the elite distancing of the landed classes from the rural community through the accumulation of capital in and its repatriation from empire. They were also a corrective to class consciousness arising from industrialization and agricultural transformation in town and country, and, above all, to the removal and relocation of people through Lowland and Highland clearances. These changes, which became particularly pronounced after the eclipse of Jacobitism, would not necessarily have been checked by a Stuart restoration.

Burns, Hogg and Lady Nairne had different approaches to Jacobite Romanticism, however. The approach of Burns was primarily radical, that of Hogg commercial, while that of Lady Nairne was conservative.

Burns did not support Jacobite doctrines ('Ye Jacobites By Name'), such as the acclaimed prerogative powers of the Stuarts to suspend or dispense with laws. He primarily saw Jacobitism as justifying popular resistance to usurpers ('Scots Wha Hae'), to political corruption ('There'll Never Be Peace Till Jamie Comes Hame') and to social exclusion from the body politic ('Honest Poverty'), which extended beyond the middle classes to the economically marginalized. Hogg, from a sheep-farming background in Ettrick Forest, liked to portray himself as an uncouth shepherd even though he had become a full-time writer of poems, songs, short stories and novels from 1810. Like his mentor, Sir Walter Scott, he was a literary entrepreneur who took up Jacobite songs as a short-term commercial opportunity. His two-volume edition of *Jacobite Relics of Scotland* (1819–21), which served as a literary preamble to the visit of George IV to Edinburgh in 1822, included works by Burns and Lady Nairne that were categorized as anonymous. In his extensive notes, Hogg echoed James Macpherson by claiming that some of the songs were transcribed and translated from privately held Gaelic manuscripts. But unlike the instigator of the Ossianic controversy, Hogg's claims for authenticity were wholly fabricated. These songs, among the strongest in the collection ('Cam Ye o'er frae France' and 'The Piper o' Dundee'), were seemingly written by himself.

Carolina, Lady Nairne, had a considerable portion of her work also included in the otherwise nondescript six-volume edition of *The Scottish Minstrel* (1821–4), whose publication straddled the visit of George IV. The editor was Robert Smith, an acclaimed precentor and church musician in Edinburgh who appreciated Lady Nairne's knowledge of music for songs, which was far more extensive than that of either Burns or Hogg. Unlike either, Lady Nairne was determined to maintain her anonymity, even going to the extent of disguising her handwriting and meeting publishers incognito. Her desire for anonymity, which she started as Carolina Oliphant to ensure that her sex did not prejudice opportunities to publish, continued after she married in 1806, when she did not wish to compromise her husband, who was then a serving British Army officer. Their grace and favour apartment in Holyroodhouse had to be vacated and refurbished for the visit of George IV. However, her husband was compensated when the king restored him to the title of

Lord Nairne in 1824. But the new lord and his lady were not restored to his family's Perthshire estate.

Lady Nairne viewed Jacobitism through a more conservative lens than Burns. What made her work Romantic rather than hymns to nostalgia was her moral perspective on the passage of time and her retrospective emphasis on scenes from childhood. She took an organic view of society under monarchy, but she also emphasized the import-ance of loyalty ('The Land o' the Leal') to the rightful monarch and his supporters which transcended death. They would achieve redress and contentment not in this world but in the next. Her family home in Gask, like the cause of the royal Stuarts, was lost by 1800 ('The Auld House'). Traditional means of protection ('Oh! Rowan Tree') could not save it from rodent infestation any more than it could sustain an idyllic infancy or reverse the fallen hopes of the Stuarts. Lady Nairne also had a social conscience that lambasted the pretensions of pompous members of the landed elite ('The Laird o' Cockpen'). She castigated their snobbery towards poorly remunerated workers, such as the women who sold herring around the countryside carrying creels of fish on their backs from ports such as Newhaven near Edinburgh ('Caller Herrin').

Lady Nairne's anonymity as a major composer of national song was broken by the posthumous publication of *Lays from Strathearn* (1846), a compilation she had been working on prior to her death on 28 October 1845. She died two days short of the centenary of Prince Charles Edward's fatal decision to overrule dissent in his Council of War that his army should leave Edinburgh rather than consolidate their hold on Scotland. This decision, taken in the absence of any verifiable evi-dence that English Jacobites would flock to his banner, set his cause on a course that snatched defeat from victory and ensured that he would never return ('Will Ye No Come Back Again').

# Valedictory:
# Conflicted Loyalties

In essence, Jacobitism was motivated by dynastic, confessional and patriotic commitment. But Jacobitism also entailed civil war which divided families for and against the exiled Stuarts, whose cause in Scotland, England and Ireland was hidebound with intrigues and hampered by conflicted loyalties. Nevertheless, Jacobitism, particularly in Scotland, lasted politically for seven decades after the Revolution of 1688–91 and culturally well into the nineteenth century, and still gains traction from historical novels, Hollywood movies and television blockbusters.

For those who went out for the cause, Jacobitism was a high-risk venture. Those who avoided death or mutilation often faced imprisonment, trial and execution or transportation overseas. Those who escaped judicial reprisals were usually forced into exile with limited prospects of returning home to Scotland, England or Ireland. Leading Jacobites, whether executed or exiled, were also liable to have their estates forfeited. Collective amnesties and individual pardons for the rank and file were of limited value to those transported overseas beyond Europe to the Americas, Africa or Asia. Those who returned with fortunes from the Caribbean, the Guinea coast or India were exceptions rather than the rule.

As well as being high risk, Jacobitism was a venture in which loyalties were conflicted both among those who went out for the cause and those who opposed the risings. This can be particularly illustrated with reference to the clans. A common theme in Whig ideology in the aftermath of the three major risings in 1689–91, 1715–16 and 1745–6, as in the minor risings of 1708 and 1719, was to denigrate Highland clans on three principal grounds: first, for their tangible commitment to Jacobitism; second, for their proclaimed aversion to Whig principles of Protestantism, property and progress; and third, for their purported reluctance to abandon their traditional tribalism for commerce and industry. This denigration – promoted not only by politicians and journalists who can be considered Whig careerists, but even by covert Jacobites – favoured the eradication of clanship in the interests of civility. Chiefs and clan gentry also saw political mileage in denigrating clanship as a Scottish anachronism that hindered the formation of a unified and imperial British state. The suppression of Jacobitism in the wake of the Forty-Five required that chiefs and clan gentry demonstrate their patriotism in a British imperial rather than in a Scottish national context. Imperial security necessitated the emasculation of the clans, which had formed the front lines of the Jacobite forces in battle, as the enemy within.

This Whig ideology of negativity has had a lasting influence on the historiography. Jacobites in general have been deemed as desperate and mercenary opportunists whose loyalty could be purchased. Continuing in this accusatory rather than analytical vein, the motivation of the clans in particular has been attributed primarily to their traditional predatory inclinations as bandits or caterans. Alternatively, ordinary clansmen who fought for the Jacobite cause were either ignorant or forced out: charges that were reputedly justified by the high rates of desertion reported in the major campaigns, especially the Forty-Five. Furthermore, Whig polemicists upholding the Enlightenment rationalized clanship as a martial society in an arrested stage of development which threatened not just to subvert constitutional liberties, but to impede the progress of commerce and manufactures. Such militant Jacobitism has led to the ready affirmation that poverty and warfare were the mutual supports of clanship. But conflicted loyalties were evident among Whig as well as Jacobite clans. Moreover, these were conflicted not just on account of political polarization. There were mounting tensions within clans – Whig as well as Jacobite – over the commercialization of estate management, alternatively known as commercial landlordism. Strained relationships between the clan elite and their rank-and-file followers in the seventeenth century became evident at the Revolution.

With respect to predatory behaviour, the deliberate confusion of clans with caterans was a core dogma of anti-Jacobite propaganda. The tradition of cattle reiving within the Highlands and on the Lowland peripheries was largely confined to the most inaccessible districts of Lochaber and Rannoch in the central Highlands and was practised by freelance bandits rather than as a covert clan enterprise. Banditry was a peripheral activity of Jacobite clansmen, notably confined to the MacDonalds of Keppoch in the first major rising and to Rob Roy MacGregor and his associates in the Fifteen. However, the lifting of cattle and the destruction of fishing boats were major Whig pursuits to promote starvation before and after the battle of Culloden in the Forty-Five. That the political association of banditry with Jacobitism was notably lacking in credibility was evident in relation to the Campbells of Glenorchy. This clan had remained neutral during the first major rising at the Revolution but had actively declared for the Jacobite cause at the Fifteen, which led them to be branded as prone to banditry by the British forces occupying the Highlands during the 1720s. At this juncture, their effective leader, John Campbell, Lord Glenorchy (later 3rd Earl of Breadalbane), was a leading British diplomat at the Danish royal court in Copenhagen. Their name was cleared of all bandit aspersions when they mobilized for the British government in the Forty-Five.

The fluctuating nature of clan support in all three major risings should neither be interpreted as a mercenary desire to return home with booty nor be magnified as persistent desertion. Fluctuating support can be attributed more to the clans' aversion to disrupt the agrarian cycles for arable and pastoral farming and in coastal areas to the seasonal patterns for inshore and deep-sea fishing. Prolonged absence from clan territories through sustained Jacobite campaigning left them exposed to reprisals by their Whig opponents, as happened in all three risings. Variant explanations of desertions from Jacobite campaigns due to ignorance or forcing out also lack substance. Charges of ignorance can be readily reversed when account is taken of the phenomenal growth of vernacular Gaelic poetry since the civil wars of the three kingdoms in the mid-seventeenth century. This poetry propagated political and social criticism of the clan elite; such criticism was not suspended during the Jacobite risings. Three instances will suffice. During the major rising at the Revolution, Kenneth MacKenzie, 4th Earl of Seaforth, was viewed as having dallied overlong with James VII & II on his Irish campaign. He faced far from muted criticism for failing the cause and forsaking honour from his clansmen, who remained reluctant to rally to his banner after he returned to Scotland in June 1690. The continuing reluctance of MacKenzies in Wester Ross and the isle of Lewis to support their errant chief obliged him to surrender to forces loyal to William of Orange within four months. Voices from within Clan Donald launched swingeing attacks on the less than heroic conduct of clan leadership in allowing the Fifteen to peter out following the inconclusive battle of Sheriffmuir. Chiefs and clan gentry attempted to enforce discipline at the outset of major campaigns to prevent precipitate enlistment in Jacobite forces, particularly in clans where the elite were sympathetic to Jacobitism but were not prepared to hazard their estates and fortunes. Despite endeavours to enforce neutrality, the Atholl men along with the Grants of Glenmoriston and Glenurquhart mobilized for the Jacobite cause in all three major risings.

The counterpoint to enforced neutrality was enforced recruitment. Claims for forced recruitment in Arrochar, Badenoch, Breadalbane and the Trossachs during the Fifteen have some foundation, albeit with the caveat that where clans were divided, the majority usually sided with the Jacobites rather than accept neutrality or join the Whigs. Enforced recruitment can be sustained during the Forty-Five in Wester Ross, Abertarff, Stratherrick, the Aird, Lochaber, Rannoch and Badenoch again. However, Jacobite intimidation of clansmen was usually to replenish rather than to instigate recruitment: a situation which contrasted markedly with the Lowland peripheries. Here intimidation was notably used to instigate recruitment on the Braes of Mar during the Fifteen and on the Gordon estates in the shires of Aberdeen and Banff during the Forty-Five. Highlanders were certainly used to force out reluctant tenants of Jacobite landlords throughout the Lowland peripheries. Yet of the 2,950 prisoners listed after Culloden, only 200 (less than 7 per cent) claimed to have been forced out – although the lack of fluency of clansmen when interrogated in English rather than Gaelic may have deflated this number.[1] Conversely, during the Forty-Five, clansmen mobilized in defiance of their chiefs and clan gentry to go out for Jacobitism in Easter and Wester Ross, Skye, Strathnairn and Badenoch. Chiefs also disowned clansmen mobilizing for Jacobitism without their approval in Morar, Moidart, Knoydart, Glengarry, Strathglass and Appin. There are no reported instances of clans defying their chiefs and leading gentry to side with the Whigs.

Much has been made of deserters swarming back to Scotland when the Jacobite Army moved into England during the Forty-Five. As in the other two major risings, desertions from the Jacobites were frequently manufactured to boost morale among the Whigs. Indeed, Jacobite desertions were more than matched on the Whig side, with the additional difference that clansmen deserted from the Whig to the Jacobite Army. The most spectacular instance of wholescale desertion during the Forty-Five occurred among the Clan Chattan. Their chief, William Mackintosh of Mackintosh, was commissioned to raise an Independent Company for the Hanoverians, of whom all bar a handful deserted to join the regiment of around six hundred clansmen raised for the Jacobite cause by their chief's wife, Lady Anne Mackintosh. The leading vernacular Gaelic poet, Dunnchadh Bàn Mac an t-Saoir (Fair-Haired Duncan Macintyre), agreed to act as substitute in the Argyllshire Militia raised for the Whigs in return for a gratuity of £200 Scots (under £17 sterling) and a broadsword. He fled from the field at the battle of Falkirk in January 1746, dropped his sword, and committed to verse his regrets over his decision to fight against the Jacobites – regrets that were compounded by the indiscriminate impact of state terrorism instigated by William, Duke of Cumberland at the conclusion of the Forty-Five:

An là sin a thug iad Cùil-lodair,
Cha robh 'm fortan ud ach searbh dhuinn,
Choisinn Diùc Uilleam 'san droch-uair,
'S mór an rosad è do dh'Alba!

[That day when they fought Culloden/ Fortune to us was but bitter,/ In an ill hour won Duke William,/ Great the harm he's been to Scotland!][2]

Desertion was but one of the major difficulties encountered by Whig commanders attempting to mobilize clans for the Hanoverian cause. It took John Campbell, Earl of Loudoun, over four months to raise the full complement of eight Independent Companies for his Highland regiment. British government plans to raise an additional twenty Independent Companies from clans they deemed loyal, first enunciated in September 1745, were still two short of completion at the outset of February 1746. Whig clans were markedly reluctant to mobilize for fear of being transported from Scotland to continental theatres of war. This fate had occasioned mutiny and desertion from the Black Watch, despatched to Flanders in 1743. Although the regiment was brought back from the Continent by November 1745, trust in its loyalty was undermined by continuous desertions from Scottish regiments in Dutch service to join the Jacobite Army advancing on England. For the remainder of the Forty-Five, the Black Watch was confined to barracks at Camberwell outside London – although three additional companies raised at the outset of 1746 were retained in Scotland for the duration of the rising.

Every Scottish rising originated in the Highlands and each campaign deliberately promoted a Highland identity. Nevertheless, the militarism of the clans can be overplayed. Before the battle of Killiecrankie in July 1689, Jacobite officers were particularly concerned that the Highlanders were predominantly raw, undisciplined troops who had never seen blood. Technological changes in weaponry meant that bows and arrows fashioned from trees were giving way to flintlocks and other guns that were more expensive to manufacture at costs the clan elite were increasingly reluctant to meet for their followers. Want of arms and ammunition, no less than money, greatly hindered the recruitment of clansmen for the Jacobites as for the Whigs during the Fifteen. Despite their limited effectiveness, the Disarming Acts of 1716 and 1725 ensured that arms and ammunition were again at a premium in the Forty-Five. Prior to the battle of Prestonpans in September 1745, Donald Cameron of Lochiel actually dismissed 150 of his Lochaber clansmen for their want of weapons.

Charges that successive risings represented not only a political contest between Jacobites and Whigs but a social contest between traditionalism and commerce are simplistic and misleading. No more excusable is the subtle variant that Jacobite officers were often desperate bankrupts who had failed to adjust to the commercial climate in post-Union Scotland. On the Jacobite side, polemical appeals for unity among the clans should not be written off as wishful thinking on the part of the vernacular Gaelic poets. They were recalling and appealing to a mythic tradition of a golden age whose actual existence was immaterial. Such a tradition was used as a moral counterpoint to the irrevocable switch towards the commercialization of clanship from the seventeenth century. The poets' defence of a traditional society masked the social tensions between the clan elite and their clansmen, who were bearing the escalating costs of absenteeism, rent raising and the accumulation of debts. During the Forty-Five, not only were some clansmen defying the clan elite in siding with the Jacobites, but some were prepared to take up arms against their chiefs and leading gentry. This was particularly noted among the MacKenzies in Lewis and Ross, where doubts about the political sympathies of the clan elite were coupled to their rack-renting under the guise of improvement.

The commercialization of clanship manifest in the reconstruction of estate management before the Revolution can be associated specifically with the profitability of cattle droving, which was a significant growth point in the Scottish economy in the wake of Union. The droving trade was dominated by black cattle from Jacobite no less than Whig clans, and led to profitable diversification into extractive industries and the timber trade, dabbling in colonial land markets, and acquiring footholds in plantations exploiting tobacco, sugar and rum. Conflicted loyalties within clans that were aggravated by commercial landlordism were compounded by mercantile and military adventuring, imperial service and Jacobite rehabilitation in the aftermath of Culloden.

The dearth of career opportunities at the courts in exile for Jacobite refugees expanded the long-established Scottish presence in Europe primarily through mercantile and military adventuring from Iberia to Russia. At the same time, placement, clientage and enterprise opened up new horizons which facilitated capital accumulation and repatriation from commissions in the army and navy, from plantations in the American South and the Caribbean, and from tramp trading as well as the civil service in India. Imperial benefits accruing to the clan elite were not necessarily passed on to the clan rank and file. Highlanders enlisting in British regiments in the Seven Years War and later in the American War of Independence were rewarded with grants of frontier land in North America from the 1760s to the 1780s. Thus, the clan elite were rewarded by episodic imperial service, while the rank and file only gained by converting their episodic into permanent migration.

In the interim, however, imperial service was linked to the removal and relocation of people from the Highlands. Wholescale agrarian transformation promoted as improvement was accomplished by Clearance. In the first phase of the Clearances, which lasted from the 1730s to the 1820s, communal townships were broken up in favour of single-tenant holdings for cattle and sheep farming. Retained tenantry were removed into crofting communities: rural ghettos geared to fishing, burning of seaweed for kelp, slate and lime quarrying, charcoal burning and timber extraction. Crofting, in turn, facilitated the retention of labour pools that provided soldiers and sailors for imperial service. Subsistence agriculture was a secondary pursuit. Although the Lowlands as well as the Highlands were affected by Clearances, the conversion of Scottish Jacobites into British imperialists came at a poignant cost to erstwhile clansmen. This was articulated particularly by Iain MacFhearchair (John MacCodrum) writing prior to a fresh round of military recruitment for the American War of Independence, when rents in his native North Uist were being driven up exponentially and forcing extensive emigration to the Carolinas at the outset of the 1770s. Effectively this was permanent rather than episodic exile.

> On as fheudar dhuibh seòladh
> ('S nach ann do ur deòin e)
> Do rioghachd nach eòl duibh
> > Mar a thòisich ur càirdean.
> O nach fuiling iad beò sibh
> Ann an crìochaibh ur n-eòlais,
> 'S fheàrr dhuibh falbh do ur deòin
> > Na bhith fodha mar thràillean.

[Because you must sail/ (Though it's not what you want)/ To a kingdom unknown to you/ In the wake of your kinsfolk./ Since they won't let you live/ In the country you know,/ You had better leave willingly/ And not be trampled like slaves.][3]

Clearances notwithstanding, the rehabilitation of the Highlander from Jacobite rebel to imperial hero dates to the Seven Years War when much was made of former clansmen serving loyally in North America as light infantry in the British Army. This rehabilitation was furthered by the notable contributions of Highland regiments as the most reliable light infantry in the service of the British Empire on a global scale from the American Revolution to the Napoleonic Wars. Rehabilitation had been facilitated by James 'Ossian' Macpherson, a prominent public intellectual with a Jacobite pedigree. This moral aspect of Romanticism was taken up generally for Scotland in poems and songs, particularly those by Robert Burns and Carolina Oliphant, Lady Nairne. Burns composed during the first phase of industrialization and large-scale urbanization that overlapped with the first phase of Clearances and was dominated by textiles, chemicals and the factory system. Lady Nairne continued to write into the second phase of Clearances from the 1830s to the 1880s that expanded sheep farming and introduced shooting estates at the expense of crofting communities. Such agrarian change dovetailed with a second phase of industrialization and urbanization occasioned by coal, iron, steel, shipbuilding and railways. Both Burns and Lady Nairne saw Jacobitism as a means of upholding community over class interests, the latter being particularly evident among landed and urban elites by their privileged social posturing and by their social distancing in town and country from urban and rural ghettos. Burns, like many radical Scots, was initially sympathetic to the French Revolution in 1789. His Scottish patriotism served as a bridge between Jacobitism and Jacobinism. Such radicalism was not a consideration for Lady Nairne. For her, Jacobitism was an antidote to the class-based political and industrial conflicts which were a notably disruptive feature in Britain in the decades following the ending of the Napoleonic Wars in 1815.

Similar conservative sentiments influenced the work of Sir Walter Scott to restore an appreciation of the enduring validity of rural community values. But his primary interest was to rehabilitate the former Jacobite clans that were now at the disposal of the British Empire. He certainly exercised considerable dramatic licence in his sympathetic portrayal of *Rob Roy* (1817), which took little account of the bandit proclivities of his immediate family and the MacGregor clan during the Jacobite risings. Three years earlier in *Waverley*, he partially based the fictional Fergus MacIvor on Colonel Alasdair MacDonnell of Glengarry, a foolhardy and mendacious martinet who instigated swingeing Clearances of his erstwhile clansmen in Lochaber at the outset of the nineteenth century. Notwithstanding Scott's glossing of the Highland Clearances, he instigated a rich tradition of historical novels involving clanship, Jacobitism, conflicted loyalties, political ambivalence and moral ambiguity.

Since Scott, the foremost practitioners of the historical Jacobite novel have been Robert Louis Stevenson, John Buchan, Neil Munro and S. G. Maclean. Stevenson's *Kidnapped* (1886) and its sequel *Catriona* (1893) are focused on the Appin Murder of 1752 that exposed Whig as much as Jacobite conflicts of interest over the trial, conviction and execution of Seumas a'Ghlinne ( James Stewart of Glenduror) for a crime he most certainly did not commit or knowingly assist. In between, Stevenson wrote the more dark and disturbing *The Master of Ballantrae* (1889), where the action moves from Culloden to the Caribbean and on to North America in the Seven Years War. Buchan's best work on Jacobitism is focused on the Forty-Five; *A Lost Lady of Old Years* (1899) concerns the intrigues surrounding John Murray of Broughton, the duplicitous secretary to Prince Charles Edward, and the more celebrated *Midwinter* (1927) about double-dealing, treachery and betrayal on the march of the Jacobite Army to Derby. Munro has masterful treatment of Jacobite intrigues in *Doom Castle* (1901) as the cause was on its last legs in the 1750s, and in the only novel set between the Fifteen and the Forty-Five, *The New Road* (1914). Most recently, Shona Maclean compellingly interlaces Jacobitism with crime and the settling of old scores six years after Culloden in *The Bookseller of Inverness* (2022).

In transposing Jacobitism to the film screen and television, the most successful author has undoubtedly been Robert Louis Stevenson. The Walt Disney production of *Kidnapped*, released in 1960 and directed by

Robert Stevenson (no relation to the author), was remarkable for three reasons. First, it was shot in 1959 in authentic locations, reconnoitred by Stevenson himself in Glencoe, Appin and Lochaber. Second, the film has a strong cast of Scottish character actors to support the leading men: Alan Breck Stewart, an actual historical figure played with swagger by Peter Finch as the Jacobite veteran of Culloden who had returned to Scotland as a French agent, and David Balfour, played more reticently by James MacArthur as a committed Lowland Whig whose Uncle Ebenezer had attempted to deprive him of his inheritance by having him shipped off to America as an indentured servant. When the ship in which he was kidnapped was wrecked in the Inner Hebrides, he was rescued by Alan Breck, who set aside their conflicting loyalties to team up on a Highland venture. Third, not only was the author's ambivalent attitudes to Jacobitism, morally and intellectually, transferred to the screen, but this was accomplished with dramatic panache and a high degree of technical skill.

The technological revolution in electronic communications from the late twentieth century has paved the way for television blockbusters of the stamp of *Outlander*, based on the romantic historical writing of Diana Gabaldon that has been developed by Ronald D. Moore. Launched initially in the United States by Starz in association with Sony Pictures Television in 2014, it was released the following year in the United Kingdom through Amazon Prime Video. It is currently preparing for its eighth series combining Jacobitism and time travel. Its leading roles are played by Caitriona Balfe as Claire Randall, a nurse in London at the end of the Second World War who is transposed back in time to Scotland prior to the Forty-Five, where she consorts with Sam Heughan playing Jamie Fraser, a warrior in the Frasers of Lovat, the epitome of a clan with conflicted loyalties. The action moves on from Culloden and its bloody aftermath to migration into North Carolina via a piratical episode in the Caribbean. The lead characters and their extended family are caught up in the American War of Independence, in which conflicted loyalties are again to the fore, while planning their return to Scotland.

However outlandish the current vogue for Jacobite adventure at home and abroad, there was much more to the cause than political intrigues, warfare and Romanticism. The final say on the essence of Jacobitism should go to Field Marshal James Keith. He participated in the Fifteen and the minor rising of 1719. He left to further his military schooling in France and to a less fulfilling extent in Spain before moving on to become a military commander of international standing in Russia and Prussia. He declined to serve in the Forty-Five. Keith was adamant that Jacobitism should be focused on the pursuit of political virtue, particularly with regard to state formation. The failure of the cause to live up to his enlightened expectations meant he was far less concerned with conflicting loyalties than with the purposeful reordering of priorities. Like other political exiles from Scotland by necessity rather than by choice, he practised pragmatism to grasp rewarding opportunities – whether military and mercantile or commercial and cultural – that opened up in Europe and beyond.

# REFERENCES

## Introduction

1 Aberdeen University Library (hereafter AUL), Macbean Collection, Scraps on the Jacobite Episode, 1688–1746, 13 vols: Highlanders as Turkish Captives, vol. II, pp. 168–70. See also Royal Archives, State Papers Online (gale.com), MS Stuart Papers [SP]/Main/199, fols 167–8 and 311, 133–7.
2 Royal Archives, State Papers Online (gale.com), MS Stuart Papers [SP]/Main/199, fols 167–8 and 311, 133–7.

## 1 The Cause of the Exiled Stuarts

1 Anon., *Britain's Alarm, or Seasonable Warning to Secure British Protestants* ([Edinburgh], 1713).
2 Mr Adam Ferguson, Chaplain to the Regiment, *A Sermon preached in the Ersh Language to His Majesty's First Highland Regiment of Foot commanded by Lord John Murray at the Containment at Camberwell on 18 December 1745* (London, 1746), p. 11.
3 National Records of Scotland, Edinburgh (hereafter NRS), Miscellaneous Small Collections, Papers of the Logan Home family of Edrom, GD1/384/34.
4 *Scots Magazine* (November 1746), p. 2.

## 2 Scottish Jacobitism

1 *Highland Songs of the 'Forty-Five*, ed. John L. Campbell (Edinburgh, 1984), pp 90–91.
2 AUL, MacBean Collection, C5, 'Copy Letter from King James Pretender to the Duke of Argyle, 1741'.
3 NRS, Miscellaneous Small Collections, Papers on the 1715 Jacobite Rising, GD1/616/46, 'Account of the Number of Men the Highland Chieftains and Superiors of the Several Clans can bring to the Field to carry Arms'.
4 NRS, Breadalbane MSS, GD112/47/1/13: 'List of Clan Chiefs with Numbers of Men raised by them in the '15 and the '45'.

5 These three tables are taken from Allan I. Macinnes, *Clanship, Commerce and the House of Stewart, 1603–1788* (East Linton, 1996), pp. 180, 190–91.

## 3 Risings and Reprisals

1 David Wemyss, Lord Elcho, *A Short Account of the Affairs of Scotland in the Years 1744, 1745, 1746* (1903; repr. Edinburgh, 1973), pp. 336–41.
2 Huntington Library, San Marino, California, Loudoun Scottish Collection, Box 47, LO 9505.
3 Bishop Forbes's work was eventually published in its entirety as *The Lyon in Mourning*, ed. Henry Paton, 3 vols (Edinburgh, 1895–6).
4 Thomas Crawford, 'Political and Protest Songs in Eighteenth Century Scotland: 1. Jacobite and Anti-Jacobite', *Scottish Studies*, XIV (1970), pp. 1–33; Murray G. H. Pittock, *Poetry and Jacobite Politics in Eighteenth Century Britain and Ireland* (Cambridge, 1994), pp. 13–17.
5 NRS, Papers of the Society of Antiquaries of Scotland, Indenture of Apprenticeship, GD103/2/382.

## 4 Jacobite Diaspora in Continental Europe

1 NRS, Miscellaneous Small Collections, Papers on the 1715 Jacobite Rising, GD1/616/44.
2 *A Fragment of a Memoir of Field-Marshal James Keith Written by Himself, 1714–1734*, ed. Thomas Constable (Edinburgh, 1843), p. 76.

## 5 Adventuring in the American Colonies

1 NRS, Clanranald Papers, GD201/4/64.
2 *Colonial Records of North Carolina*, vol. IV [1734–53], ed. William L. Saunders (New York, 1968), pp. 940–41.
3 *The Colonial Records of the State of Georgia*, vol. III: *The General Account of the Monies and Effects received and expended by the Trustees for establishing the Colony of Georgia in America*, ed. Allan D. Candler (New York, 1970), pp. 427–8.
4 In 1938 the Glenfinnan Monument was taken into the care and custody of the National Trust for Scotland.

## 6 Africa, Asia and Global Adventuring

1 Rigsarkivet, Copenhagen, Det vestindisk-guineske kompani: Guvernnement paa Guineakysten Breveboger, 1703–1754, 446/887.
2 NRS, Abercairny Papers, GD24/1/464n/67–70, fols 522–7.
3 Allan I. Macinnes, Marjory-Ann D. Harper and Linda G. Fryer, eds, *Scotland and the Americas, c. 1650–c.1939: A Documentary Source Book* (Edinburgh, 2002), pp. 75–7.

## 7  Enlightenment and Romanticism

1  NRS, Records collated by Bishop Andrew Jolly, CH12/19/3, pp. 1–6.
2  AUL, Keith, James Francis Edward, Correspondence with Chevalier Colonel John Drummond (photocopies of MSS in Berlin State Library), MS 2709, pp. 28–9, 33–4.

## Valedictory: Conflicted Loyalties

1  *The Prisoners of the '45*, ed. Sir B. G. Seton and J. G. Arnot, 3 vols (Edinburgh, 1928–9), vol. I, pp. 270, 306–7, 316, 310; vols II and III passim.
2  *Highland Songs of the 'Forty-Five*, ed. John L. Campbell (Edinburgh, 1984), pp. 210–11.
3  *An Lasair: Anthology of 18th Century Scottish Gaelic Verse*, ed. Ronald Black (Edinburgh, 2001), pp. 286–7, 495.

# BIBLIOGRAPHY

## Archives

### Aberdeen City Archives

Council Register, 1741–53, CAI/61
Miscellaneous 1745 Rebellion, CA25/5
Outletters, vol. II, 1738–47, CA/8/3/2

### Aberdeen University Library

Collection of Letters, 1747–1813, relating to Jacobite Affairs, MS 95
Duff House (Montcoffer Papers), MS 3175
Duff of Meldrum Collection, MS 2778
Erskine, Charles, Lord Justice Clerk, 'Letter on Pacification of the Highlands, 14 May 1752', Safe Box B, 954
Historical Papers, MS 3163
Keith, James Francis Edward, Correspondence with Chevalier Colonel John Drummond (photocopies of MSS in Berlin State Library), MS 2709
Keith-Falconer (Earls of Kintore), MS 3064
MacBean Collection, C5, Copy Letter from King James Pretender to the Duke of Argyle, 1741, C5/46; Scraps on the Jacobite Episode, 1688–1746, 13 vols
MacBean, William M., A Contribution to a Jacobite Iconography, part of MacBean Collection
Miscellaneous Personal Papers MS
Pitsligo Papers, MS 2740
Ramsay, Allan, 'The Royall Youth many now Advance', MS955
Records of the Scottish Episcopal Church: Diocesan Office – Aberdeen and Orkney, MS 3320
William Duff of Braco, MS 2727

### Archivio del Palazzo di Propaganda Fide, Rome

Congregazione Particolari, Scozia, vols 32 (1696–1707), 34A (1707–12), 50 (1694–1719), 86 (1735–6), 87 (1737–41)
Scritture riferite nei Congressa, Scozia, first series, 2 vols (1623–1760)

## Argyll and Bute District Archives

Argyll Papers
Burgh of Inveraray Minute Book, 1741–75, BI/1/2
Minute Book of the Commissioners of Supply of Argyllshire, 1744–95

## Beinecke Rare Books and Manuscripts Library, Yale University, New Haven, CT

Papers of the Earl of Morton, Osborn Collection, OSB MSS 72
Stair Papers, Osborn Collection, OSB MSS 24/box 1

## Bodleian Library, Oxford University

Carte Papers (1701–19), MS Carte 180
Nairn's Papers, vol. II (1689–1706), MS Carte 209

## British Library, London

Athenian Letters, Miscellaneous Papers: Birch Collection, Add. MS 4326A
Blenheim Papers, vol. DXXXI, Add. MS 61,631
Hardwicke Papers, vol. XCIX, Correspondence of the Lord Hardwicke on Scotch Affairs, 1741–53, Add. MS 35,447; vol. C, Correspondence of Lord Hardwick on Scotch Affairs, 1753–5, Add. MS 35,448; vol. DX, Political Tracts relating to Scotland, 1745–52, Add. MS 35,858; vol. DXXIX, Papers relating to State Trials, 1748–88, Add. MS 35,887; untitled vols: CCXLIII, Add. MS 35,591; DL, Add. MS 35,898; DLI, Add. MS 35,899; DCCLXXX, Add. MS 36,128
Hodgkin Papers, vol. VI, Papers relating to the Pretender, 1688–1746, Add. MS 38,851
Leeds Papers, vols CX and CXI, Edgerton MS 3433–34
Letters and Papers of Sir Robert Walpole, vol. CCLXXIV, Add. MS 74,053, and vol. CCXCVII, Add. MS 74,066
Liverpool Papers, vol. CLIII, Official Papers of the 1st Earl, 1773–7, Add. MS 38,342
Miscellanea, Stowe MS 1083
Newcastle Papers, vol. XXIV, Add. MS 32,709; vol. XXVII, Add. MS 32,712; vol. XXVIII, Add. MS 32,713; vol. XLVII, Add. MS 32,733
Papers relating to Scotland, Stowe MS 158
Papers relating to the West Indies, America Sixteenth–Eighteenth Centuries, Africa and the Canaries, 1696–1726, Add. MS 14,034
Public Debts, 1748–51, Add. MS 50,203
Scotch Plot, 1702–4, Papers of Simon Fraser, Lord Lovat, Add. MS 31,250
Sidney, 1st Earl of Godolphin, Official Correspondence, Home, 1701–10, Add. MS 28,055
State Papers, 1631–1727, Stowe MS 186
Strang, Sir John, Brief on the Trials of the Scotch Rebels, 1746, Egerton MS 200
Supplementary Walpole Papers, vol. I, Add. MS 78,913
Townshend Papers, vol. XVI, Miscellaneous Papers, 1707–83, Add. MS 38,507
Walpole Papers, vol. XLIX, Lord Waldegrave, 1736, Add. MS 73,818; vol. CVCVI, Add. MS 73,965; unnumbered vols, Add. MS 73,993 and Add. MS 74,002

Whiteford Papers, vol. C, Whiteford Correspondence, 1738–52, Add. MS 36,592
Windham Papers, vol. XL, Add. MS 37,881

**Centre historique des Archives Nationales, Paris**

Affaires Estrangers (consulats) Etates Unis, Etates de commerce et de navigation des ports, 1697–1830, B/III/444

**Dundee University Archives**

Brechin Library Manuscripts, BR MS 3/DC 89 and BR MS 2/1/11

**Dunollie Castle, Oban**

MacDougalls of Dunollie, Eighteenth-Century Papers

**Glasgow City Archives**

Campbell of Shawfield, TD1619
Campbell of Succoth and Garscube Records, TD219
Hamilton of Barns Papers, TD589
Messrs Mitchells, Johnston & Co., MacLeod Family Papers, T-MJ377
Records of the Lennox Family of Woodhead, T-LX
Records of the Maxwells of Pollok, T-PM 115
Stirlings of Keir Papers, vol. II, 1702–53, T-SK 11/2; John Stirling of Keir, Memorandum Book, 1728–41, T-SK 14/1; John Stirling of Keir, Expenses Book, 1729–31, T-SK 14/2; Archibald Stirling, Account Book as an East Indian Merchant, 1747–54, T-SK 15/1

**Huntington Library, San Marino, California**

Bridgewater and Ellesmere MSS
Hastings Irish Papers, boxes 31–4
Huntington Manuscripts, Itinerarium of Alexander Hamilton, 1744, HM 922
Loudon Papers Americana, 1682–1784, Boxes 9–10
Loudoun Scottish Collection, Boxes 1–48
Newsletters from London to Tamworth (1690–1704), HM 30,659; Shirley Papers; Stowe Americana; Sunderland Collections I and II; Upcot-Bixby Collection
Papers of James Abercromby, AB976
Papers relating to African Affairs, ST 9
Stowe Papers, Brydges Family Papers, ST 57/vols 1–33 (1706–33); ST 58/vols 1–14 (1700–1712)

**Inveraray Castle Archives**

Argyll Papers
Miscellaneous Argyll Letters
Miscellaneous Eighteenth-Century Papers

**Mount Stuart House, Rothesay**

Loudon Papers

## The National Archives, London

Secretaries of State, State Papers Scotland, Series Two (1688–1788), SP54,
    vols 1–41
Treasury Board, Papers and In-Letters (1745–52), T 1/348; (1753) T 1/353
Treasury Solicitor and HM Procurator General Papers (1746), TS 11/1081

## National Library of Scotland, Edinburgh

Cameron of Fassifern Papers, Brodrick Haldane Collection, Acc. 11,337
Jacobite Letters and Papers, MS 295
Lauriston Castle Collection, Delvine Papers, Family Correspondence,
    MS 1118–24, 1128, 1136; Baillie MS 1230; Elphinston–Easdaile MS 1263;
    Mackintosh MS 1378; Jacobites–Peers MS 1498
Mackintosh Genealogies, Farr Manuscript, MS 9854
Saltoun Papers, vol. XII, MS 175,222
Some Remarks on the Highland Clans and Methods proposed for Civilizing
    Them, Adv. MS 16.1.14
Yester Papers, MS 7044–7046

## National Records of Scotland, Edinburgh

Abercairny Papers, GD24
An Account of the Surveys made on the Forfeited Estates in Scotland
    and returned unto the Court of Exchequer, 1749, E707/7/3
Breadalbane MSS, GD112
Boyd Alexander Papers, GD393
Bruce of Airth Papers, GD37
Campbell of Barcaldine Papers, GD170
Campbell of Dunstaffnage Papers, GD202
Clanranald Papers, GD201
Clerk of Penicuik Papers, GD18
Dalhousie Papers, GD45
Dundas of Arniston Papers, GD235
Episcopal Church of Scotland Records, Charter Chest, CH12/12; Bishop Andrew
    Jolly, Miscellaneous Correspondence, CH12/14
        Folio Volumes, CH12/19
        Letters, CH12/23
Forfeited Estates Papers 1715, Burleigh and Fernie, E619/64; Unsold Estates,
    Lochiel E682/5
Forfeited Estates Papers 1745, Replies from Sheriffs, 1747–8, E706/1
Gilmour of Craigmillar Correspondence, GD123
Grant of Monymusk Papers, GD345
Hall of Dunglass Papers, GD206
Hamilton Papers, GD406
Hawthorn of Castlewigg Papers, GD455
Innes of Stow Papers, GD113
Journal of W. Simpson, Merchant, Aberdeen, CS 96/957
Keith Papers, GD156
Kennedy of Dalquharran Letters and Papers, GD241

Kinross House Papers, GD29
Leven and Melville Papers, GD26
Mar and Kellie Papers, GD12
Miscellaneous Papers, Alexander Campbell, Merchant in Edinburgh, RH15/14;
    Sir Andrew Home, Lord Kimmerghame, RH15/15; Cunningham of
    Cunninghamhead, RH15/28; James Carnegie W. S., RH15/56
Miscellaneous Small Collections, Papers of Sir John Erskine of Alva, GD1/44;
    St Andrews Papers, GD1/50; Irvine Robertson Papers, GD1/153; Papers of
    the Logan Home Family of Edrom, GD1/384; Papers on the 1715 Jacobite
    Rising, GD1/616; Papers on Kelso Burgh, GD1/811
Miscellaneous Transcripts, Individual Documents, RH1/2; Volumes, RH2/2
Montrose Muniments, GD220
Morton Papers, GD150
Papers of the Society of Antiquaries of Scotland, GD103
Records of Brodie, W. S., GD247
Records of Thomson and Baxter, W. S., GD241
Roberston of Lude Papers, GD132
Ross of Pitcalnie Papers, GD 199
Scot of Gala Papers, GD477
Scottish Society for the Propagation of Christian Knowledge Records, GD59
Seafield Papers, GD248
Shairp of Houston Papers, GD30
Smythe of Methven Papers, GD19
State Papers of Scotland, Series II, RH2/4/305
Stonehaven Sheriff Court, Papers relating to James Grant, Merchant in Montrose,
    SC5/75
Supplementary Parliamentary Papers, PA7/17
Warrant of Bught Correspondence, GD23

### Newberry Library, Chicago

Edward E. Eyer Manuscript Collection, Memoranda on French Colonies in
    America, including Canada, Louisiana, and the Caribbean (1702–50), 4 vols,
    Ayer MS 827

### Orkney Archives, Kirkwall

Kirkwall Town Council Minute Books (1659–1716), B1/12–14
Sheriff Court Records, SC 11/86

### Perth and Kinross Council Archives

Fergusson of Baldemond, MS 79
Perth Burgh Records, B59/30
Perth Town Council 'Mass', PE 15/4
Threipland of Gask, MS 169

### Public Record Office of Northern Ireland, Belfast

Londonderry Papers, Papers of Sir Robert Cowan, Outward Bound Letter
    Books, 1721–35, D654/B/1AA – /1P; Europe Letter Books, 1728–34, D654/
    B/1/2A – /2D; Gather of Original Inward Letters, 1725–8, D654/B/1/4B

Miscellaneous Letters from Captains of Sea Vessels, 1725–34, D654/B/1/5C
Reports from George Morton Pitt, 1724–33, D654/B/1/5K

**Rigsarkivet, Copenhagen**

Det vestindisk-guineske kompani, Guvernnement paa Guineakysten
    Breveboger, 1703–54, 446/886–9
Guvernor Michel Crones og Knud Helmers dodsboer, 1713–37, 446/232

**Stirling District Council Archives**

Blair Drummond Printed Pamphlets, PD 17
Murray Family of Polmaise and Touchadam Papers, PD 189
W. B. Cook Collection, PD 16

# Printed Sources


*1715: The Story of the Rising*, ed. Alistair and Henrietta Tayler (London, 1936)
*An Abridgement of the Public Statutes in force and in use relative to Scotland from the Union to 1783*, ed. J. Swinton, 2 vols (Edinburgh, 1788)
Abudacnus, Joseph, *The True History of the Jacobites of Aegypt, Lybia, Nubia, of their Origin, Religion, Ceremonies, Laws and Customs, whereby you may see how much they differ from the Jacobites of Great Britain* (London, 1692)
*The Albemarle Papers: Correspondence of William Anne, Second Earl of Albemarle, Commander-in-Chief in Scotland, 1746–47*, ed. Charles S. Terry, 2 vols (Aberdeen, 1902)
Anders, John, *The Book of the Chronicles of His Royal Highness William, Duke of Cumberland: Being an Account of the Rise and Progress of the Present Rebellion* (Edinburgh, 1746)
Anon., *Britain's Alarm, or Seasonable Warning to Secure British Protestants* (1713)
Anon., *An Enquiry into some things that concern Scotland* (Edinburgh, 1734)
Anon., *A Full and Impartial Account of the Company of Mississippi, otherwise called the French-East-India Company. Projected and Settled by Mr Law* (London, 1720)
Anon., *The Occasional Patriot, written in Plain Scotch* (Edinburgh, 1734)
Anon., *Reflections upon the Constitution and Management of the Trade to Africa* (London, 1709)
Bayse, S., *An Impartial History of the Late Rebellion in 1745: From Authentic Memoirs particularly the Journal of a General Officer* (London, 1748)
Bentley, R., *An Attempt towards an Apology for His R.H. the Duke of Cumberland* (London, 1751)
*The Best of our Owne: Letters of Archibald Pitcairne, 1652–1713*, ed. W. T. Johnston (Edinburgh, 1979)
*The Book of the Duffs*, ed. Alistair and Henrietta Tayler, 2 vols (Edinburgh, 1914)
*Caledonian Mercury* (1739–45)
*The Chevalier de Johnstone: A Memoir of the 'Forty-Five*, ed. Brian Rawson (London, 1958)
*Chronicles of the Atholl and Tullibardine Families*, ed. James J.H.H. Stuart-Murray, 7th Duke of Atholl, 5 vols (Edinburgh, 1908)
*Colin Campbell 1686–1757: His Will – Annotated*, ed. Alexander A. Cormack (Aberdeen, 1960)

*Collected Papers on the Jacobite Risings*, ed. Rupert C. Jarvie (Manchester, 1972)

*A Collection of Scarce and Valuable Tracts on the Most Interesting and Entertaining Subjects, but chiefly such as relate to the History and Constitution of these Kingdoms*, vol. III (London, 1745)

*Colonial Records of North Carolina*, vol. IV [1734–53], ed. William L. Saunders (New York, 1968)

*The Colonial Records of the State of Georgia*, vol. III: *The General Account of the Monies and Effects received and expended by the Trustees for establishing the Colony of Georgia in America*, ed. Allan D. Candler (New York, 1970)

*The Correspondence of Colonel N. Hooke, Agent for the Court of France to the Scottish Jacobites in the years 1703–1707*, ed. W. D. MacKay, 2 vols (London, 1870–71)

[Couper, Patrick,] *Jacobite Loyalty: Or a Letter to North-British Jacobites about their taking the Oaths to King George and the Government* (Edinburgh, 1724)

*Darien Shipping Papers, 1696–1707*, ed. George P. Insh (Edinburgh, 1924)

[Defoe, Daniel,] *The History of the Jacobite Clubs* (London, 1712)

*Extracts from the Records of the Burgh of Glasgow 1718–38*, ed. R. Renwick (Glasgow, 1909)

Ferguson, Mr Adam, Chaplain to the Regiment, *A Sermon preached in the Ersh Language to His Majesty's First Highland Regiment of Foot commanded by Lord John Murray at the Containment at Camberwell on 18 December 1745* (London, 1746)

Ferguson, Andrew, *A Genuine Account of All of the Persons of note in Scotland, who are now engaged in the service of the Chevalier* (Edinburgh, 1745)

*The Forty-Five: A Narrative of the Last Jacobite Rising by Several Contemporary Hands*, ed. Charles S. Terry (Cambridge, 1922)

*A Fragment of a Memoir of Field-Marshal James Keith Written by Himself, 1714–1734*, ed. Thomas Constable (Edinburgh, 1843)

Fraser-Mackintosh, Charles, *Antiquarian Notes* (Inverness, 1865)

Hamilton, Captain Alexander, *A New Account of the East Indies*, 2 vols (London, 1744)

[Hayes, Charles,] *The Importance of Effectually Supporting the Royal Africa Company of England impartially considered* (London, 1745)

*Highland Songs of the 'Forty-Five*, ed. John L. Campbell (Edinburgh, 1984)

*Historical Papers relating to the Jacobite Period*, ed. Col. J. Allardyce, 2 vols (Aberdeen, 1895)

*House of Commons Sessional Papers of the Eighteenth Century: Reports and Papers, 1717–25 (Scotland)*, ed. Sheila Lambert (Wilmington, DE, 1975)

*The Jacobite Cess Roll for the County of Aberdeen, 1715*, ed. Alistair and Henrietta Tayler (Aberdeen, 1932)

*Jacobite Correspondence of the Atholl Family during the Rebellion, 1745–1746*, ed. J. H. Burton and D. Laing (Edinburgh, 1840)

*The Jacobite Court at Rome in 1719*, ed. Henrietta Tayler (Edinburgh, 1938)

*Jacobite Letters to Lord Pitsligo 1745–1746*, ed. Alistair and Henrietta Tayler (Aberdeen, 1930)

'Jacobite Papers at Avignon', ed. Henrietta Tayler; 'Marchmont Correspondence relating to the '45', ed. G.F.C. Hepburne Scott; and 'The Fragments of Autobiography, by George Keith, 10th Earl Marischal of Scotland', ed. J.Y.T. Greig, in *Scottish History Society Miscellany V* (Edinburgh, 1933)

*The Jacobite Risings of 1715 and 1745*, ed. Rupert C. Jarvie (Carlisle, 1954)

*The Jacobite Threat: Rebellion and Conspiracy 1688–1759; England, Ireland, Scotland and France. A Source Book*, ed. Bruce P. Lenman and John S. Gibson (Edinburgh, 1990)

*The Jacobites and the Union: Being a Narrative of the Movements of 1708, 1715, 1719 by Several Contemporary Hands*, ed. Charles S. Terry (Cambridge, 1922)

*An Lasair: Anthology of 18th Century Scottish Gaelic Verse*, ed. Ronald Black (Edinburgh, 2001)

*The Letter Book of Bailie James Steuart of Inverness, 1715–52*, ed. J. Mackay (Edinburgh, 1915)

*The Letter Book of James Abercromby, Colonial Agent 1751–1773*, ed. J. C. Van Horne and G. Reese (Richmond, va, 1991)

*Letters of George Lockhart of Carnwath 1698–1732*, ed. Daniel Szechi (Edinburgh, 1989)

'Letters of Lord Balmerino to Harry Maule, 1710–1713 & 1720–1722', ed. Clyve Jones, in *Scottish History Society Miscellany* xii (Edinburgh, 1944)

*A List of Persons Concerned in the Rebellion 1745–46*, ed. W. Muirhead (Edinburgh, 1890)

*A List of the Scots Noblemen and Gentlemen that are designed for England* (Edinburgh, 1717)

*Lists of Scottish Noblemen and Gentlemen attainted of High Treason in the last Session of Parliament* (Edinburgh, 1716)

Lockyer, Charles, *An Account of the Trade in India* (London, 1711)

*London Magazine* (1745)

[Lyndsey, Patrick,] *The Interest of Scotland Considered* (Edinburgh, 1734)

*The Lyon in Mourning: Or a Collection of Speeches Letters Journals etc relative to the Affairs of Prince Charles Edward Stuart by the Rev. Robert Forbes, Bishop of Ross and Caithness, 1746–1775*, ed. Henry Paton, 3 vols (Edinburgh, 1895–6)

*The Memoirs of John Ker of Kersland in North Britain*, 3 vols (London, 1727)

*Memoirs of John Murray of Broughton, Sometime Secretary to Prince Charles Edward, 1740–1747*, ed. R. F. Bell (Edinburgh, 1898)

Meston, William, *The Poetical Words of the Ingenious and Learned William Meston, sometime Professor of Philosophy in the Marischal College of Aberdeen*, 6th edn (Edinburgh, 1767)

[Murray, Lord George,] *A Particular Account of the Battle of Culloden, April 16, 1746, in a Letter from an Officer of the Highland Army to his Friend at London* (London, 1749)

*Muster Roll of Prince Charles Edward Stuart's Army 1745–46*, ed. Alistair Livingstone of Bachuil, Christian W. H. Aikman and Betty Stuart Hart (Aberdeen, 1984)

*The Oliphants of Gask: Records of a Jacobite Family*, ed. E. M. Graham (London, 1910)

*Origins of the Forty-Five and Other Papers relating to that Rising*, ed. Walter B. Blaikie (Edinburgh, 1916)

*The Prisoners of the '45*, ed. Sir B. G. Seton and J. G. Arnot, 3 vols (Edinburgh, 1928–9)

*A Report from the Commissioners appointed to Enquire of the Estates of Certain Traitors in that part of Great Britain called Scotland* (Edinburgh, 1717)

Robertson [of Strowan], Alexander, *Poems on Various Subjects and Occasions* (Edinburgh, 1749)

*Scotland and the Americas, c.1650–c.1939: A Documentary Source Book*, ed. Allan I. Macinnes, Marjory-Ann D. Harper and Linda G. Fryer (Edinburgh, 2002)

*'Scotland's Ruine': Lockhart of Carnwath's Memoirs of the Union*, ed. Daniel Szechi (Aberdeen, 1995)

*Scots Magazine*, vols I–XV (1739–53)

*Secret History of Colonel Hooke: Negotiations in Scotland in 1707* (Edinburgh, 1760)

*The Stirlings of Keir and their Family Papers*, ed. Willliam Fraser (Edinburgh, 1858)

*Virginia Gazette of Williamsburg* (1745–6)

[Wemyss,] David, Lord Elcho, *A Short Account of the Affairs of Scotland in the Years 1744, 1745, 1746* (1903; repr. Edinburgh, 1973)

*Witness to Rebellion: John Maclean's Journal of the 'Forty-Five*, ed. Iain Gordon Brown and Hugh Cheape (East Linton, 1996)

Wood, William, *Survey of Trade* (1718)

## Digital Databases

ANOM (Archives Nationales d'Outre-Mer), archivesnationales.culture.gouv.fr

Layne, Darren S., The Jacobite Database of 1745, jdb1745.net

Legacies of British Slave-Ownership Databases, LBS Centre, UCL, ucl.ac.uk/lbs

MS Stuart Papers, Royal Archives, State Papers Online, gale.com

*Oxford Dictionary of National Biography*, online edition, 2018–24, oxforddnb.com

Records of the Parliaments of Scotland to 1707, ed. K. M. Brown et al., online edition, 2007–10, rps.ac.uk

## Books

Banks, Kenneth J., *Chasing Empire Across the Sea: Communications and the State in the French Atlantic, 1713–1763* (Montreal, 2003)

Bernard, Toby C., and Jane Fenlon, eds, *The Dukes of Ormonde, 1610–1745* (Woodbridge, 2000)

Calder, Angus, *Revolutionary Empire: The Rise of the English-Speaking Empires from the Fifteenth Century to the 1780s* (London, 1998)

Checkland, S. G., *Scottish Banking: A History, 1695–1973* (Glasgow and London, 1975)

Clark, Jonathan D. C., *Revolution and Rebellion: State and Society in England in the Seventeenth and Eighteenth Centuries* (Cambridge, 1986)

Clyde, Robert, *From Rebel to Hero: The Image of the Highlander 1745–1830* (East Linton, 1995)

Colley, Linda, *Britons: Forging the Nation, 1707–1837* (London, 1992)

Cruickshanks, Evelyn, ed., *Ideology and Conspiracy: Aspects of Jacobitism, 1689–1739* (Edinburgh, 1982)

——, and Jeremy Black, eds, *The Jacobite Challenge* (Edinburgh, 1988)

——, and Edward Corp, eds, *The Stuart Court in Exile and the Jacobites* (Rio Grande, OH, 1995)

Devine, Thomas M., *Scotland's Empire, 1600–1815* (London, 2003)
——, ed., *Scottish Elites* (Edinburgh, 1994)
——, and John R. Young, eds, *Eighteenth Century Scotland: New Perspectives* (East Linton, 1999)
Donaldson, William, *The Jacobite Song: Political Myth and National Identity* (Aberdeen, 1988)
Duffy, Christopher, *The '45: Bonnie Prince Charlie and the Untold Story of the Jacobite Rising* (New Haven, CT, and London, 2006)
Dunyach, Jean-François, and Anne Thomson, eds, *Scotland and Enlightenment: National and International Perspectives* (Oxford, 2015)
Dunyach, Jean-François, Richard Sher and Allan I. Macinnes, eds, 'Enlightenment and Empire' special issue, *Journal of Scottish Historical Studies*, XXXVIII/1 (2018)
Dziennik, Matthew P., *The Fatal Land: War, Empire, and the Highland Soldier in British America* (New Haven, CT, and London, 2015)
Eriksonas, Linas, *National Heroes and National Identities: Scotland, Norway and Lithuania* (Brussels, 2004)
Farrington, Anthony, *Trading Places: The East India Company and Asia, 1600–1834* (London, 2002)
Finn, Margot, and Kate Smith, eds, *East India Company at Home, 1757–1857* (London, 2018)
Forsyth, David, ed., *Bonnie Prince Charlie and the Jacobites* (Edinburgh, 2017)
Fraser, Sarah, *The Last Highlander: Scotland's Most Notorious Clan Chief, Rebel and Double Agent* (London, 2013)
Fritz, Paul S., *The English Ministers and Jacobitism between the Rebellions of 1715 and 1745* (Toronto, 1975)
Frost, Robert I., *The Polish Portrait of Bonnie Prince Charlie* (Basingstoke, 2022)
Fry, Michael, *The Scottish Empire* (Edinburgh, 2001)
Genet-Rouffiac, Nathalie, *Le Grand Exil: Les Jacobites en France, 1688–1715* (Paris, 2007)
Gestrich, Andreas, and Michael Schaich, eds, *The Hanoverian Succession: Dynastic Politics and Monarchical Culture* (Farnham, 2015)
Gibson, John S., *Playing the Scottish Card: The Franco-Jacobite Invasion of 1708* (Edinburgh, 1988)
Gooch, Leo, *The Desperate Faction? The Jacobites of North-East England, 1688–1745* (Hull, 1995)
Graham, Eric J., *A Maritime History of Scotland, 1650–1790* (East Linton, 2002)
Hancock, David, *Citizens of the World: London Merchants and the Integration of the British Atlantic Community, 1735–1785* (Cambridge, 1997)
Harris, Tim, *Revolution: The Great Crisis of the British Monarchy, 1685–1720* (London, 2006)
Holmes, Geoffrey, *The Making of a Great Power: Late Stuart and Early Georgian Britain, 1660–1722* (Harlow, 1993)
Hont, I., and Michael Ignatief, eds, *Wealth and Virtue: The Shaping of Political Economy in the Scottish Enlightenment* (Cambridge, 1983)
Hopkins, Paul, *Glencoe and the End of the Highland War* (Edinburgh, 1986)
Humm, Louisa, John Lowrey and Aonghus MacKechnie, eds, *The Architecture of Scotland, 1660–1750* (Edinburgh, 2020)

Israel, Jonathan I., *Radical Enlightenment: Philosophy and the Making of Modernity, 1650–1750* (Oxford, 2001)

Jacob, Margaret C., *The Radical Enlightenment: Pantheists, Freemasons and Republicans* (London, 1981)

Jones, Peter, ed., *Philosophy and Science in the Scottish Enlightenment* (Edinburgh, 1988)

Kidd, Colin, *Subverting Scotland's Past: Scottish Whig Historians and the Creation of an Anglo-Scottish Identity, 1689–c. 1830* (Cambridge, 1999)

Lenman, Bruce, *The Jacobite Risings in Britain, 1689–1746* (London, 1980)

——, *The Jacobite Clans of the Great Glen, 1650–1784* (London, 1984)

——, *Britain's Colonial Wars, 1688–1783* (Harlow, 2001)

Livesey, James, *Civil Society and Empire: Ireland and Scotland in the Eighteenth-Century Atlantic World* (New Haven, CT, and London, 2009)

McGilvary, George, *East India Patronage and the British State: The Scottish Elite and Politics in the Eighteenth Century* (London, 2008)

——, *All for Union, Empire and Homeland: The Labours of 'Honest John' Drummond of Quarrel* (New York and London, 2019)

McInally, Thomas, *The Sixth Scottish University: The Scots Colleges Abroad, 1575–1799* (Leiden and Boston, MA, 2012)

Macinnes, Allan I., *Clanship, Commerce and the House of Stewart, 1603–1788* (East Linton, 1996)

——, *Union and Empire: The Making of the United Kingdom in 1707* (Cambridge, 2007)

——, and Douglas J. Hamilton, eds, *Jacobitism, Enlightenment and Empire, 1680–1820* (London, 2014)

Macinnes, Allan I., Kieran German and Lesley Graham, eds, *Living with Jacobitism, 1690–1788: The Three Kingdoms and Beyond* (London, 2014)

Macinnes, Allan I., Patricia Barton and Kieran German, eds, *Scottish Liturgical Traditions and Religious Politics: From Reformers to Jacobites, 1540–1764* (Edinburgh, 2021)

MacKenzie, John M., and Thomas M. Devine, eds, *Scotland and the British Empire* (Oxford, 2011)

Mackillop, Andrew, *'More Fruitful than the Soil': Army, Empire and the Scottish Highlands, 1715–1815* (East Linton, 2000)

——, and Steve Murdoch, eds, *Military Governors and Imperial Frontiers c. 1600–1800: A Study of Scotland and Empires* (Leiden and Boston, MA, 2003)

MacLean, Christopher, and Ronald W. Renton, eds, *Gael and Lowlander in Scottish Literature: Cross-Currents in Scottish Writing in the Nineteenth Century* (Glasgow, 2015)

McLynn, Frank, *The Jacobites* (London, 1985)

Mann, Alastair J., *James VII: Duke and King of Scots, 1633–1701* (Edinburgh, 2014)

Mansfield, Andrew, *Ideas of Monarchical Reform: Fénelon, Jacobitism and the Political Works of the Chevalier Ramsay* (Manchester, 2015)

Marshall, P. J., ed., *The Oxford History of the British Empire*, vol. II: *The Eighteenth Century* (Oxford and New York, 1998)

Mather, James, *Pashas: Traders and Travellers in the Islamic World* (New Haven, CT, and London, 2009)

Mijers, Esther, 'News from the Republick of Letters': Scottish Students, Charles Mackie and the United Provinces, 1650–1750 (Leiden, 2012)

Monod, Paul K., Jacobitism and the English People, 1688–1788 (Cambridge, 1995)

Murdoch, Steve, Network North: Scottish Kin, Commercial and Covert Associations in Northern Europe, 1603–1746 (Leiden, 2006)

Ó Baoill, C., and N. R. McGuire, eds, Rannsachadh na Gaidhlig 2000 (Aberdeen, 2002)

Ó Buachalla, Brendan, Aislig Ghear: Na Stiobhartaigh Agus An Taos Leinn, 1603–1788 (Dublin, 1996)

Ó Ciardha, Éamonn, Ireland and the Jacobite Cause, 1685–1766: A Fatal Attachment (Dublin, 2002)

Orr, Julie, Scotland, Darien and the Atlantic World, 1698–1700 (Edinburgh, 2018)

Paquette, Gabriel, The European Seaborne Empires: From the Thirty Years' War to the Age of Revolutions (New Haven, CT, and London, 2019)

Parrish, David, Jacobitism and Anti-Jacobitism in the British Atlantic World, 1688–1727 (Woodbridge, 2017)

Patton, Norrie, The Jacobites: Their Roots, Rebellions and Links with Freemasonry (London, 1994)

Petrie, Sir Charles, The Jacobite Movement: The First Phase, 1688–1716 (London, 1948)

——, The Jacobite Movement: The Last Phase, 1716–1807 (London, 1950)

Philipson, Nicholas T., and Rosalind Mitchison, eds, Scotland in the Age of Improvement (Edinburgh, 1970)

Pincus, Steve, 1688: The First Modern Revolution (New Haven, CT, and London, 2009)

Pittock, Murray G. H., Poetry and Jacobite Politics in Eighteenth Century Britain and Ireland (Cambridge, 1994)

——, The Myth of the Highland Clans (Edinburgh, 1995)

——, Inventing and Resisting Britain: Cultural Identities in Britain and Ireland, 1685–1789 (Basingstoke, 1997)

——, Jacobitism (Basingstoke, 1998)

Raffe, Alasdair, Scotland in Revolution, 1685–1690 (Edinburgh, 2018)

Rapport, Michael, Nationality and Citizenship in Revolutionary France: The Treatment of Foreigners, 1789–1799 (Oxford, 2000)

Ritchie, Robert C., Captain Kidd and the War against the Pirates (Cambridge, MA, 1986)

Shaw, John S., The Management of Scottish Society, 1707–1764 (Edinburgh, 1983)

Sirota, Brent S., The Christian Monitors: The Church of England and the Age of Benevolence, 1680–1730 (New Haven, CT, and London, 2014)

——, and Allan I. Macinnes, eds, The Hanoverian Succession in Great Britain and its Empire (Woodbridge, 2019)

Smith, Annette M., Jacobite Estates of the Forty-Five (Edinburgh, 1982)

Smout, T. Christopher, A History of the Scottish People, 1560–1830 (London, 1970)

Stephen, Jeffrey, Defending the Revolution: The Church of Scotland, 1689–1716 (Farnham, 2014)

Stern, Philip J., The Company-State: Corporate Sovereignty and the Early Modern Foundation of the British Empire in India (Oxford, 2011)

Stevenson, David, *The First Freemasons: Scotland's Early Lodges and their Members* (Aberdeen, 1988)

Storrs, Christopher, *The Spanish Resurgence, 1713–1748* (New Haven, CT, and London, 2016)

Stroh, Silke, *Gaelic Scotland in the Colonial Imagination: Anglophone Writings from 1600 to 1900* (Evanston, IL, 2016)

Swingen, Abigail L., *Competing Visions of Empire: Labor, Slavery, and the Origins of the British Atlantic Empire* (New Haven, CT, and London, 2015)

Szechi, Daniel, *The Jacobites: Britain and Europe, 1688–1788* (Manchester, 1994)

——, *1715: The Great Jacobite Rebellion* (London, 2007)

——, ed., *The Dangerous Trade: Spies, Spymasters and the Making of Europe, 1688–1788* (Dundee, 2010)

——, *Britain's Lost Revolution? Jacobite Scotland and French Grand Strategy, 1701–8* (Manchester, 2015)

[——, ed.], *State Papers Online: The Stuart and Cumberland Papers from the Royal Archives, Windsor Castle* (London, 2017)

Vaughn, James M., *The Politics of Empire at the Accession of George III: The East India Company and the Crisis and Transformation of Britain's Imperial State* (New Haven, CT, and London, 2018)

Watt, Douglas A., *The Price of Scotland: Darien, Union and the Wealth of Nations* (Edinburgh, 2007)

Whatley, Christopher A., *The Scots and the Union* (Edinburgh, 2007)

Williams, Kelsey Jackson, *The First Scottish Enlightenment: Rebels, Priests, and History* (Oxford, 2020)

Wills, Rebecca, *The Jacobites and Russia, 1715–1750* (East Linton, 2002)

Wilson, David, *Suppressing Piracy in the Early Eighteenth Century: Pirates, Merchants and British Imperial Authority in the Atlantic and Indian Oceans* (Woodbridge, 2021)

Zimmermann, Daniel, *The Jacobite Movement in Scotland and Exile, 1746–1759* (Basingstoke, 2003)

## Journal Articles

Behre, Göran, 'Sweden and the Rising of 1745', *Scottish Historical Review*, LI/1 (1972), pp. 148–71

——, 'Scots in "Little London": Scottish Settlers and Cultural Developments in Gothenburg in the Eighteenth Century', *Northern Scotland*, VII/2 (1987), pp. 133–50

——, 'Jacobite Refugees in Gothenburg after Culloden', *Scottish Historical Review*, LXX/1 (1991), pp. 58–65

Broad, John, 'Cattle Plague in Eighteenth-Century England', *Agricultural History Review*, XXXI (1983), pp. 104–15

Bryant, J. G., 'Scots in India in the Eighteenth Century', *Scottish Historical Review*, LXIV/1 (1985), pp. 22–41

Carmichael, Elizabeth K., 'Jacobitism in the Scottish Commission of the Peace, 1707–1760', *Scottish Historical Review*, LVIII/1 (1979), pp. 58–69

Chaussinand-Nogaret, G., 'Une Élite Insulaire au Service de l'Europe: Les Jacobites au XVIIIe Siècle', *Annales*, XXVIII (1973), pp. 1097–122

Corp, Edward, 'James II and David Nairne: The Exiled King and his First Biographer', *English Historical Review*, CXXIX (2014), pp. 1383–411

Crawford, Thomas, 'Political and Protest Songs in Eighteenth Century Scotland: 1. Jacobite and Anti-Jacobite', *Scottish Studies*, XIV (1970), pp. 1–33

Doyle, Thomas, 'Jacobitism, Catholicism and the Irish Protestant Elite, 1700–1710', *Eighteenth Century Ireland*, XII (1997), pp. 28–59

Fisher, Samuel, 'Fit Instruments in a Howling Wilderness: Colonists, Indians, and the Origins of the American Revolution', *William and Mary Quarterly*, LXXIII/4 (2016), pp. 58–65

Genet-Rouffiac, Nathalie, 'Les Britanniques du Roi Soleil: La Cour Jacobite à Saint-Germain-en-Laye', *Annuaire-Bulletin de la Société de l'histoire de France* (2012–13), pp. 167–200

Gillies, William, 'Gaelic Songs of the 'Forty-Five', *Scottish Studies*, XXX (1991), pp. 19–58

Hoppit, Julian, 'Compulsion, Compensation and Property Rights in Britain, 1688–1833', *Past and Present*, CCX (2011), pp. 93–128

Johnsen, Arne Odd, 'Jacobite Officers at Bergen, Norway, after the Battle of Culloden', *Scottish Historical Review*, LXVII/2 (1978), pp. 186–96

Kaiser, Thomas E., 'The Drama of Charles Edward Stuart, Jacobite Propaganda, and French Political Protest, 1745–1750', *Eighteenth Century Studies*, XXX/4 (1997), pp. 365–81

Kidd, Colin, 'North Britishness and the Nature of Eighteenth-Century British Patriotism', *Historical Journal*, XXXIX (1996), pp. 361–82

Lenihan, Patrick, 'The "Irish Brigade" 1690–1715', *Eighteenth Century Ireland*, XXXI (2016), pp. 47–74

McGuirk, Carol, 'Jacobite History to National Song: Robert Burns and Carolina Oliphant', *Eighteenth Century*, XLVII/2–3 (2006), pp. 253–87

Macinnes, Allan I., 'Jacobitism in Scotland, an Episodic Cause or National Movement?', *Scottish Historical Review*, LXXXVI/2 (2007), pp. 225–52

——, 'The Appin Murder: Jacobite Assassins or Campbell Killer?', *Transactions of the Gaelic Society of Inverness*, LXVIII (2015–17), pp. 324–58

——, 'Los jacobitas y el nacionalismo escoces', *Desperta Ferro: Historia moderna*, XXVIII (2017), pp. 62–5

——, 'Political Virtue and Capital Repatriation: A Jacobite Agenda for Empire', *Journal of Scottish Historical Studies*, XXXVIII (2018), pp. 36–54

Mackillop, Andrew, 'Accessing Empire: Scotland, Europe, Britain and the Asia Trade, 1695–c. 1750', *Itinerario*, XXIX (2005), pp. 7–30

Maclean-Bristol, Nicholas, 'Jacobite Officers in the Scots Brigade in Dutch Service', *Journal of the Society for Army Historical Research*, LXXXII (2004), pp. 97–108

Monod, Paul, 'Dangerous Merchandise: Smuggling, Jacobitism, and Commercial Culture in Southeast England, 1690–1760', *Journal of British Studies*, XXX/2 (1991), pp. 150–82

Morley, Vincent, 'The Continuity of Disaffection in Eighteenth-Century Ireland', *Eighteenth Century Ireland*, XXII (2007), pp. 365–81

Murphy, Sean, 'Irish Jacobitism and Freemasonry', *Eighteenth Century Ireland*, IX (1994), pp. 75–82

Oates, J. D., 'Jacobitism and Popular Disturbances in Northern England, 1714–1719', *Northern History*, XLI (2004), pp. 111–12

Pentland, Gordon, '"We Speak for the Ready": Images of Scots in Political Prints, 1707–1832', *Scottish Historical Review*, XC/1 (2011), pp. 64–95

Pincus, Steve, 'Rethinking Mercantilism: Political Economy, the British Empire, and the Atlantic World in the Seventeenth and Eighteenth Centuries', *William and Mary Quarterly*, LXIX/1 (2012), pp. 3–34

Pittock, Murray G. H., 'The Political Thought of Lord Forbes of Pitsligo', *Northern Scotland,* XVI (1996), pp. 73–86

Robinson, Daniel, 'Giving Peace to Europe: European Geopolitics, Colonial Political Culture, and the Hanoverian Monarchy in British North America, ca 1740–63', *William and Mary Quarterly*, LXXIII/4 (2016), pp. 291–332

Sankey, Margaret, and Szechi, Daniel, 'Elite Culture and the Decline of Scottish Jacobitism, 1716–1745', *Past and Present*, CLXXIII (2001), pp. 90–128

Smith, Hannah, 'The Idea of a Protestant Monarchy in Britain, 1714–1760', *Past and Present,* CLXXXV (2004), pp. 91–118

Soubigou, Gilles, 'Héroes en Tartan', *Cahiers d'études nodiéristes*, 1/3, L'Écosse des Romantiques (2017), pp. 197–216

Steele, Margaret, 'Anti-Jacobite Pamphleteering, 1701–1720', *Scottish Historical Review*, LX/1 (1981), pp. 140–55

Stephen, Jeffrey, 'Scottish Nationalism and Stuart Unionism: The Edinburgh Council, 1745', *Journal of British Studies*, XLIX (2010), pp. 47–72

Sullivan, C. R., 'The First Chair of Political Economy in France: Alexandre Vandermonde and the "Principles" of Sir James Steuart at the École Normale of the Year III', *French Historical Studies*, XX (1997), pp. 635–64

Szechi, Daniel, 'Constructing a Jacobite: The Social and Intellectual Origins of George Lockhart of Carnwath', *Historical Journal*, XL (1997), pp. 977–96

——, '"Cam Ye O'er Frae France?" Exile and the Mind of Scottish Jacobitism 1716–1727', *Journal of British Studies*, XXXVII/4 (1998), pp. 357–90

Talbott, Siobhan, '"Such unjustifiable practices"?: Irish Trade, Settlement, and Society in France, 1688–1715', *Economic History Review*, LXVII/2 (2014), pp. 556–77

Waddell, Brodie, 'The Politics of Economic Distress in the Aftermath of the Glorious Revolution, 1689–1702', *English Historical Review*, CXXX (2015), pp. 318–51

Wagner, Michael, 'Misunderstood and Underappreciated: The Russian Company in the Eighteenth Century', *Russian History*, XLI/3 (2014), pp. 393–422

Walsh, Patrick, 'The Bubble on the Periphery: Scotland and the South Sea Bubble', *Scottish Historical Review*, XCI/1 (2012), pp. 106–24

Wendell, Thomas, 'Jacobitism Crushed: An Episode Concerning Loyalty and Justice in Colonial Pennsylvania', *Pennsylvania History: A Journal of Mid-Atlantic Studies*, XL/1 (1973), pp. 58–65

Whatley, Christopher A., 'Reformed Religion, Regime Change, Scottish Whigs and the Struggle for the "Soul" of Scotland, c. 1688–c. 1788', *Scottish Historical Review*, XCII/1 (2013), pp. 66–99

Zook, Melinda S., 'Turncoats and Double Agents in Restoration and Revolutionary England: The Case of Robert Ferguson, the Plotter', *Eighteenth Century Studies*, XLII/3 (2009), pp. 363–78

# ACKNOWLEDGEMENTS

I owe a considerable debt of gratitude to colleagues, former students and friends and to my family in both Scotland and Denmark. I should like to give specific mention to the following:

For engagement in editing projects and organizing seminars which helped shape my views on Jacobitism: Ali Cathcart, Neil Mcintyre, John Young, Kieran German, Lesley Graham, Doug Hamilton, Jean-François Dunyach, Ann Thomson, Brent Sirota, Tim Harris, Daniel Szechi, David Forsyth, Tricia Barton, Aonghas MacKechnie, Steve Pincus, Ronnie Renton, Ronnie Black and Darren Layne.

For access to new sources on and new approaches to Jacobitism: Michelle Gait, Linda Fryer, Esther Mijers, Emsley Nimmo, Douglas Kornahrens, Catriona MacDonald, Nicola Cowmeadow, Robert Frost, Michael Brown, Linas Eriksonas, Steve Murdoch, Billy Kay, Peter Davidson, Jane Stevenson, Anna Groundwater, Emma Macleod and Roy Ritchie.

For productive discussion and occasional amicable dissent on Jacobitism: Éamonn Ó Ciardha, George McGilvary, Michael Broers, Tom McInally, Michael Fry, Abby Swingen, James Vaughn, Stephen Mullen, David Wilson, Amy Watson, Liam McIlvanney, Ranald MacInnes, Murray Pittock, Sarah Barber, Andrew Mackillop, Nicola Martin, Jeff Stephen and Chris Whatley.

For his constructive expertise in mapping, Jamie Bowie, cartographer in Geography, University of Aberdeen.

I should also like to thank, for his persistently entertaining confusion of myth and history, my brother, Dougie Macinnes, and for their technical and moral support, my wife, Tine Wanning, and our best man, Liam Hamilton.

As the COVID-19 pandemic was abating, I was privileged to be given access to Aberdeen University Library, the National Records of Scotland and the National Library of Scotland in Edinburgh, Stirling District Council Archives and Inveraray Castle Archives. The service in all was excellent. I have also enjoyed open access to the following archives and libraries: the Huntington Library, San Marino, California; Rigsarkivet, Copenhagen; Centre historique des Archives Nationales, Paris; Archivio del Palazzo di Propaganda Fide, Rome; Newberry Library, Chicago; the British Library and the National Archives in London; the

Public Record Office for Northern Ireland in Belfast; Beinecke Rare Books and Manuscripts Library, Yale University, New Haven, Connecticut; the Bodleian Library, Oxford University; Dundee University Archives; Aberdeen City Archives; Glasgow City Archives; Orkney Archives, Kirkwall; Perth and Kinross Council Archives; Argyll & Bute District Archives; and Mount Stuart House, Rothesay, Isle of Bute.

Finally, this book would not be possible without the constructive backing and forbearance of Michael Leaman and his team at Reaktion Books.

Abercromby, Patrick  67, 206–7
Aberdeen  15, 51, 59, 67, 131, 152
   governmental forces  95, 101, 191
   Jacobite control  59
   nonjurors in  64, 160, 208
   trade  111, 113, 128, 175
   weapon delivery  113, 154
Aberdeenshire  64, 66, 158
Ackland, Dudley, lieutenant  101–2
Africa  15, 18–19, 106, 110, 145, 175
   Company trading  145, 173–7
   Gold Coast, the  174, 176, 192
   Guinea  149, 174–7, 185, 225
   *see also* Royal African Company;
     slave trade
Aix-la-Chapelle  57
Alexander, Alexander, banker  114, 125
Alexander, Claud, merchant  177
American Colonies  18, 29–30, 32–3,
     164, 168, 173, 214
   deportations to  17, 105–6, 152
   Jacobite presence  159–60
   trade  112, 142
   *see also* Jacobite exiles in America
American Revolution/War of
     Independence  18, 37, 142,
     164–9, 196, 215–18, 232–5
Anna, empress of Russia  134–5
Anne, queen of England, Ireland and
     Scotland  21–3, 42, 50, 52, 62,
     68, 148
Annexed Estates  161, 165

anti-Jacobite propaganda  22–3, 27,
     30–33, 35–8, 95, 159, 177, 180, 227
Appin Murder  102
Arbuthnot, Robert, banker  114–16,
     122, 124, 149–50, 184
Argyll (ducal house of )  68–71, 95,
     100, 150, 152, 156
Argyll Regiment  22, 91
Asia  106, 110–11, 139, 151
   company trading  145, 173–4
   Jacobite presence in  179–84
   *see also* English East India
     Company
Atholl (ducal house of )  71–3, 75, 124
Atterbury, Francis, bishop of
     Rochester  27, 43, 137–8
Atterbury Plot, the  27, 42–3, 56
Aughrim, battle of  80–81
Austria  110–11
   *see also* foreign support/ lack of
     support of Jacobitism
Avignon  41, 44, 109, 116–17, 119, 132,
     137

Balfour, 5th Lord Balfour of Burleigh
     176
Baltic, the  57, 111, 128–9, 135, 154–5,
     185
banditry  38, 60, 91, 102
Bank of England  37, 145
Bank of Scotland  69
banking and finance  112–15

Barbados 105, 143, 145, 147, 159, 177, 185
Barbary Coast 106
Bengal 19, 179, 181–3, 188–9, 193–5, 196, 215
Bergen 111, 128
Berlin 57, 135, 211
Black Watch Regiment 31, 161–2, 201, 230
Blackwood and Cathcart, trading company 175
Blair, Alexander of Kinfauns 117
Board of Trustees for Fisheries and Manufactures 69
*Bonnie Banks of Loch Lomond, the* 104
Bordeaux 105, 111, 116, 121, 149, 210
Boston 145
    commercial network 155, 185
    Scots in 32, 141, 144, 147, 155, 159–60, 166
Boyne, battle of 80–81
Breholt, John, captain 148
British Admiralty 86
British Army 100, 123–4, 164, 185, 233–4
British Empire, the 37, 95, 151–2, 159
    ideology about 36, 70, 211–12, 215, 219, 221
    repatriating of capital from 17, 19, 174, 187, 223–4
    Scots in 69, 170, 179, 189, 193, 218–20, 222, 234
    Scots in military service 218–19, 233
British identity 201, 207, 222
Bruce, Sir William of Kinross 202
Brydges, John, Duke of Chandos 114–15, 175
Buchan, John, author 234
Buchan, Thomas, Major-General 81
Buchanan, Andrew, merchant 30, 153–4, 177
Buchanan, George, scholar 206
Burnet, Archibald of Carlops 76
Burns, Robert 221–3, 233
Butler, James, 2nd Duke of Ormonde 42, 46, 82, 84, 138

*Caledonian Mercury* 85, 207
Cameron, Dr Archibald 34–5
Cameron, Donald, of Lochiel 54, 56–7, 86, 96, 154–5, 230
Cameron, Sir Ewen of Lochiel 154–5
Cameron, John (of Lochiel) 154–5
Cameron, Reverend John 76
Cameron, John of Fassifern 154–5
Cameron, Sergeant Mor 102
Camerons of Lochiel 73, 136, 154, 177, 185
Camocke, George, captain 148–9
Campbell, Alexander, bishop of Aberdeen 64–5, 208–9
Campbell, Alexander of Fonab 147, 150
Campbell, Archibald, 10th Earl and 1st Duke of Argyll 91
Campbell, Archibald, Earl of Islay and 3rd Duke of Argyll 54, 70, 100, 103, 121, 155, 191
Campbell, Colin, trader 183–4, 198
Campbell, Colin of Glendaruel 53
Campbell, Colin of Glenure 102
Campbell, Daniel of Shawfield 28
Campbell, Sir James of Auchinbreck 55, 152–3
Campell, John, 2nd Duke of Argyll 24, 54, 68, 70, 72, 82, 93, 152, 155
Campbell, John, 4th Duke of Argyll 99
Campbell, John, 5th Duke of Argyll 99
Campbell, John, 1st Earl of Breadalbane 152
Campbell, John, 2nd Earl of Breadalbane 152
Campbell, John, 3rd Earl of Breadalbane 186, 227
Campbell, John, 4th Earl of Loudon 87, 94, 99, 161, 230
Campbell, John, cashier of RBS 186
Campbell, John of Barcaldine 186
Campbell, Mungo 102
Campbells of Argyll 22, 69–71, 95
Campbells of Barcaldine 185–6
Campbells of Cawdor 71, 183
Campbells of Glenorchy 71, 150, 186, 227

Canon, Alexander, Brigadier  81
Canton  173, 180, 183-4, 192, 195
Carlisle
    battleground  86, 98, 127
    trials and imprisonment  34, 54,
        72, 76, 92-3, 104, 191
Caribbean, the  147, 145, 149
Carnegie, George  187, 198
Carnegie, James, 5th Earl of Southesk
    198
Carnegie, James, priest  52
Caryll, John, 1st Lord Caryll of
        Durford  41-2
Catholic  25-7, 50
    clans  75-6
    converts  24, 37, 61, 205
    Highland mission  63
    Jansenism  63
    Jesuits  62-3
    see also Propaganda Fide; Scots
        Colleges
cattle
    droving  97, 154, 231
    reiving  227
    trade  54, 87, 122
Charles I  67, 84, 105
Charles II  142
Charles Edward Stuart  15, 40, 170,
    206
    arrival in Scotland  31, 55-6, 113,
        125, 157
    commanding the Forty-Five  13,
        55, 77, 85-8, 94, 126, 164, 224
    conversion to Anglicanism  57, 62
    death  21, 198, 216
    escape to France  56, 88, 97, 127,
        157, 164
    exile  34, 44-5, 57, 61
    papal recognition, lack of  39, 136
Charleston  165
    Scots in  141, 144, 166
    slave trade  155
Charitable Company of London, the
    29
Cherokees  18, 142, 167-8
China  19, 173, 178, 182, 184, 186, 192,
    215
Chisholms of Strathglass  100

Church of England  65
    Anglicans  25-6, 32, 63
    dissenters from  25, 27, 32
Churchill, John, Earl and 1st Duke of
        Marlborough  50, 114
civil wars in Britain  32, 48, 80, 86,
    225, 227
'Clan Act', the  69
Clan Chattan  38, 59, 75, 90-91, 100,
    151, 229
Clan Donald  39
Clan Gregor  55
clans
    bandits  226
    caterans  226-7
    confessional allegiances  75-6
    internal conflicts  226-9, 231-2,
        235
    political affiliations  74
    political continuity  75
    Whig denigration of  226
Claude, Comte de Forbin  82
clearances  97, 100, 152, 198, 222,
    232-4
Clive, Robert  194, 196
colonial settlers  141, 150-52, 163-5
commercial landlordism  226, 231
commercial networks  110-12, 128,
    132-3, 149, 153-5, 157-8, 231
Commission of Trustees in Scotland
    53, 119-20
Commissioners for Forfeited Estates
    154
Commissioners of the Customs  146
Convention of Royal Burghs  101
Cornwallis, Edward, colonel  97
Cope, Sir John  86-7
Coptic Christianity  64, 208
Council for Trade and Plantations
    146
Country Party  23-4, 49, 51
Covenanters  57-8, 60, 67-8, 81, 84,
    105
Cowan, Robert, colonial governor
    180-81
Craftsman, the  35
Cromdale, battle of  82
Court party  24, 50-52

Company of Scotland  18, 145–6, 148, 174, 178
Culloden  13, 17, 32–6, 56, 58, 77, 88, 94, 235

Dalrymple, Sir John, Master (later 1st Earl) of Stair  22, 91–2, 122–3, 161
Dalrymple, John, 2nd Earl of Stair  30, 43, 70, 119–20
Dalrymple and Graham, shipping agents  175, 188
Dalzell, Frances  192–3
Danish East India Company  183, 186
Darien scheme  14, 18, 23, 49, 145–8, 150, 174
De Ginkel, Godert  80–81
Deacon, Thomas, bishop of Manchester  98
Deacon, Thomas, captain  98
Defoe, Daniel  26–7, 51
Derby  86, 94, 188, 234
Derry, siege of  80, 89
desertions  226–7, 229–30
Dillon, General Arthur  42, 114
Disarming Acts  93, 102–3, 230
Dominion of New England  144–5
Douai  50, 62–3, 191, 206
Douglas, James, 2nd Duke of Queensberry  24, 50–51
Douglas, James, 11th Earl of Morton  148
Douglas-Hamilton, James, 4th Duke of Hamilton  24, 49
Drummond, Alexander, banker  122
Drummond, Andrew, banker  114, 122, 125, 179, 191
Drummond, James, 6th Earl of Perth and 3rd Duke of Perth  54, 144
Drummond, Lord John, 4th Earl of Perth and 4th Duke of Perth  40–41, 87, 110, 126
Drummond, John, 7th Earl of Perth  55
Drummond, Chevalier John  212–13
Drummond, John of Quarrel  115, 179–83, 188, 195

Drummond, William, 1st Earl and Duke of Melfort  40–41, 91, 129, 144, 212
Drummond, William, 4th Viscount of Strathallan  115
Drummond, William of Balhaldy  55–6
Duff, Archibald  192
Duff, George  192–3
Duff, Patrick of Premnay  101, 190–91
Duff, Robert, admiral  192
Duff, William of Dipple, Lord Braco and Earl of Fife  190–93
Dundas, Henry (Viscount Melville)  195
Dundas, Robert, Crown Solicitor  66
Dundas, William  114, 116–17
Dundee  24, 59, 64, 111, 128
Dunkeld, battle of  8
Dutch Republic, the  17, 19, 23, 31, 60 Jacobite exiles in  117, 120, 123, 125 *see also* foreign support/ lack of support of Jacobitism

East Indies  18–19, 23, 111, 148, 173–4, 177, 183, 185–6, 198
    Scottish presence  179
Edgar, James, Jacobite secretary  44
Edinburgh  64, 83
    Castle  72, 220
    commerce  111, 113, 175, 210
    Enlightenment  19, 200–201
    Forty-Five  59, 77, 85–6, 96, 224
    riots  26, 29, 93
    royal visits  60, 143, 220, 223
Eigg, island of  90
Elibank Plot, the  34–5, 39, 45, 47, 57, 120, 18
Elizabeth Farnese, queen of Spain  39
Elphinstone, Arthur, 6th Earl of Balmerino  33
enforced recruitment  228
English Act of Settlement  50
English East India Company (EIC)  19, 115–16, 145, 173–4, 178–80, 195
    civil service  193, 197, 232

political impact of Asia  181
   Scots serving in  179, 181–2, 186,
     196–7
   territorial expansion  193–5
English Parliament  179
English Press, licensing  22
Enlightenment, the  15–16, 19–21, 31,
    36, 136
   architecture and design  202
   art  216
   constitutional ideas  206–7, 211–13,
    217
   deism  202, 204–5
   economy models  204, 214–16
   engineering  203
   Edinburgh  200–201
   history writing  207
   Jacobite contribution  200–201,
    211
   land management  203
   patriotism  200, 206–7, 212, 214
   philosophy  210
   Republic of Letters  201, 207
   science  216
   spirituality  204–5, 208–9
   stadial development  213, 220
   Whig contribution  200–201, 217,
    226
Episcopalians  26, 34, 43, 65, 136
   College of Bishops  65, 209
   jurors  63–4, 208
   liturgical matters  208–10
   nonjurors  17, 26, 30, 33, 64–6,
    97–8, 153, 157–8, 187, 208–9
   usagers  64–5, 209
Eriskay, island of  55
Erskine, Charles, Lord Justice Clerk
   118
Erskine, James Lord Grange  30, 70,
   118, 120
Erskine, John, 6th Earl of Mar  52–3,
   119–20, 130, 190, 202
   British informer  120, 43, 70
   economic transactions  113–14,
    116
   exile  42–2, 123, 137
   leading the Fifteen  42, 53, 77,
    82–3, 85, 130

Erskine, Sir John of Alva  118–19, 132
Erskine, Dr Robert  132
Erskine, William, merchant  114
Ethiopia  13–15, 106
Eugene, Prince of Savoy  80
exiles  50, 58, 92, 114, 119, 152–3
expulsions  104

Falkirk, battle of  34, 87, 96, 229
Farquharson, Francis of Monaltry  76,
   127
Farquharson, John of Invercauld  102
Fenwick, Sir John  89
Ferguson, Adam, sociologist  31, 201,
   211
Ferguson, James, major  90
Ferguson, John, captain  97
Fitz James, James, Duke of Berwick
   82, 84–5
Fitzjames, James, Duke of Liria  130,
   134
Flanders  31, 49, 116, 230
Fleming, Mary, Countess of Wigtown
   112
Fletcher, Andrew of Saltoun  68
'Flight of the Wild Geese, the'  81,
   89, 110
Fontenoy, battle of  56, 195
Forbes, Alexander, Lord Forbes of
   Pitsligo  43, 68, 122, 127, 204
Forbes, Robert, bishop for Ross and
   Caithness  97–8
   *The Lyon in Mourning*  97
foreign support/ lack of support of
   Jacobitism  86
   Austria  44, 85, 137, 173
   Bavaria  38
   Denmark-Norway  38
   Dutch Republic  38, 80
   France  21, 38, 39, 44, 46, 55, 57,
    62, 80, 82, 85, 87, 99, 213
   papacy, the  21, 38–9, 44, 57, 116,
    136
   Poland-Lithuania  28
   Prussia  34, 38, 45
   Russia  28, 38, 130, 137
   Spain  38–9, 42, 46, 57, 62, 84–5,
    110, 118, 130, 137

Sweden  27, 38–9, 85, 118, 130, 183,
    198
Forster, Thomas MP  35, 83, 85, 92
Fort Augustus  87, 99, 202
Fort William  87, 99, 154–5
Fotheringham, John, merchant  182
France  15, 17, 45, 54, 60, 82, 217
    (Jacobite) exiles in  24, 56, 119,
        123–7, 130, 149, 155–6, 182
    intellectual links  204–6, 214–15
    Irish brigades in  46, 56, 110–11
    mercantile networks  110, 112,
        114–15, 118–19, 121, 127, 184
    relations with exiled Stuarts  26,
        36, 38–9, 41, 57, 97, 99, 126
    Royal Scots in  55, 57
    wars against  22–3, 25, 45, 54,
        80–81, 91, 151, 161–2
    see also foreign support/ lack of
        support of Jacobitism
Fraser, Simon, Master of Lovat  162
Fraser, Simon of Beaufort (later Lord
    Fraser of Lovat)  23–4, 181
Frasers of Lovat  74, 87, 23
Frederick II of Prussia  45, 103, 135,
    211
Freebairn, Robert, printer  22, 83,
    206–7
Freemasonry  17, 21, 136–8, 166, 197,
    201, 205
French East India Company  115, 184,
    194
French Revolution, the  127, 198, 215,
    217, 222, 233

Gadderar, Thomas, bishop of
    Aberdeen  64, 208–9
Gallicanism  39, 72
George I  21–2, 27, 43, 76, 120, 122,
    130, 137
George II  22, 28, 32, 35, 45, 103, 130,
    134
George III  103, 168, 216
George IV  20, 198, 217, 220, 223
Georgia  105, 141, 151–2, 166–8, 178
general amnesty of 1726  123, 157
general indemnity of 1747  34, 157,
    164, 182, 188, 191, 213, 216

Gibraltar  134, 137, 192
Glasgow  25, 28, 32, 52, 64, 93, 96, 155
    Forty-Five  96
    riots  28, 93
    slave trade  175, 177
    tobacco trade  153–77
    trade  111–13, 153, 155–6, 203
Glen, James, colonial governor  159
Glencoe, massacre of  22, 91–2, 145
Glenfinnan  85, 157, 170
Glenshiel, battle of  84, 93
Global enterprises  185–93
    repatriating capital from  187–90,
        192, 196–8, 211–12, 215, 231
Gordon (ducal house of )  40, 52, 59,
    71, 196
Gordon, Alexander, major general
    129–30
Gordon, Alexander, Marquess of
    Huntly and 2nd Duke of Gordon
    72
Gordon, Andrew, professor of
    Philosophy  216
Gordon, Cosmo 3rd Duke of Gordon
    72
Gordon, George, 1st Duke of Gordon
    72
Gordon, Ludovic, merchant  72, 155
Gordon, James, coadjutor bishop  62
Godon, John, merchant  131
Gordon, John of Glenbucket  53–4,
    131, 190
Gordon, Patrick of Auchleuchries
    129, 131
Gordon, Robert, merchant and
    Jacobite agent  149–50
Gordon, Thomas, naval commander
    130–31
Gordon, William, 6th Viscount of
    Kenmure  33, 36
Gordon, William, banker  116–18,
    122
Gordon, Sir William of Park  191
Gothenburg  85, 111, 128–9, 174,
    183–4, 192, 198
Graham, Dugald, author  36
Graham, James, 1st Marquess of
    Montrose  67, 87

Graham, John, Viscount Dundee 81,
91
Graham, Mungo, trader to Persia
132–3
Grant, Alexander of Dalvey, slave
trader 178
Grant, Alexander of Knockando,
captain 97
Grant, Ludovic of Strathspey 100
Grant, Peter, abbé 14
Grants of Glenmoriston and
Glenurquhart 73, 75, 228
Grants of Monymusk 184
Green, Thomas, captain 178–79
Great Northern War, the 130, 133,
135
Gualterio, Francesco, Cardinal 24
Gyllenbourg, Count, Swedish
ambassador 27

Hamilton 52
Hamilton (ducal house of ) 52, 71
Hamilton, Lord Archibald, colonial
governor 159
Hamilton, Reverend Ezekiel 138
Hamilton, John, Lord Belhaven 50
Hamilton, Margaret, Lady Orbiston
112
Hanoverian monarchy 14, 15, 17, 21,
26, 34, 38, 94–6
succession 21, 26–8, 37, 42, 44, 50,
52–3, 60, 62, 69, 82, 119
troops 33, 54, 70
Hawley, Henry, general 87
Hay, Charles, 13th Earl of Erroll 49,
68
Hay, James of Cromlix, titular Earl
and Duke of Inverness 43–4,
136, 138
Hay, Marjorie 43
Henderson, William (or Harrison),
priest 14
Henry Benedict, Prince, Cardinal
Duke of York 16, 22, 44, 57, 111,
198, 200, 217
Highland 17, 28–31, 34, 47, 51, 53–4,
56, 69, 82, 218
Army 88

emigration 163–4
regiments 18–19, 161–2, 164–5,
168, 174, 196, 219, 230, 233
Hogg, James, poet 221–3
Holker, John, manufacturer 127
Honours of Scotland, the 220
Hooke, Captain Nathaniel 40, 84
Hudson's Bay Company 143
Hume, Abraham, trader 183
Hume, Alexander, trader 183
Hume, David, Jacobite 34
Hume, David, philosopher 210,
213–14
Hume, John, Whig polemicist 36
Hume, William of Broomhouse 34
Hunter, Robert, colonial governor 159

Imperial service 141, 151–2, 160–64
*see also* clan regiments
Independent Companies, the 31, 75,
152, 161, 164, 186, 229–30
India 19, 116, 178–80
economical returns from 179–80
Seven Years War, the 194–6
tramp trading in 180
industrialization 167, 222, 233
Innes, James, rector 125
Innes, Lewis, rector 207
Innes, Thomas, priest 207
Inverurie, battle of 87
Inverness 91, 112
colonial ventures 151, 155, 167, 175,
185
Jacobite control 59, 82, 87–8
reprisals in 96, 98–9
Irish Brigades (in France/Spain)
55–6, 81, 87, 110, 195
Irvine, Charles, colonial trader 184

Jacobite agents and agencies 48, 51,
53–5, 132, 157
couriers 49–50, 56, 112
Jacobite Army, the 32, 36, 87, 91,
93–4, 98, 188, 213, 229
Jacobite clans 52, 90, 92, 163, 177,
180, 196, 218
divided loyalties 71, 73–6, 226
polemical attacks on 96, 102

rehabilitation of 181, 185–6, 219, 234

reprisals against 94, 99, 102, 160, 165

Jacobite clubs 136

Jacobite diaspora 17, 105–6, 109

Jacobite diplomatic activity 110, 213

Jacobite extra-parliamentarism 49, 51–2

Jacobite rehabilitation 162, 174, 231, 233–4

Jacobite relations with Native Americans 142, 167–8

Jacobitism, England 15–16, 21, 35, 45–7, 56–7, 86

Jacobitism, Ireland 15–16, 21, 45–6, 79

Jacobitism, Scotland 15–16, 20–21, 26–7, 45, 4–8

confessional commitments 61–6

constitutional reformers 67–8, 211

dynastic commitments 60–61, 77, 83, 85–7, 206

family divisions 70–73

patriotic commitments 66–8, 77, 82–7, 212

poetry 60–61

Jamaica 98, 143, 147, 150, 152–3, 155–6, 159, 169–70, 176–8, 185–7, 189, 192–3

James VI & I 67

James VII & II 22, 33, 37, 48, 136, 202, 217

campaigns in Ireland and Scotland 80–82, 228

Court in exile 40–41, 44, 49–50

revolution against 16, 21, 25, 62, 67, 145

Scottish colonies in America 18, 105, 142–4

James VIII & III 14, 50, 53, 56, 58, 62, 216

courts in exile 16, 40–44, 68, 137–8

diplomatic recognition of 21, 23, 39–40, 51, 82

in the Fifteen 72, 77, 84, 118, 130, 134

Hanoverian Succession 23, 26–8, 51, 71

manifestos 22, 27, 59

setting intellectual agenda 200, 207–8

Johnson, Gabriel, colonial governor 159

Johnson, Sir Nathaniel, colonial governor 158

Johnstone, James, lieutenant 162

Johnstones of Westerhall 170, 197

Keith, George, 10th Earl Marischal 42–3, 45, 54, 84, 103, 134–5, 138–9, 192, 212

Keith, James, Field Marshal 134–5, 137, 139, 211–14, 216, 236

Keith, John, 3rd Earl of Kintore 135

Keith, William, 9th Earl Marischal 49, 68

Keith, Sir William, governor of Pennsylvania 70

Kelly, George 56–7

Keppell, William, Earl of Albemarle 97, 101

Ker, Henry of Graden, colonel 99

Ker, John of Kersland 51–2, 183

*Kidnapped* 55, 234–5

Killiecrankie, battle of 81, 90, 230

Kinloch, James of Kinloch 191

Knight, Joseph, former slave 169–70

Lacy, Peter, general 133

Laffeldt, battle of 56

Lally, Thomas, Count Tollendall 195

Lang, Andrew 15

Law, James of Lauriston 195

Law, John, banker 114–15, 117, 196, 203–4, 214

Law, William, banker 117, 121, 125

Lemnoa, isle of 13

Leslie, Charles Jacobite polemicist 22

Limerick

siege of 80–81

Treaty of 89

Lochaber 74, 99, 102, 165, 227–8, 230

Lockhart, George of Carnwath 52–3, 119, 202

Logan, William of Logan  30
London  57, 80, 89
    central administration  66, 68–9,
        144, 146
    commercial hub  111–12, 154, 160,
        173, 175, 177, 179, 180, 185
    Forty-Five  86–7
    Jacobites in  47, 58, 64, 130, 159
    propaganda  32, 34–5
    Scots in  24, 114, 122, 145, 188, 191,
        208
    Whig base  23, 25
*London Magazine*, the  33
Louis XIV, king of France  23–4, 37,
        39–42, 68, 80, 146
Louis XV, king of France  14, 55, 57
Louis XVI  195, 199
Lowther, Robert, colonial governor
        159
Loyalists  95, 161, 164–6, 168–9
Lumisden, Andrew  44
    Jacobite secretary  216
Lyall, David, merchant  198
Lyon, Patrick of Auchterhouse  53
Lyon, Robert, priest  34

Mac an t-Saoir, Dunnchadh Bàn
        (Fair-Haired Duncan Macintyre)
        229
MacBean, William Munroe, collector
        15
MacDaniell, James, plotter  24
MacDonald, Aeneas, banker  125, 127,
        156
MacDonald, Alexander, merchant  156
MacDonald, Alexander of Glenaladale
        156–7, 163, 170
MacDonald, Sir Alexander of Sleat
        152
MacDonald, Allan of Kingsburgh
        164–5
MacDonald, Angus of Glengarry  76
MacDonald, Coll of Keppoch  76,
        90–91
MacDonald, Etienne, Duke of
        Taranto  127
MacDonald, Flora  164–5
MacDonald, Hugh, bishop  63

MacDonald, John of Glenaladale
        163
MacDonald, Neil MacEachen  127
MacDonalds of Clanranald  14, 90,
        100, 163
MacDonalds of Glencoe  58, 91–2
MacDonalds of Keppoch  38, 90–91,
        93, 227
MacDonalds of Sleat  99
MacDonnell, Alexander of Glengarry
        15, 38
MacDonnell of Scotus, Donald  13–14
MacDonnells of Glengarry  13, 73,
        100, 165
MacDougall, Alexander, of Dunollie
        156
MacDougall, Duncan, merchant  156
MacDougall, Iain Ciar of Dunollie
        156
MacFarlane, John of Arrochar  119
MacFhearchair, Iain (John
        MacCodrum)  232
McGill, James, informer  49–50
MacGillivray, Alexander of
        Drumnaglass  167
MacGillivray, John, Creek chief  167
MacGregor, Rob Roy  54, 93, 220,
        227, 234
Mackay, Donald, 3rd Lord Reay  99
MacKay, Hugh of Scourie  81, 91
MacKenzie, Alexander of Prestonhall
        181
MacKenzie, George, 1st Earl of
        Cromartie  148
MacKenzie, George, 3rd Earl of
        Cromartie  123
MacKenzie, George, author  67,
        206–8
MacKenzie, George (of Delvine),
        Jacobite exile  121–3
MacKenzie, Hugh of Fraserdale  181
Mackenzie, Kenneth, 6th Earl of
        Seaforth  123, 228
Mackenzie, William, 5th Earl of
        Seaforth  76, 94, 123–4
Mackenzies
    of Easter and Wester Ross  99, 231
    of Seaforth  74, 87

Mackintosh, Lady Anne  75, 229
Mackintosh, John Mor  151, 166, 168
Mackintosh, Lachlan of Torcastle
    90
Mackintosh, William of Borlum,
    brigadier  59, 83, 92, 151, 155, 166,
    202, 207
Mackintosh, William of Mackintosh
    75, 229
MacLachlan, John, priest  58
MacLachlans of Ardgour  30, 58
Maclean, Shona, author  234
Macleans of Duart  30
MacLeod, Alexander, captain
    196-7
MacLeod, John of Dunvegan  152
MacLeods of Dunvegan  74, 99, 196
MacMaighstear, Alasdair (Alexander
    MacDonald)  61, 77
MacPherson, James, poet  197, 218,
    233
MacPherson, Sir John, colonial
    governor  197
MacRae, James, colonial governor
    180-82
Madagascar  148, 178
Manchester Regiment, the  34, 85,
    98, 127
Mary, queen of England, Ireland and
    Scotland  21, 80
Mary of Modena, queen mother  50,
    116-17, 134, 148
Maryland  142, 145, 151, 153, 185
Maule, Harry/Henry of Kelly, 5th
    Earl of Panmure  114, 120
Maule, James, 4th Earl of Panmure
    119
Maule, John of Inverkeillor, MP  101,
    121
Maule, Countess Margaret of
    Panmure  112, 120
Maxwell, William, 5th Earl of
    Nithsdale  92
Mercer, Hugh, general  166
Meston, William  77
Middleton, Charles, 2nd Earl of
    Middleton  40-42, 91, 129
Middleton, George of Seaton  101

military service abroad  110, 128-31,
    133-4, 141, 151-2, 212, 231
Militia Act, the  161
Mississippi Project, the  114-16,
    120-21, 179, 190, 195, 204
Moir, James of Stoneywood, merchant
    128, 198
Monro, Hector of Nevar, major  196
Mordaunt, Henrietta, duchess of
    Gordon  72
Morgan, Henry, captain  101-2
Mughal Empire, the  194
Mullany, John, bishop of Killalie  24
Mulroy, battle of  38, 91
Munro, George of Culcairn, captain
    97, 101
Munro, Neil, author  234
Murchieson, Donald, chamberlain  94
Murray, Alexander (of Elibank
    House)  34, 57
Murray, Sir Alexander of Stanhope  30
Murray, Charles  73
Murray, David, 5th Earl of Stormont
    43
Murray, Elizabeth, dowager Countess
    of Lauderdale  49
Murray, Lord George  73, 85, 87-8,
    95, 124-6, 162
Murray, James, 2nd Duke of Atholl
    72, 124-5, 132
Murray, James, Earl of Dunbar  43-4,
    138
Murray, John, 1st Duke of Atholl  24,
    49-50, 72-3, 124, 131
Murray, John, 3rd Duke of Atholl  73
Murray, John of Broughton  39, 55,
    234
Murray, Lord John  73
Murray, William, Marquess of
    Tullibardine  42, 54, 73, 84,
    124-5
Murrays of Glen Girnaig  197
Muscovy Company, the  133
mysticism  43, 64, 205, 208

Nairn, Thomas, captain  158
Nairne, Sir David  44
Nairne, Lady Margaret  221

Nairne, Lord William  221, 223
Napier, George, merchant  132–3
Native Americans  18, 142–3, 147, 151,
    160, 167–8
Navigation Acts, the  142, 144–5, 153,
    175
neo-Stoicism  67
Netherlands, the *see* Dutch Republic
New Jersey  60, 141, 143–4, 154–5,
    158–9, 166, 186
New York  145
    colony  142, 144, 152, 163
    commercial network  141, 144, 147,
        155
    Scots in  157–9, 166, 185
Newcastle  83–6, 112, 146
Nicholson, Thomas, vicar-apostolic
    62
Nine Years War, the  22, 41, 49,
    80–81, 91
nonjurors  27, 64
    English  25–7, 65, 158–9, 208–9
    Irish  56
    Scottish  17, 26, 64–6, 75, 157–8,
        160, 208–9
North Carolina  55, 105, 141, 143, 152,
    159, 163–4, 169, 235
Northumberland  83, 85
Nova Scotia  151–2, 160, 162–3, 165

Ogilvy, David, 4th Earl of Airlie  126,
    128
Oglethorpe, James, general  151–2,
    168
Oldmixon, John, author  27
Oliphant, Carolina, Lady Nairne,
    poet  221–4
Order of Toboso  17, 138
Orthodoxy, Greek and Russian  64,
    208
Ostend East India Company, the  19,
    174, 183, 186
O'Sullivan, John William  56, 88
Oswald, Grant and Company  177
Oswald, Richard  177
Ottoman Empire, the  106, 212
Ouchterlony, Alexander, investor  116,
    122, 175–6, 179, 188, 192

Ouchterlony, Georg, investor  116,
    122, 179, 184, 188–9, 192
Ouchterlony, Thomas, trader  184
Outlander  235

Pain, Neville, priest  90
papacy, the  14, 21, 38–9, 43–4, 57, 72,
    116, 136
pardons  122–4, 126–7
Paris  29, 41–2, 52, 57, 62–3
*Paris Gazette*  22
Parliament of Great Britain  68
Paterson, Sir Hugh of Bannockburn
    119, 122
Paterson, William, merchant  145
Patriot Party, the  29–30, 35, 70, 151,
    154
patriotism  20, 38, 200, 212–13
    British  36, 201, 207–8, 226
    Scottish  15, 48, 66, 68, 77, 206–7,
        221–2, 233
Patriots  164–9
Patten, Robert, Whig polemicist  35
Penn, William, Quaker and colonizer
    144
Pennsylvania  70, 144–5, 158, 166, 185
pensions  114, 116–17, 126, 149–50
Persia  132–3
Perth  59, 82–4, 162
Peter the Great of Russia  28, 42, 64,
    129–30, 132–3, 135, 203, 213
Philadelphia
    commercial network  144
    Scots in  32, 141, 160, 165–6
Philippe, Duke of Orléans  39, 82,
    114–16
piracy  13, 17–18, 79, 106, 147–50, 178,
    180
Pitcairne, Dr Archibald, physician
    203, 206
Pitt, William the Elder, prime
    minister  161
Pitt, William the Younger, prime
    minister  194
planters  143, 147, 152, 170
Plenderleith, David, minister  32
Polish-Lithuanian Commonwealth
    44, 128, 131

Porteous Riot, the  29
Pottinger, Edward, naval commander
    90
Presbyterians
    Cameronians  51–2, 81
    Nonconformists  143
    Scotland  25, 29, 32, 51, 61, 63–5,
        161
    United Societies  81
    *see also* Covenanters
Preston, battle of  35, 76, 83, 86, 92
Prestonpans, battle of  86–7, 182, 201,
    230
Propaganda Fide (Sacred College of
    Propaganda)  62–3, 65
Prussia  45, 103–4, 135, 137–9, 212–13,
    236
    *see also* foreign support/ lack of
        support of Jacobitism support to
        Jacobitism

Quiberon Bay, battle of  40
Quietism  204–5

Radcliffe, James, 3rd Earl of
    Derwentwater  33, 35, 82, 85
Rae, Peter, printer  36
Ramsay, Allan, poet  66
Ramsay, Chevalier Andrew Michael
    136, 205–6, 210
Rattray, Thomas, bishop  65, 209
reprisals in America  95
reprisals in England and Ireland
    89–90
reprisals in Scotland  90–102, 227
    executions  104–5
    expulsions  104–6
    forfeitures  79, 91–4
    Scotophobia  96
    show trials  92, 102, 104
    starvation  97
    state terrorism  93–9, 102, 161, 196,
        229
Republic of Letters  19, 201, 207
Revolution (the Glorious) of 1688–91
    15–16, 21, 39, 48, 208
    Dutch intervention  80–82
    impact on American colonies  205

polemics of  22, 31–2, 34, 37–8,
    205
Three Kingdoms impact  21, 76,
    79–82, 129
Rising of 1689–91  16, 38, 54
Rising of 1708  16, 21, 24, 40–41, 53,
    69, 77, 82
Rising of 1715–16 (the Fifteen)  16, 18,
    21–2, 27–8, 30, 32, 35, 41–3, 47–8,
    53–4, 59, 73–7
    course and participants  82–3, 85
Rising of 1719  16–17, 21, 27, 46, 53,
    84, 110
Rising of 1745–6 (the Forty-Five)
    16–18, 21, 30–33, 35–6, 38, 44–8,
    55–7, 59, 62, 73–7
    course and participants  85–8
Robertson, Alexander of Strowan  77,
    123, 152
Robertson, William, historian  201,
    211, 218
Romanticism  15, 19–21, 136
    British Empire, views on  220–22
    Gaelic oral tradition  218
    historical novel, the  220
    Jacobite  170, 200, 222–3
    'Ossianic controversy'  218, 223
    poetry and songs  221–3
    rural community values  219
    Scottish distinctiveness  220
    Scottish patriotism  219, 222
    social conscience  222–4
    Union, the views on  217–22
Rome
    Catholic mission  62–3, 65, 126
    court in exile  14, 27, 29, 39, 41–5,
        54–5, 117, 119, 131–2, 136, 205
    cultural centre  216–17
    Jacobite community  138–9, 43
Ross, John, Cherokee chief  167
Rouen  114, 122, 124, 127, 149, 184
Royal African Company (RAC)  18–19,
    115, 173, 175–7, 191
Royal Bank of Scotland  69, 186
Royal Danish West India and Guinea
    Company  176–7
Royal Navy, the  82, 84, 86, 90, 95,
    123–4, 128, 149, 155, 175, 185, 192

Royal Scots/Royal Ecossais
  (regiment) 55, 87, 126
Ruddiman, Thomas, printer and
  bookseller 206–7
Russia 17, 127–8, 212–13
  Jacobite exiles in 127–34
  *see also* foreign support/ lack of
    support of Jacobitism
Russia Company, the 133
Ruthven 87–8, 99

Sacheverell, Henry, priest 25
Sacred College of Propaganda 14,
  62–3, 65
Saint Germain 24, 26, 40–41, 44,
  50–51, 77, 91, 114, 116, 118,
  129–30, 208
St John, Henry, Viscount Bolingbroke
  42–4, 46, 118
St Petersburg 29, 111, 128–9, 132–4,
  155, 203
Sarsfield, Patrick 1st Earl of Lucan 81
scaffold statements 32–4
Scandinavia 17, 127–8
Scotch Plot of 1703 23
Scots Colleges on the continent 50,
  52, 62–3, 125–6, 206–7, 217
*Scots Magazine*, the 33, 35, 85
Scott, Caroline, captain 97
Scott, Christian (Lady Largo) 50, 112
Scott, David, lawyer 207
Scott, Sir Walter 170, 218–21, 223, 233
Scottish Estates/ Parliament, the 51,
  77, 91, 204
  Darien Scheme 145–6, 148
  making the Union 23, 52, 82, 179,
    211, 218–19
Scottish Jacobite Association 54, 56,
  136
Scottish Privy Council 49, 59, 68
Scottish Society for the Propagation
  of Christian Knowledge
  (SSPCK) 150, 161
Seabury, Samuel, bishop 210
Sempill, Francis, 2nd Lord Sempill
  55–7
Seton, George, 5th Earl of Winton
  92

Seven Years War, the 18–19, 40, 45,
  103, 161–4, 166, 194–6, 211, 218,
  232–4
  Plassey, battle of 194, 196
Shawfield Riot, the 28–9, 54
Sheriffmuir, battle of 72, 76–7, 83–4,
  129, 228
  plundering before and after 93
Shirley, William, colonial governor
  161
Simon, Lord Fraser of Lovat 54
Simpson, William, merchant 154
Sinclairs (Caithness and Orkney) 74
slave trade and slavery 19, 142, 155,
  168–70, 175–8
  Spanish *assiento* 175, 185, 188
Smith, Adam 201, 211, 214–15
Smith, James, architect 202
Smith, Samual, London merchant
  105
smuggling 47, 112, 153–4, 184, 198
  160
Sobieska, Maria Clementine 43–44,
  113
Sobieski, James, Polish prince 43
South Carolina 60, 105, 116, 141,
  143–4, 150–52, 158–9, 178, 185
South Sea Bubble, the 27, 30, 120, 137,
  183, 190, 204
South Sea Company, the (SSC) 19,
  115, 173, 175, 185, 192
Spain 62
  Darien 23, 146
  diplomacy with Jacobites 103, 118
  trade 110, 112, 142, 145
  *see also* foreign support/ lack of
    support of Jacobitism
Spotswood, Alexander, colonial
  governor 159
Steuart, Sir James of Goodtrees 211,
  213–16
Stevenson, Robert Louis, author 234
  *Kidnapped* and *Catriona* 55, 234–5
Stewart, Alexander of Ballachulish 85
Stewart, Archibald, lord provost of
  Edinburgh 210
Stewart, Charles of Ardshiel 123
Stewart, Duncan of Appin 123

Stewart, governor of Lemnoa 13–14
Stewart of Glenbuckie 14
Stewart, James of Glenduror 102, 234
Stewart, John of Acharn 13–14
Stewart, John Roy, captain and poet 77
Stewart, Patrick, Earl of Orkney 151
Stewart, Robert of Appin 123
Stewarts of Appin 58, 73, 100
Stewarts of Atholl 13
Stirling, Archibald (of Keir) 187–9
Stirling, Sir Henry of Ardoch 131–3, 135, 139
Stirling, Hugh (of Keir) 188
Stirling, James of Keir 187–9
Stirling, James 'the Venetian' 203
Stirling, John of Keir 187–9
Stirling, Robert (of Keir) 187, 189
Stirling, William (of Keir) 188–9
Stirlings of Keir 186–7, 203
Strange, Robert, engraver 216
Straton, Captain Henry, Jacobite agent 51
Stuart, Charles, Lord Linton and Earl of Traquhair 54
Stuart, John, frontier promotor 151, 161
Stuart courts in exile 15–16, 19, 41, 54, 64, 68, 109–10, 113, 136, 200, 202
    agents/ambassadors for 44, 52, 55, 132, 135, 137, 157, 208, 213
    coordination with Scotland 40, 45, 48, 54–5
    correspondents 39, 44
    courtiers 17, 41, 43, 45, 50, 68, 91, 122, 212
    diplomacy 38, 103, 110, 131–2
    economical transactions 114, 117
    informants 50, 137, 151
    political activity 22, 24, 27–8
    Scots at court 40–43, 44–6, 53, 109, 118, 129, 205, 216, 231
    see also Jacobite agents and agencies
Stuart Restoration 16, 40, 43, 48, 68, 206

military commitment to 48, 51, 55–7, 79, 83
    religious support for 26, 33, 66
Sutherland, Kenneth, 3rd Lord Duffus 128, 190
Sutherland, William of Roscommon 190
Sweden 54, 111, 118, 128, 134–5, 137
    see also foreign support/ lack of support of Jacobitism
Swedish East India Company 19, 174, 183–4, 192, 198
Swedish Plot, the 41–2, 53

taxes 28, 59
Thomson, John, fraudster 29
Threipland, Sir David of Fingask 181
Toboso, Order of 17, 138
Toland, John, Whig intellectual 25
Toleration Act, the 26
Tories 22–7, 46, 53, 71, 158–9, 195, 211
    Scottish 27, 52
Tower of London 34–5, 92, 164
trade
    sugar 17, 113, 153, 169, 180, 183, 186, 215
    tobacco 17, 113, 141–2, 153–4, 157, 169, 177, 215, 231
    tramp trading 111, 113, 173, 180, 231
    see also cattle

Union, Treaty of 1707 16, 23, 25, 30, 201
    access to American colonies 18, 26
    extra-parliamentary protest 23–5, 38, 48, 52
    moves to revoke 26–7, 53, 66, 68–9, 77
    parliamentary passage 49–51, 71
Universal Catholic Church, the 65, 209
Urbino 41, 44, 117, 119–20
Urquhart, John, captain 191–2

Valladolid 62–3
vernacular poetry 60–61, 66, 77, 227, 229, 231–2
Victoria, queen 20, 220

Virginia  95, 105, 116, 142, 145, 151,
    153–4, 177–8

Wade, George, general and field
    marshal  28–31, 54, 85, 87, 123,
    152, 155
Walpole, Sir Robert, prime minister
    29–30, 46, 70, 116, 122, 135, 137,
    151, 179, 190
Walsh, Anthony, transatlantic trader
    56
War of the Austrian Succession,
    the 54, 57, 84, 134–5, 160, 186,
    194
War of the Polish Succession, the  131,
    134
War of the Spanish Succession, the
    18, 23, 25–6, 41, 114–15, 175
Wars of Independence, the  26, 67
Washington, George, general and
    president  166–8
Wedderburn, Alexander, tramp-trader
    182
Wedderburn, James of Inveresk
    170
Wedderburn, John of Ballidean
    169–70
Wedderburn, John of Blackness
    170
Wemyss, David, Lord Elcho  87, 126
Wentworth, Thomas  137
West Indies, the  19, 145, 166
    destination for prisoners  137, 149
    trade  113, 149, 155, 168, 174, 177,
        179, 186

Westminster  25, 34, 53
    House of Lords  53, 71
Wharton, Philip, Duke of Wharton
    and Duke of Northumberland
    137–8
Whig  46, 69–70, 72, 85, 124, 152,
    161, 210
    ascendancy  30, 46, 102, 137, 151,
        195, 197, 218
    clans  71, 74–5, 99–100, 160, 163,
        181, 230–31
    colonial ventures  180–81, 184–6
    forces  82–4, 86, 91, 93–4
    polemics  19, 22–3, 25, 27, 32, 36–7,
        211, 226
Whitehaven  153–4, 175, 177
Wightman, Joseph, general  84, 93
William Augustus, Duke of
    Cumberland  13, 35–6, 56, 72,
    87–8, 94–6, 98–100, 161, 195, 229
William of Orange  18, 21, 38–9, 63,
    145, 228
    accession  68, 80, 145
    assassination plots  22, 33, 47, 49,
        89, 129, 145, 202
    Darien scheme  18, 23, 49, 145–8
    famine  23, 145
    Massacre of Glencoe  22, 91–2, 145
    *see also* Revolution 1688–91
Williams-Wynn, Sir Watkins, MP  86
Wolfe, James, major  97
Wray, James, Whig agent  36

York Buildings Company  93, 103, 115,
    120–21